HOME
INSULATION

D O - I T - Y O U R S E L F

HOME
INSULATION

Mike Lawrence
Consultant Editor: Ian Penberthy

LORENZ BOOKS

This edition is published by Lorenz Books,
an imprint of Anness Publishing Ltd,
Blaby Road, Wigston,
Leicestershire LE18 4SE;

info@anness.com

www.lorenzbooks.com;
www.annesspublishing.com

If you like the images in this book and
would like to investigate using them for
publishing, promotions or advertising,
please visit our website
www.practicalpictures.com for more
information.

© Anness Publishing Ltd 2013

A CIP catalogue record for this book is
available from the British Library.

Publisher: Joanna Lorenz
Project Editor: Felicity Forster
Editor: Ian Penberthy
Photographers: Colin Bowling & John Freeman
Designer: Bill Mason
Production Controller: Mai-Ling Collyer
Additional text: Diane Carr, Mike Collins,
David Holloway & Brenda Legge

NOTES
The author and publishers have made
every effort to ensure that all instructions
contained within this book are accurate and
safe, and cannot accept liability for any
resulting injury, damage or loss to persons
or property, however it may arise. If in any
doubt as to the correct procedure to follow
for any home improvements task, seek
professional advice.

CONTENTS

INTRODUCTION

Insulation is a means of preventing heat from escaping from a house. Heat loss can occur through roofs, walls, floors, doors and windows, and each of these can be insulated in different ways – with loose-fill or blanket insulation, or by installing double glazing, to name a few.

Related to insulation is draughtproofing, which is also a method of reducing heat loss, particularly under doors, through letter plate openings and keyholes, and through gaps in windows.

Insulating and sealing a house totally is not the answer, however, as there always needs to be some air ventilation to prevent condensation, which can lead to mould and structural damage. So a combination of insulation, draughtproofing and ventilation is required.

This book shows how to insulate, draughtproof and ventilate the main areas of the home where heat loss can be a problem. Doing this will save energy and money, and will also cut down on unnecessary wastage of fossil fuels, which in turn causes the widespread environmental problems associated with the release of carbon dioxide into the atmosphere.

CAUSES OF HEAT LOSS

The primary areas of heat loss are through the roof, walls and floors – around 25 per cent of heat is lost through the roof and pipework, 35 per cent through the walls, and 15 per cent through the floors – so these are the first areas to work on.

Doors and windows are the next most likely places where heat is lost, due to draughts coming through gaps and cracks. About 15 per cent of heat loss is attributed to poor draughtproofing.

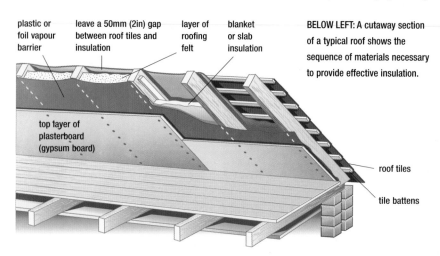

plastic or foil vapour barrier

leave a 50mm (2in) gap between roof tiles and insulation

layer of roofing felt

blanket or slab insulation

BELOW LEFT: A cutaway section of a typical roof shows the sequence of materials necessary to provide effective insulation.

top layer of plasterboard (gypsum board)

roof tiles

tile battens

ABOVE: Draughts can enter your home through the smallest of gaps. You can easily prevent draughts through keyholes by installing keyhole covers.

CAUSES OF CONDENSATION

Condensation can be caused by a lack of ventilation and over-insulation in properties not designed for it, both inside the rooms and within the building's structure. When water vapour condenses, the water runs down windows and walls, and causes mould, health problems, and even damage to the structure of the home.

People themselves are a major source of the moisture in the air inside a building. Breath is moist and sweat evaporates; one person gives off 250ml (½ pint) of water during eight hours of sleep, and three times as much during an active day.

Domestic activities create even more moisture. Cooking, washing up, bathing, washing and drying clothes can create as much as a further 10 to 12 litres (about 3 gallons) of water a day, and every litre of fuel burnt in a flueless oil or paraffin (kerosene) heater gives off roughly another litre of water vapour.

The air in the house is expected to soak up all this extra moisture invisibly. It may not be able to manage unaided. However, a combination of improved insulation and controlled ventilation will help eliminate condensation. An electric dehumidifier can also help in soaking up excess moisture.

ABOVE: A significant cause of condensation in the kitchen is cooking. Steam rises from pans and the vapour then condenses, forming droplets on walls and ceilings.

ABOVE: Constant condensation ruins paintwork and will eventually cause wooden window frames and sills to rot, unless action is taken to increase ventilation.

PROVIDING GOOD INSULATION

Good insulation reduces the rate at which expensive domestic heat escapes through the fabric of your home and helps to protect vulnerable plumbing systems from damage during cold weather. The different parts of your home can be insulated by various methods, and most jobs can be handled by a competent person.

ROOFS AND PIPEWORK

The roof is a good place to start your insulation project. This is where pipework is at greatest risk of freezing, so pipes must be tackled as well. The main options for roof insulation are loose-fill, blanket and slab insulation, and pipes are best insulated with foam taped around them.

WALLS

The best solution for cavity walls is a job that must be left to the professionals. Despite the extra outlay, the work is very cost-effective, and you can expect to see a return on your investment after a few years. The usual procedure is to pump foam, pellets or mineral fibres into the cavity through holes drilled in the outer leaf of the wall. Make sure that the work is carried out by an approved contractor.

Applying insulation to the inner faces of walls is well within the scope of most people. One possibility is to use thermal plasterboard (gypsum board) to dry-line external walls. Another is to add a framework of wood strips to the wall, infill with slab or blanket insulation and face it with plasterboard. To prevent condensation, plastic sheeting should be stapled to the insulating material.

FLOORS, DOORS AND WINDOWS

Suspended floors can be insulated by fixing sheets of rigid polystyrene (plastic foam) between the joists, and solid floors can be lined with a vapour

ABOVE: Installing cavity wall insulation is a specialist job that can take up to three days.

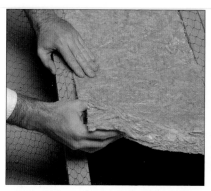

ABOVE: You can insulate a suspended floor by laying loft (attic) or wall insulation batts between the joists.

ABOVE: Glass is an extremely poor insulator, and double glazing can cut down on heat loss. It can also help to reduce noise penetration from outside and will give added security against burglars.

ABOVE: To control ventilation in steamy rooms, such as kitchens and bathrooms, extractor fans can be fitted. The types linked to humidity detectors are ideal, as they activate automatically.

barrier of heavy-duty plastic sheeting, topped with a floating floor of tongued-and-grooved chipboard (particle board) panels. Draughty floorboards can easily be repaired by applying silicone sealant (caulking) to small cracks, or by tapping slivers of wood into larger gaps.

Doors and windows are the two main sources of draughts in the home, and many products have been designed to deal with the problem. For example, gaps under doors and around windows can be sealed with draught excluder strips. Some are self-adhesive and easy to apply, while others can be fixed with screws. Make sure you choose the correct size for your doors and windows.

Windows can also be insulated by installing double glazing, either as a thin film stuck to each window frame or by fitting sliding units on to separate tracks within the window frames.

PROVIDING GOOD VENTILATION

A free flow of fresh air, ventilation is essential in a home, not only for humans to breathe, but also to prevent condensation occurring. There are many types of extractor fan that will help air to circulate. These can be fitted to ceilings, windows and walls, and can be installed by any competent do-it-yourselfer. For underfloor ventilation, airbricks are a good solution: ideally there should be an airbrick every 2m (6ft) along an external wall.

OVERCOMING DAMP

The best way of dealing with damp is to install a damp-proof course, but seek professional guidance before carrying out this work yourself. Other solutions include waterproofing exterior walls, installing ventilation fans and buying an electric dehumidifier.

MATERIALS & EQUIPMENT

There are three basic aspects involved in saving energy in your home: insulation to prevent heat from escaping; draughtproofing to prevent cold air from seeping into your home; and ventilation to prevent condensation from forming and causing problems. Various types of insulation material are made to cope with different situations; all are easy to use. Likewise, draughtproofing materials are easy to install, although ventilation devices require a bit more effort to fit. None of this work is beyond any competent do-it-yourselfer equipped with a relatively small collection of basic tools. As with all do-it-yourself work, due regard for your own safety, and that of others who may be nearby, is essential.

INSULATION MATERIALS

Before thinking about individual types of insulation, it is important to understand the concept of cost-effectiveness. Insulation costs money to install, and can bring benefits in two main ways.

It can reduce heating bills, since the home will waste less heat and the same internal temperatures can be maintained without burning so much fuel. The annual saving on the heating bill will therefore "pay back" the cost of the extra insulation. Also, when replacing a heating system, having better standards of insulation allows a less powerful, and less expensive, boiler to be used – an indirect saving, but valuable none the less.

ESSENTIAL BUYS

Good insulation need not mean great expenditure. The most effective items are relatively cheap and could save you a great deal in the long term. Any water storage tanks in the roof must be insulated to protect them from freezing. Padded jackets are available for the purpose. Likewise, any exposed pipework in the roof should be fitted with insulating sleeves.

ABOVE: Fix reflective foil between rafters to act as a vapour barrier over insulation.

ABOVE: Split foam pipe insulation comes in sizes to match standard pipe diameters.

ABOVE: Secure an insulation blanket to a hot water cylinder.

ABOVE: Insulate a cold water cistern with a purpose-made jacket.

LAYING LOOSE-FILL INSULATION

Lay loose-fill insulation by pouring the material between the joists. Spread it out so that it is level with the tops of the joists to ensure a thick and effective layer.

LOOSE-FILL INSULATION
This is sold by the bag and is simply poured between the joists and levelled off with their top surfaces. The dustier varieties, such as vermiculite, can be unpleasant to work with.

BLANKET INSULATION
This consists of rolls of glass fibre, mineral fibre or rock fibre, in standard widths to unroll between the joists. A typical roll length would be 6–8m (20–26ft), but short lengths are also available, known as batts. Always wear a face mask, gloves and protective clothing when laying the insulation.

SLAB INSULATION
These products are light and easy to handle, but as with the blanket versions some types may cause skin irritation. The slab widths match common joist spacings.

LAYING BLANKET INSULATION

If the roof of the house is pitched (sloping), blanket insulation can be laid over the loft (attic) floor. This is one of the most cost-effective forms of insulation.

PAY-BACK PERIODS

Hot water cylinder jacket *****
Pay-back period: less than 1 year.
Loft (attic) insulation ****
Pay-back period: 1–2 years.
Reflective radiator foil ****
Pay-back period: 1–2 years.
Draught excluders ***
Pay-back period: 2–3 years.
Flat roof insulation **(*)
Pay-back period: 2–4 years.
Floor insulation **
Pay-back period: 3–5 years.
Cavity wall insulation **
Pay-back period: around 5 years.
Double glazing **(*)
Pay-back period: 5 years or more.
Solid wall insulation *
Pay-back period: over 10 years.

* Star rating indicates cost-effectiveness.

DRAUGHT EXCLUDERS

Draught excluder strips are an inexpensive method of sealing gaps around windows and doors. The strips are self-adhesive and easy to apply, although foam strips offer variable levels of success. Avoid the cheapest varieties, as they may soon become compressed and will not do the job properly. Look for products that are guaranteed for between two and five years. These will be easy to remove and replace if you wish to upgrade the draughtproofing system.

Rubber strips, commonly with E- or P-shaped profiles, are dearer, but are better in terms of performance and longevity. Normally, casement windows are easier to draughtproof than the sash variety.

The most effective way of keeping draughts out at the sides of sashes is to fix nylon pile brush strips to the window frame. The top and bottom do not need special treatment, as any of the products recommended for casement windows can be used.

The gap between the bottom of a door and the threshold (saddle) can be draughtproofed by attaching a solid blade or brush strip to the bottom edge of the door, so that it meets the floor or sill, or by fixing a special strip across the threshold so that it is in contact with the underside of the door.

Unused chimneys can be sealed, or a temporary solution is to block off the flue with a "balloon" device which can be removed when a fire is needed.

V-strip metal draughtproofing strip with brush

ABOVE: A metal draughtproofing strip can be fixed to a door frame, such as the example shown here, a V-strip type. The insert shows where the brush strip should be fixed.

ABOVE: A brush-type strip fitted at the base of the door works well on uneven surfaces.

ABOVE: A flexible rubber blade held in a plastic or aluminium extrusion, secured by screws.

EXTRACTOR FANS AND AIRBRICKS

There are several options for ensuring a constant circulation of air in the home. Each works by providing ventilation, thus preventing condensation and its associated problems.

Extractor fans can be fitted in ceilings, windows or walls. Ceiling fans are particularly effective in bathrooms and kitchens, where warm water vapour rises. Window fans need care when installing; you can either cut a hole in a single-glazed window or order a new pane with the hole already cut by a glass supplier. Wall extractor fans are fixed to an outside wall. Always check for pipes before cutting into brickwork.

Airbricks are installed into external walls to ventilate the space below suspended wooden floors.

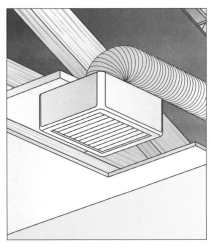

ABOVE: A ceiling-mounted extractor fan works by extracting the moist air that tends to collect just below the ceiling. A fan like this extracts this air to an outlet.

ABOVE: It is best to install a wall extractor fan as high as possible, where rising steam collects. Employ an electrician if you are unsure about how to install the wiring.

ABOVE: An airbrick contains perforated openings that allow ventilation in rooms and under wooden floors. It is important to keep them clear of earth, leaves and other debris, so clean them regularly.

TOOLS

Measuring and marking out are common tasks. A retractable steel measuring tape will take care of the former, while a combination square will allow you to mark cutting lines at 90 and 45 degrees. A craft knife can be used for marking the cutting lines as well as for cutting soft sheet materials.

A spirit (carpenter's) level is essential for finding a true horizontal or vertical.

For driving nails, a claw hammer is the ideal general-purpose tool, but for small pins (brads), the narrow end of a cross-pein hammer is better. You will need a nail punch to punch nail heads below the surface of the work, and a nail puller to remove nails or pins.

Various sizes of screwdriver for slotted, Phillips and Pozidriv screws will be necessary, while an adjustable spanner can be used on nuts and bolts.

Saws are also essential. Choose a general-purpose hand saw for large sections of wood and a tenon saw for smaller work. A mitre box will allow you to make 45-degree cuts.

For drilling holes, a cordless drill will be most convenient.

Use a jack plane for shaping wood, and bevel-edged chisels to make cutouts and recesses. Abrasive paper is essential for giving a final finish to wood.

When filling cracks and holes, use a putty knife for small repairs and a small trowel for larger ones. Use a caulking gun to apply silicone sealants.

A heavy-duty stapler is ideal for securing netting to joists for insulating.

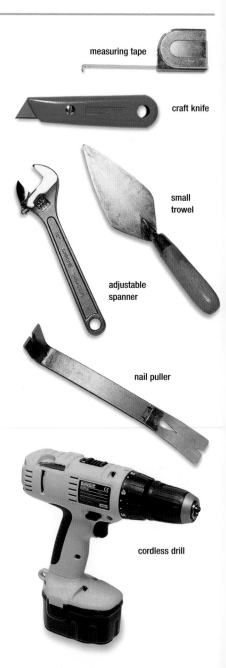

measuring tape

craft knife

small trowel

adjustable spanner

nail puller

cordless drill

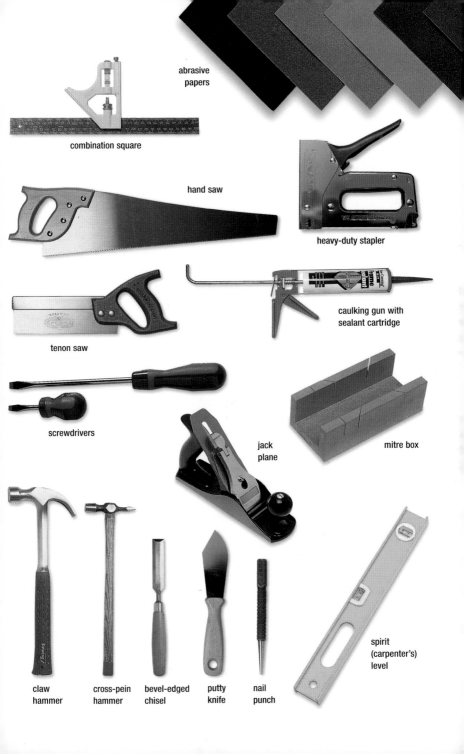

abrasive
papers

combination square

hand saw

heavy-duty stapler

tenon saw

caulking gun with
sealant cartridge

screwdrivers

jack
plane

mitre box

claw
hammer

cross-pein
hammer

bevel-edged
chisel

putty
knife

nail
punch

spirit
(carpenter's)
level

AWARENESS AND CLOTHING

A complete book could be devoted to the subject of safety in the home, and there is a wide range of equipment designed to minimize our capacity for hurting ourselves. Nevertheless, there is one requirement that we cannot buy, without which all that equipment is virtually useless, namely concentration. This is particularly important when working alone.

AWARENESS

Concentration is essential when using any form of power tool, especially a saw, where one slip can mean the loss of a finger, or worse. The dangers of accidents involving electricity are well

documented, as are those involving falls from ladders, spillages of toxic materials, and burns and injuries caused by contact with fire or abrasive surfaces. In almost every case, there is a loss of concentration, coupled with poor work practices and inadequate protective clothing or equipment. So, although the items shown here are all useful forms of protection, concentrating on what you are doing is the best advice to prevent accidents from occurring around the home.

CLOTHING

Overalls are a good investment because they not only protect clothing, but also most are designed to be close-fitting to prevent accidental contact with moving machinery. Industrial gloves, although not worn by those engaged in fine work, can provide very useful protection against cuts and bruises when doing rougher jobs. Similarly, safety boots should be worn when heavy lifting or the use of machinery is involved.

Knee pads are necessary for comfort when working on a floor or carrying out any other job that requires a lot of kneeling. They will also protect the wearer from injury if a nail or similar projection is knelt on accidentally.

Finally, a bump cap is worth considering. This will protect the head from minor injuries and bumps, but is not so cumbersome as the hard hat required on building sites. It is ideal for working in the close confines of a roof.

ABOVE: Wear overalls to protect your clothes when carrying out any dirty or dusty job. Disposable types are available for one-off jobs.

ABOVE: A pair of thick gloves will be essential when handling rough materials such as sawn wood or sharp objects such as broken glass. Make sure they fit well.

ABOVE: If you have to do a job that involves a lot of kneeling, rubber knee pads will be invaluable. They provide comfort and protection from sharp projections such as nail heads.

ABOVE: Safety boots with steel caps will protect your feet from injury when working with heavy items such as large sections of wood, bricks and concrete blocks.

ABOVE: When working in situations where you may hit your head accidentally, the bump cap will provide protection without being as cumbersome as a conventional hard hat.

SAFETY

Make sure you have the appropriate safety equipment to hand when carrying out do-it-yourself tasks, and always use it. Doing so can prevent nasty accidents and serious injury.

FIRST AID

Keeping a basic first aid kit is a common and wise precaution even before any do-it-yourself work is envisaged. It should always be kept where it can be reached easily.

You can buy a home first aid kit that will contain all the necessary items to cope with minor injuries, or you can assemble your own, keeping it in a plastic box with an airtight lid.

You should include items such as bandages, plasters, wound dressings, antiseptic cream, eye pads, scissors, tweezers and pins.

If you have cause to use your first aid kit, replace the items you have removed as soon as possible.

AIRBORNE DANGERS

When you are working with wood, the most common airborne danger is dust, mainly from sawing and sanding. This can do long-term damage to the lungs.

A simple face mask, however, will offer adequate protection for occasional jobs. These can also be purchased for protection against fumes, such as from solvents, which can be very harmful. Dust, of course, also affects the eyes, so it is worth investing in a pair of impact-resistant goggles, which will protect the wearer from both fine dust and flying debris. Full facial protection is available as a powered respirator for those working in dusty conditions over long periods.

When carrying out insulation work it is particularly important to wear a face mask to avoid inhaling glass fibre, mineral wool or loose-fill material. It is also important to wear gloves to avoid skin irritation.

RIGHT: Typical personal safety equipment – first aid kit, impact-resistant safety spectacles, ear protectors, two types of dust mask and sturdy industrial-type gloves.

LEFT: A simple circuit breaker can save a life by cutting off the power to faulty equipment.

ELECTRICAL SAFETY

If used incorrectly, electrical equipment can be life-threatening, and the dangers of fire are obvious. Always treat the former with respect, and take sensible precautions against the latter.

Some tools have removable switches that allow the user to immobilize them and prevent any unauthorized use.

To safeguard against electrocution, which can occur if the flex (power cord) is faulty or is cut accidentally, the ideal precaution is a residual current device (RCD). This is simply plugged into the main supply socket (electrical outlet) before the flex and will give complete protection to the user.

The danger of electrocution or damage caused by accidentally drilling into an existing cable or pipe can be largely prevented by using an electronic pipe and cable detector, which will locate and differentiate between metal pipes, wooden studs and live wires through plaster and concrete to a depth of approximately 50mm (2in). These are not too expensive and will be very useful around the home.

SAFE ACCESS

Steps and ladders can be hazardous, so make sure they are in good condition. Accessories include a ladder stay, which spreads the weight of the ladder

ABOVE: A ladder platform will provide a firm footing, especially if heavy footwear is worn.

ABOVE: Platforms supported by trestles, or step-ladders, are the safest way to work at a height.

across a vertical surface, such as a wall, to prevent slippage; and a standing platform, which is used to provide a more comfortable and safer surface to stand on. The last often has a ribbed rubber surface and can be attached to the rungs of almost all ladders. Even more stable is a movable workstation or a board or staging slung between two pairs of steps or trestles. These can often be used with a safety rail, which prevents the operator from falling even if a slip occurs.

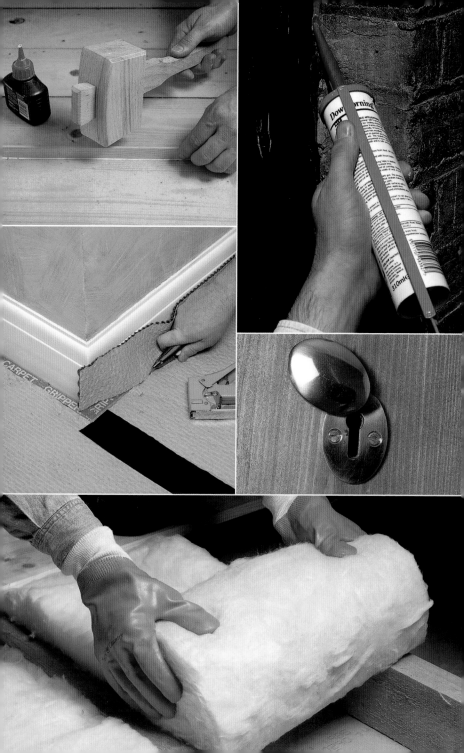

INSULATION &
DRAUGHTPROOFING

Heat rises, so the most important area of your home to insulate is the roof. Fortunately, this is very easy to do, although working in a small roof space can be difficult. Keeping the heat below the ceiling may have unforeseen consequences, however, in that any pipes and water tanks in the roof may freeze, so these too must be wrapped in insulating material. Once you have dealt with the roof, turn your attention to the walls and floors, since both can be insulated to provide a real bonus in energy saving. Floors not only act as heat sinks, but if boarded, they can allow in cold draughts. Sealing the gaps between boards will make your rooms feel cosy, as will draughtproofing the doors and windows. For extra comfort, opt for double glazing.

INSULATING ROOFS

In a building with a pitched (sloping) roof, where the loft (attic) space is used only for storage, it is usual to insulate the loft floor. To do this, use either blankets of glass fibre or mineral wool, sold by the roll, or else use loose-fill material (vermiculite, a lightweight expanded mineral, is the most widely used). Some kinds of loose-fill insulation, usually mineral wool or fireproofed cellulose fibres, can be blown into the loft by specialist professional contractors.

Blanket materials are generally easier to handle than loose-fill types unless the loft is awkwardly shaped, contains a lot of obstructions or has irregular joist spacings. The rolls are generally 600mm (24in) wide to match standard joist spacing, and common thicknesses are 100mm (4in) and 150mm (6in).

Choose the latter unless there is already thin sonic loft insulation, and ensure that it is laid with eaves baffles to allow adequate ventilation of the loft, otherwise condensation may form and lead to rotting of the wood. It is essential to wear protective clothing when handling glass fibre insulation. Wear a face mask, gloves and cover any exposed skin with suitable clothing.

Apart from being awkward to handle, loose-fill materials have another drawback. To be as effective as blanket types, they need laying to a greater depth – usually at least an extra 25mm (1in). With few ceiling joists being deeper than about 150mm (6in), there is nothing to contain the insulation and allow for maintenance access, unless strips of wood are fixed along the top edge of every joist.

LAYING LOOSE-FILL INSULATION

1 Lay loose-fill insulation by pouring the material between the joists. Prevent it from running out at the eaves by fixing lengths of wood between the joists.

2 Level it off with a spreader, which you can make from chipboard (particle board). You may need to add strips of wood to the joists to obtain the required depth of insulation.

LAYING BLANKET ROOF INSULATION

1 Clear all stored items from the loft (attic) area, then put down a sturdy kneeling board and use a heavy-duty vacuum cleaner to remove dust and debris.

2 Always put on gloves and a face mask, and wear long sleeves, to handle the insulation. Unroll it between the joists, leaving the eaves clear for ventilation.

3 Butt-join the ends of successive lengths of blanket. To cut the material to length, either use long-bladed scissors or simply tear it.

4 While working across the loft, make sure that any electrical cables are lifted clear of the insulation so they cannot overheat.

5 Insulate the upper surface of the loft hatch by wrapping a piece of blanket in plastic sheeting and stapling this to the hatch door.

6 Do not insulate under water tanks. If the tank has a lid, blanket insulation can also be wrapped around the tank and tied in place.

INSULATING PIPEWORK

When the loft (attic) floor is completely insulated, remember to insulate any water tanks and pipework within the loft, since they are now at risk of freezing. For this reason, do not lay insulation under water tanks.

FOAM PIPE INSULATION

Exposed pipework in the loft can easily be protected by covering it with proprietary foam pipe insulation. Basically, this comprises lengths of foam tubing, which have been split along the length and which come with inside diameters to match common domestic pipe sizes. All that is necessary is to open the split to allow the foam to be fitted over the pipe.

PIPE BANDAGE INSULATION

An alternative method is to use pipe bandage, but this is more labour intensive, since it must be wrapped around the pipe, although the fibrous material is useful for pipes with awkward bends. To secure it, tie each end firmly with a short length of string.

JACKETS FOR TANKS

Tanks can be insulated with proprietary jackets, or you can tie lengths of blanket insulation around them, or tape on thick rigid foam sheets. Alternatively, you can build a plywood box around the tank and fill the gap between it and the tank with loose-fill insulation material.

INSULATING PIPES WITH BANDAGE

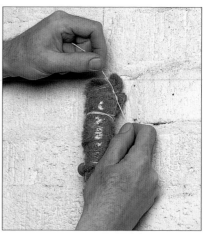

1 Pipe bandage can be used instead of foam insulation. Wrap it around the pipe in a spiral, with successive turns just overlapping. Don't leave any pipework exposed.

2 Tie the insulation bandage in place at the end of each length, or where the pipe passes through a wall. Simply tear the material to length as necessary.

INSULATING PIPES WITH FOAM

1 The quickest and easiest way of insulating pipework is to slip on lengths of foam pipe insulation, which is slit lengthways. Join the lengths with PVC (vinyl) tape.

2 To make neat joins in the insulation at corners, cut the ends at 45 degrees, using a mitre box and a carving knife or hacksaw blade. Tape the corner joint.

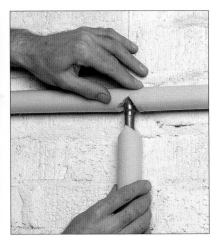

3 Make a V-shaped cutout in the insulation at a tee joint, then cut an arrow shape to match it on the end of the insulation which will cover the branch pipe.

4 As with butt and corner joints, use PVC tape to secure the sections of insulation together and prevent them from slipping out of position. In time, you may need to renew this.

BOXING-IN PIPES

Some people regard visible pipes in the home as an eyesore. Moreover, where the pipes are in rooms that are unheated, or where they run against external walls, there is a possibility that they may freeze during a severe winter. Fortunately, with a little time and minimal woodworking skills, exposed pipes can be hidden successfully from view and protected from freezing at the same time, by building boxing around them and filling it with loose-fill insulation. If the boxing is decorated to match the room, the pipes can be concealed completely. Be sure to allow for the boxwork to be easily removed in situations where it may be necessary to gain access.

ACCESSIBILITY

Bear in mind that stopcocks, drain taps, pumps, hand-operated valves and the like will need to be readily accessible and require some form of removable box system. For this reason, the boxing around them should be assembled with screws rather than nails. If a panel needs to be regularly or quickly removed, turn buttons or magnetic catches are a good idea.

BOXING BASICS

Steel anchor plates and screws can be used to secure the sides of boxing to walls, and these will be easy to remove when necessary. Battens (furring strips), either 50 x 25mm (2 x 1in) or 25 x 25mm (1 x 1in), can be used to fix boards at skirting (baseboard) level.

Disguise the boxing by decorating it to match the rest of the room. If pipework is running along a panelled or boarded wall, construct the boxing so that it follows the general theme, using similar materials and staining and varnishing the boxes accordingly.

WALL PIPES

Measure the distance the pipes project from the wall, taking account of any joints and brackets. Cut the side panels from 25mm (1in) board slightly over this measurement and to their correct length. Fix small anchor plates flush with the back edge of each panel and spaced at about 600mm (24in) intervals.

If using plywood, you may need to drill pilot holes. Hold the panels against the wall and mark the positions of the screw holes on the wall. Drill the holes and fix the panels to the wall with rawl plugs and screws.

Cut the front panel to size from 6mm (¼in) plywood. Drill evenly spaced screw holes in the front panel and fix it in position with 19mm (¾in) No. 6 screws. Use cup washers underneath the screw heads to protect the panel if it is likely to be removed often. Trim the edges flush with a block plane.

With horizontal pipes, arrange the boxing so that you can remove the top panel to make filling with loose-fill insulation easy. For vertical pipes, leave a small access panel at the top of the box and pour the insulation through this, tapping the boxing to make sure that it fills the void completely.

BOXING-IN WALL PIPES

1 Measure how far the pipes protrude from the face of the wall.

2 With a pencil, mark the positions for the side batten fixings.

3 Attach the side battens, screwing them firmly into position.

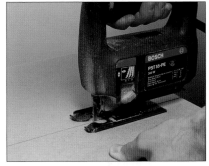

4 Cut the front panel of the box to size with a jigsaw. Use 6mm (¼in) plywood.

5 Drill pilot holes and screw the front panel into position, using 19mm (¾in) No. 6 screws.

6 Trim the edges of the front panel with a block plane. Add loose-fill insulation from the top.

INSULATING SOLID WALLS

House walls are the most extensive part of the whole building and absorb a lot of heat, which is why a house takes so long to warm up once it has become cold. Some of the lost heat can be retained by insulating the walls.

For solid walls, the most economical solution is to dry-line them on the inside with insulating plasterboard (gypsum board), fixed directly to the wall with panel adhesive or nailed to a supporting framework of treated wood strips. Alternatively, ordinary plasterboard sheets can be used, with insulation blanket or boards placed between the support strips and covered with a plastic vapour barrier.

INSULATING CAVITY WALLS

The cavity wall consists of two "leaves" of masonry with a gap, usually of 50mm (2in), between them. Their insulation performance can be improved by filling the cavity with insulating material. This is done by specialist installers who pump treated fibres, pellets or insulating foam into the cavity through holes drilled in the wall's outer leaf.

For wood-framed walls, the best alternative is to remove the interior finish, install insulation batts and cover these with a vapour barrier, such as plastic sheeting. Then add a new inner skin of plasterboard.

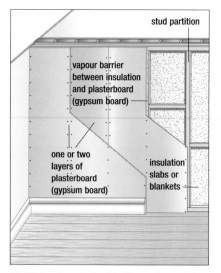

stud partition

vapour barrier between insulation and plasterboard (gypsum board)

one or two layers of plasterboard (gypsum board)

insulation slabs or blankets

ABOVE: A wall can be insulated by erecting a stud partition wall in front of it, the void being filled with blanket or slab insulation, while two layers of plasterboard (gypsum board) are added to the framework.

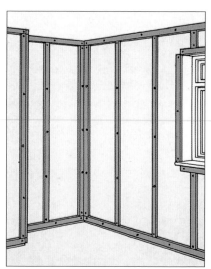

ABOVE: Fix a framework of 50 x 25mm (2 x 1in) softwood strips to the walls with masonry nails to support the edges and centres of the insulating boards.

ADDING THE DRY-LINING

1 Mark cutting lines on the board surface in pencil, then cut along the line with the insulation facing downwards, using a fine-toothed saw.

2 Use a simple lever and fulcrum to raise the boards to touch the room ceiling as they are fixed. A skirting (baseboard) will cover the gap.

3 Fix the boards by positioning them against the supporting framework so that adjacent boards meet over a strip, and nail them in place. The nail heads should just "dimple" the surface.

4 At external corners, remove a strip of the polystyrene (plastic foam) insulation as wide as the board thickness so the edges of the plasterboard (gypsum board) can meet in a butt joint.

5 Arrange the boards at external corners so that a paper-covered board edge conceals one that has its plaster core exposed. Finish off all joints with plasterboard tape and filler.

6 To make cutouts for light switch boxes, plug sockets and similar obstacles, mark their positions on the boards and cut them out with a padsaw.

INSULATING SUSPENDED FLOORS

Few people think of ground floors when considering insulation, yet a surprisingly large amount of heat can be lost through both solid and suspended wood floors. Insulating a suspended floor will involve disruptive work, since the floorboards will need lifting. However, if you are prepared to do this, the methods are very similar to laying roof insulation.

INSULATION METHODS

With suspended wood floors insulation can be fixed between the joists after lifting the floorboards. One method is to cut strips of rigid expanded polystyrene (plastic foam) and rest them on nails driven into the sides of the joists, or on battens nailed to the sides of the joists. Bear in mind that the material is very light and may be dislodged by severe draughts caused by windy weather; a few nails driven into the joists to "pinch" the edges of the insulation will help.

Another method of treating a suspended floor is to fill the gaps between joists with lengths of insulation blanket, supported on nylon garden netting stapled to the joists. Pull up the netting tightly before

LIFTING FLOORBOARDS

Unless you have a basement that allows you to reach the underside of a suspended floor, to insulate it you will have to lift all of the floorboards.

To lift a board, tap the blade of a bolster (stonecutter's) chisel into the gap between two boards, close to the end of the board you want to lift, and lever the board upward; repeat for the other side.

Continue levering until the end of the board is clear of the floor and you can insert the claw of a hammer beneath it.

Use the hammer to lever the end high enough to insert a length of wood beneath the board to hold the end clear of the floor. Continue in this way along the board until you can lift it completely.

nailing down the boards so that the blanket does not sag and let cold air through. The insulation is then covered with a vapour barrier.

USING INSULATION BLANKET

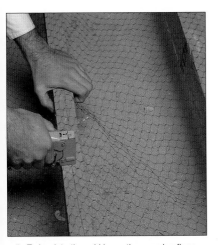

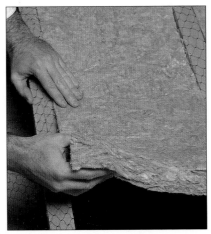

1 To insulate the void beneath a wooden floor, lift all the floorboards. Then drape lengths of garden netting loosely over the joists and staple them in place.

2 Lay lengths of loft (attic) insulation blanket or wall insulation batts in the "hammocks" between the joists. If the netting sags, pull it up a little and staple it again.

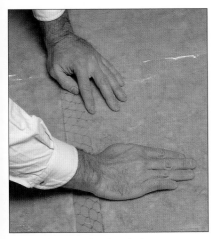

3 To prevent moisture from the house condensing within the insulation, cover the insulation with a vapour barrier of heavy-duty plastic sheeting.

4 Re-lay the floorboards by nailing them to the joists. Take this opportunity to close up any joints between the boards for a neat finish and to cut down draughts.

INSULATING SOLID FLOORS

With direct-to-ground concrete floors (slab on grade), the commonest method of insulation involves lining the floor with a vapour barrier of heavy-duty plastic sheeting, and installing a floating floor of tongued-and-grooved chipboard (particle board) panels. If additional insulation is required, place rigid polystyrene (plastic foam) insulation boards directly on top of the vapour barrier, then lay the new flooring on top of them.

Treat damp floors with one or two coats of a proprietary damp-proofing liquid and allow to dry before laying the vapour barrier. A gap of 9mm (⅜in) should be left between the chipboard and the wall to allow for expansion. This gap will not be noticeable once a new skirting (baseboard) is installed. The layer of trapped air under the floating floor will help keep the area warm.

Since the new floor will be at a raised level, any doors will need to be removed and planed down to a smaller size. Also, the flooring will either have to be cut to fit around architraves (door trim), or the architraves will have to be shortened so that the flooring fits beneath them.

LAYING A FLOATING FLOOR

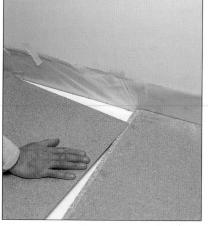

1 Remove the skirtings (baseboards) and put down heavy-duty plastic sheets. Tape the sheets to the walls; they will be hidden behind the skirting later. Then butt-joint 25mm (1in) polystyrene (plastic foam) insulation boards over the floor, staggering the joints in adjacent rows.

2 Cover the polystyrene insulation board with tongued-and-grooved flooring-grade boards. Use cut pieces as necessary at the ends of rows, and add a tapered threshold (saddle) strip at the door. When finished, replace the skirtings with hammer and nails.

DRAUGHTPROOFING FLOORS

Gaps between the boards of a suspended wooden floor can allow cold draughts to enter a room. There are various methods for coping with this problem, depending on the size of the gaps and whether you want the boards exposed as a decorative feature, or are happy to conceal them beneath a floorcovering.

EXPOSED FLOORBOARDS

Large gaps in floorboards can be filled with strips of wood, carefully cut to fit tightly. Spread adhesive on the sides of each strip and tap it into the gap. Allow the glue to set, then plane down the strip so that it is flush with the surrounding floor. The strips can then be stained to match the colour of the other floorboards.

In severe cases, and if you want the boards to be exposed, you may have no option but to lift all of the boards and re-lay them, butting them tightly together as you do so. You can hire special flooring clamps for this purpose, which attach to the joists and allow you to push the boards tightly together before you nail them down. ▶

TIP
A papier-mâché mix made from pieces of newspaper and a thick solution of wallpaper paste can be used to repair small holes in floorboards. Add woodstain to match the surrounding boards, then sand the repair smooth when dry.

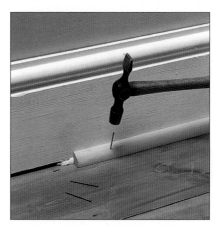

ABOVE: Tap slivers of wood in place to cure draughts through large gaps. Leave the repair slightly proud of the surface. Once the glue has set, sand down the raised area to a smooth finish with a power sander or planer.

ABOVE: Stop draughts at skirting (baseboard) level by filling any gaps with silicone sealant (caulking) and covering with quadrant (quarter-round) moulding. Secure the quadrant moulding with pins.

COVERED FLOORS

Where there are large gaps between floorboards, and especially if the boards themselves are in poor condition, you can cover the floor with sheets of hardboard to provide a sound surface for carpeting or some other form of floorcovering. At the same time, this sub-floor will eliminate draughts.

Before laying, condition the hardboard by spraying the textured side of each sheet with 450ml (¾ pint) of water. Stack the sheets back-to-back and flat, separated by strips of wood, on the floor of the room where they are to be laid. Leave them for 48 hours, until they are completely dry.

Begin laying the hardboard sheets in the corner of the room farthest from the door, fixing each sheet in place with 19mm (¾in) annular (spiral) flooring nails. Start to nail 12mm (½in) from the skirting (baseboard) edge. To ensure the boards lie flat, work across the surface in a pyramid sequence, spacing the nails 150mm (6in) apart along the edges and 230mm (9in) apart in the middle.

Butt boards edge to edge to complete the first row, nailing the meeting edges first. Use the offcut (scrap) from the first row to start the next row, and continue in this way, staggering the joins between rows.

If boards are in really poor condition, you may be better off replacing them completely with tongued-and-grooved chipboard (particle board) panels, which will eliminate draughts.

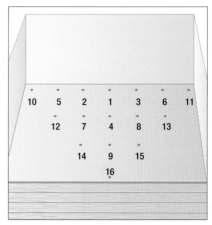

ABOVE: Nail across a hardboard sheet in a pyramid sequence to avoid creating bulges. Nails should be 150mm (6in) apart along the edges and 230mm (9in) apart in the middle.

LAYING A HARDBOARD SUB-FLOOR

1 Condition the hardboard sheets by brushing or spraying them with water, and leave them for 48 hours before laying.

CARPET

If the gaps between boards are narrow, and you don't want the boards to be exposed, the easiest method of coping with a draughty floor is to lay fitted carpet with a good underlay.

Put down the underlay and cover with double-sided adhesive tape. Unroll the carpet and butt the edges up against the walls of the room and ensure that the carpet is lying flat. Trim the edges against the skirtings (baseboards) and tape them down.

Laying carpet will effectively block the passage of air through the floor. For added protection, you can repair any major gaps between the boards with a silicone sealant (caulking).

LAYING CARPET

When the gaps between floorboards are relatively narrow, simply laying a good-quality, thick underlay beneath the carpet will prevent draughts from being a problem.

2 To ensure a secure fixing, use annular (spiral) flooring nails. A piece of wood cut to size will allow you to space nails correctly and rapidly.

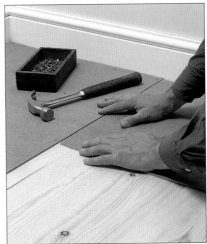

3 Use the offcut (scrap) from each row to start the next so that joins are staggered.

DRAUGHTPROOFING DOORS

Ill-fitting doors are a major source of heat loss, as well as causing cold draughts. Fitting efficient draught stripping around them will reduce the losses and cut down the draughts, and is a simple job to carry out.

Doors are best draughtproofed with pin-on (tack-on) plastic or sprung metal strips or types containing a compressible rubber seal. Special draught excluders are available for door thresholds (saddles), and can be fitted to the door bottom or across the threshold. There are even excluders designed to fit over letter plate openings.

REMEMBER VENTILATION

Don't forget that draughtproofing a home will close off many "unofficial" sources of ventilation, turning it into a well-sealed box. Fuel-burning appliances such as boilers and room heaters must have an adequate source of fresh air to burn safely, so it is wise to ask a fuel supplier to check that there is adequate ventilation in rooms containing such appliances. Often a ventilator in a window pane will solve the problem. However, you may need to take more drastic steps, such as fitting an airbrick into a wall with a vent cover that can be opened and closed.

Efficient draughtproofing may also increase condensation, especially in kitchens and bathrooms. This can be prevented by providing controlled ventilation in these rooms with an extractor fan.

ABOVE: Letter plate openings can be draught-proofed in a variety of ways. You can fit a hinged plate to the inside to provide extra protection. Alternatively, rubber and brush seals are available that will also do the job.

ABOVE: Draughts may not only pass around doors, but also through them. The problem is quite easy to solve. Keyhole covers are inexpensive. Many locks intended for external doors are provided with them as standard.

1 The simplest type of door-bottom draught excluder is a brush seal mounted in a wood or plastic strip. Simply cut it to length and screw it on to the foot of the door.

2 Alternatively, fit a threshold (saddle) strip. Cut the metal bar to length and screw it to the sill, then fit the compressible rubber sealing strip in the channel.

3 Draughtproof a letter plate opening by screwing on a special brush seal. Check beforehand that it does not foul the letter plate flap if this opens inwards.

4 Draughtproof the sides and top of the door frame by pinning (tacking) on lengths of plastic or sprung metal sealing strip. Pin the edge farthest from the door stop bead.

5 Alternatively, stick lengths of self-adhesive foam excluder to the stop bead against which the door closes. At the hinge side, stick the foam to the frame.

6 A third option is to use lengths of self-adhesive brush strip excluder. These three types can also be used for draughtproofing hinged casement windows.

DRAUGHTPROOFING WINDOWS

Windows are a major source of draughts in the home and are responsible for about ten per cent of heat loss. Many products have been designed to deal with these problems, but they vary in cost-effectiveness. The simplest are draught excluder strips, similar to those used for doors, while the most expensive remedy is to replace single-glazed units with double glazing. The latter will provide a considerable degree of comfort, as well as reducing sound transmission, but it may take up to 20 years to recoup your investment in terms of energy savings.

SEALING THE GAPS

You can choose from a variety of draught stripping products for windows, but some are more effective on certain types of window than others. For example, modern self-adhesive foams are much more efficient and longer lasting than older types, and are ideal for hinged casement windows. Simply stick strips around the rebate (rabbet) of the frame so that the opening casement compresses them when closed.

Sash windows, however, are not so easy to treat. The best solution is to use the same type of plastic or sprung metal strips that are suitable for doors. These can be pinned (tacked) around the frame to provide a seal against the sliding sashes. The job can be completed by attaching strips of self-adhesive foam to the top edge of the upper sash and bottom edge of the lower sash, so that these seal against the frame.

SASH WINDOWS

1 To fit a sprung metal strip excluder to a sliding sash window, first prise off the staff bead (window stop) that holds the inner sash in position, and swing it out.

4 Use the special wheeled springing tool provided with the draught excluder to make a small groove in the strip, causing it to spring outwards to press against the sash.

2 Measure the length of strip needed to fit the height of the window, and cut it to length with a pair of scissors. Beware of the sharp edges of the metal.

3 Pin (tack) the strip to the side of the frame so it will press against the edge of the sliding sash. Drive the pin through the edge facing towards the room.

5 Pin a length of the strip along the inner face of the top sash meeting rail (mullion), and "spring" it so it presses against the outer face of the bottom sash rail.

6 You can draughtproof the bottom edge of the lower sash and the top edge of the upper one by sticking on lengths of self-adhesive foam draught excluder.

DOUBLE GLAZING

The glass in windows is the least efficient part of the house at keeping heat in, and the only way of cutting this heat loss while still being able to see out is to add another layer of glass. Double glazing can be done in two ways: existing single panes of glass can be replaced with special double-glazed panes called sealed units, or a second pane can be installed inside the existing one – so-called secondary glazing.

SECONDARY GLAZING

This is the only practical form of double glazing for the do-it-yourselfer, and it is relatively inexpensive. There are dozens of types available, providing hinged and sliding inner panes that blend in well with most types of window; similar systems are also available from professional installers. The panes are either fixed directly to the window frame, or fitted within the window reveal on special tracks.

SLIDING UNITS

Do-it-yourself secondary glazing systems come in kit form and are easy to install. The kits provide enough materials to cover a range of window sizes; all you need do is cut the lengths of special track to fit within the window reveal and screw them in place. You do have to provide your own glass, however, and careful measurements must be taken so that you can order this from your local glass supplier. Then all you need do is fit the glazing gaskets and insert the panes in the tracks.

FITTING SLIDING UNITS

1 Measure the height and width of the window reveal at each side. If the figures differ, work from the smaller measurements for height and width. Cut the track sections to size.

4 When positioning the bottom track on the windowsill, use a straightedge and a spirit (carpenter's) level to check that it is perfectly aligned with the top track.

2 Offer up the side track sections and screw them to the window reveal. Use thin packing pieces to get them truly vertical if the walls are out of square.

3 Next, secure the top track section in place. Screw it directly to a wooden lintel or pre-drill holes in a concrete beam and insert plastic wall plugs first.

5 Measure up for the glass as directed in the kit manufacturer's instructions, and order the glass. Fit cut lengths of glazing gasket to the edges of each pane.

6 Fit the first pane into the track by inserting its top edge in the top channel, and then lowering its bottom edge. Repeat the procedure for the other pane.

CLEAR FILM

There is a particularly cheap form of secondary glazing that involves attaching a clear PVC (vinyl) film to the inside of the window with double-sided adhesive tape. This can be discarded during the summer months and fresh film applied for the winter.

A sturdier option is acrylic sheet. If you opt for this method, make sure that at least one window is easy to open in case of an emergency.

DON'T FORGET THE DOORS

Heat is lost through external doors too, and solid doors are best. If you prefer a glazed door, however, opt for a modern replacement fitted with a sealed double-glazing unit. You can reduce heat loss still further with an enclosed porch.

2 Press the film on to the tape, pulling it as taut as possible. Then play hot air from a hairdrier over it to tighten it up and pull out any wrinkles.

FITTING THIN-FILM SECONDARY GLAZING

1 Start by sticking lengths of double-sided adhesive tape to the window frame, about 12mm (½in) in from the surrounding masonry.

3 When the film is even and wrinkle-free, trim off the excess all the way around the window with a sharp knife.

APPLYING SEALANTS

Silicone sealants (caulking) are good for filling large or irregularly shaped gaps around windows and doors. They come in white, brown and clear versions. Use a caulking gun for ease of application, although products that do not require a gun are also available.

To make a repair with silicone sealant, clean the frame rebate (rabbet) and apply the sealant to the fixed frame. Brush soapy water on to the closing edge of the window or door. Close and immediately open the door. The soapy water acts as a release agent, preventing the door or window from sticking to the sealant.

Because silicone sealants are flexible, they will absorb movement in the structure of your home that otherwise would produce cracking. For particularly large gaps around frames, you can use an expanding foam filler.

TIP

For good adhesion, always clean and dry window and door frames thoroughly before applying self-adhesive sealant.

ABOVE: Fill cracks between the window frame and plasterwork with silicone sealant (caulking).

ABOVE: You can also use silicone sealant outdoors to seal gaps between frames and masonry where a rigid filler might crack.

ABOVE: Coloured silicone sealants can be used to blend in with their surroundings – or you can paint over them when a skin has formed.

VENTILATION

You can go too far in draughtproofing your home; if you seal up all the sources of outside air, you will prevent moist air from being carried away. This will cause condensation to form on any cold surfaces, such as windows, tiles and exterior walls. In severe cases, this can result in mould growth and even damage to the structure of your home. Moreover, a lack of airflow can cause problems with certain types of heater. The ideal is to keep out the cold draughts, but provide a sufficient flow of air to prevent condensation and ensure the efficient operation of heaters. The judicious use of manual vents, airbricks and electric extractor fans will provide all the ventilation you need without making you feel chilly.

FITTING A CEILING EXTRACTOR FAN

An extractor fan provides positive ventilation where it is needed, in a kitchen or bathroom, removing stale or moist air before it can cause a problem. There are three places you can fit an extractor fan: in a window, in a wall or in the ceiling, where ducts carry the stale air to the outside. In a kitchen, an extracting cooker hood can serve the same function, provided it is ducted to the outside; a recirculating cooker hood only filters the air.

It is important that an extractor fan is positioned so that the replacement air, which normally will come through and around the door leading to the remainder of the house, is drawn through the room and across the problem area. In a kitchen, the problem areas are the cooker and the sink; in a bathroom, they are the lavatory and shower unit.

Ceiling-mounted extractor fans are particularly efficient in bathrooms and kitchens, since the warm moist air will tend to collect just below the ceiling. Moreover, fitting the fan in the ceiling often makes for an easier installation, since all you need do is cut a circular hole in the ceiling with a padsaw, taking care to avoid the ceiling joists. From the fan, plastic ducting needs to be taken to an outside wall or to the eaves, where it is connected to an outlet. On no account allow it to discharge into the roof.

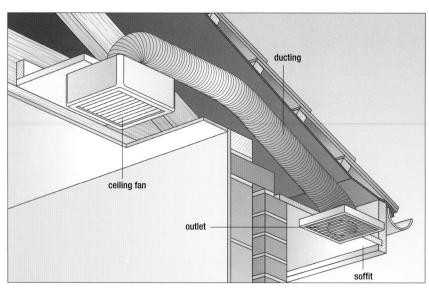

ABOVE: Fit an extractor fan in the ceiling so that it discharges via a duct to a hole with an outlet at the soffit.

FITTING A WINDOW EXTRACTOR FAN

If a simple window ventilator already exists in a fixed window, you may be able to replace it with an extractor fan. If not, you will have to cut a hole in one of the window panes. However, this will not be possible if the glass is toughened or laminated. The same applies to double-glazed units; they must be ordered with the hole pre-cut.

The only window you can cut a hole in is one made from normal glass in a single-glazed frame, and even here you may prefer to order a new pane from a glass supplier with the hole already cut. That way, the only work you will have to do is to take out the old pane and fit the new one.

Fit the extractor fan near the top of the window, since warm, moist air rises and it will do the most good at high level. Also, this will keep the fan away from inquisitive children, who may be tempted to push things into it.

To cut the hole in the glass yourself, you will need a beam circle cutter as well as a normal glass cutter. Use the beam cutter to score two circles: one the correct size for the extractor fan, and one slightly smaller inside it. Then use the normal glass cutter to make cross-hatched lines inside the inner circle, and single radial lines between the two circles. Tap out the glass from the inner circle, then use the glass breaker rack on the glass cutter to snap off the remaining margin of glass. Smooth the edge with fine abrasive paper wrapped around a circular tool handle or piece of thick dowelling rod. Once you have a hole of the correct size, fitting a window fan is simply a matter of following the instructions.

ABOVE: If the window was fitted originally with a simple ventilator unit such as this one, you may be able to remove it and fit an extractor fan in the existing hole.

ABOVE: If no ventilator is fitted, you will need to cut a hole in the glass to fit an extractor fan. For this, you will need a special tool known as a beam circle cutter.

FITTING A WALL EXTRACTOR FAN

Most designs of extractor fan will require a circular hole to be cut through the house wall. The best tool to use for this is a heavy-duty electric drill fitted with a core drill bit, both of which you can hire. These will cut a hole of exactly the right size. Make holes in both leaves of a cavity wall and fit the sleeve supplied with the extractor fan. Some fans require a rectangular hole to be cut, which may mean removing one or more whole bricks. Take care when doing this; cut through the mortar joints around the bricks with a cold chisel and club (spalling) hammer, and try to ease the bricks out in one piece. Keep as much debris as possible out of the wall cavity, since this could bridge the cavity and lead to damp problems. Once the sleeve for the fan is in place, make good the brickwork and plaster.

Fitting the fan is easy – simply drill holes for wall plugs to take the fan on the inside wall, and fit the outlet on the outer wall.

WIRING

An extractor fan needs to be wired up via a fused connection unit to the nearest power supply circuit. If you are not sure how to do this, employ a qualified electrician to do the job. In a bathroom or shower room, with no opening window, a fan is a compulsory requirement and it must be wired via the light switch so that it comes on with the light and remains on for 15 minutes afterwards.

1 The first step when fitting a wall-mounted extractor fan is to mark the exact position of the wall sleeve. Place the fan near the top of the wall for the best performance.

4 Offer up the extractor and mark its fixing-hole positions on the wall. Drill these and fit them with wall plugs so that you can screw the extractor to the wall surface.

2 Use a core drill bit, fitted to a heavy-duty electric drill, to cut a hole of the correct size through both leaves of the wall (if it is of the cavity type).

3 Check the fit of the sleeve in the hole and push it through the wall. Mark it off for length, then remove it and cut it down with a hacksaw. Replace it.

5 Wiring comes next (get help with this if necessary). Make a check that the extractor functions correctly, after which the cover of the unit can be put on.

6 Finally, fit the outlet on the outside wall. Sometimes this simply pushes into the end of the sleeve. In other cases, you may need to screw it to the wall.

FITTING EXTRA AIRBRICKS

In other rooms, fitting small "trickle" ventilators at the top of window frames and putting in extra airbricks will often supply enough ventilation to allow the moist air to disperse before condensation becomes a problem.

UNDERFLOOR VENTILATION

A suspended wooden floor consists of floorboards or sheets of flooring-grade chipboard (particle board) supported on joists. To keep the joists and the flooring dry, some kind of underfloor ventilation is essential. This takes the form of airbricks in the outer walls.

The first thing to check is that all the existing airbricks are free of debris and have not been blocked up in the mistaken belief that this will save money on heating. Next, check that there are enough airbricks – there should be one airbrick for every 2m (6ft) of wall length. Inserting a new airbrick is not difficult, as most match the size of standard bricks.

Decide where you want to put it, drill out the mortar around the existing brick and remove it. With a cavity wall, you will have to continue the hole through the inner wall and fit a terracotta liner to maintain the airflow. Use the corners of the hole in the outer wall to line up and drill four holes in the inner wall, then chip out the hole with a bolster (stonecutter's) chisel and club (spalling) hammer, working from the inside. You will need to lift floorboards to do this.

Fit the airbrick from the outside, applying mortar to the bottom of the hole and the top of the brick, pushing mortar in the sides. Point the mortar joints to the same profile as the surrounding joints. Mortar the liner in place from inside the house.

VENTILATING ROOF SPACES

If your house has a gable end wall, the roof space can be ventilated by fitting airbricks in the gable. If the house is semi-detached, ask your neighbour to do the same, and fit another airbrick in the party wall to allow air to circulate.

SAFE VENTILATION

There are two very important points to remember concerning ventilation. Firstly, many fuel-burning appliances need an adequate supply of fresh air to work efficiently and safely, so rooms where they are sited must contain provision for this if they are well sealed against natural draughts. Secondly, disused flues must be ventilated at top and bottom; if they are not, condensation can occur within the flue, which may show up as damp patches on the internal chimney walls.

TIP

You may need to install more airbricks in a room where there is a solid concrete hearth (from an old cooking range, say). This can create "dead" areas which may need extra ventilation to prevent rot.

1 Airbricks are the same size as one, two or three bricks. To fit one, start by drilling a series of closely-spaced holes through the joint around a brick.

2 Then use the club (spalling) hammer and a wide bolster (stonecutter's) chisel to cut out the brickwork. With solid walls, drill holes right through and work from inside too.

3 Fit a cavity liner through to the inner wall if the wall is of cavity construction, then trowel a bed of fairly wet mortar on to the bottom of the opening.

4 Butter mortar on to the top of the airbrick and slide in place. Push more mortar into the gaps at the sides. Inside, make good the wall with plaster and cover the opening with a ventilator grille.

5 As an alternative to the traditional terracotta airbrick, fit a two-part plastic version. The sleeves interlock to line the hole as the two parts are pushed together.

6 Slide the outer section into place, and point around it. Slide the inner section into place from the inside of the house. Make good the plaster and fit its cover grille.

OVERCOMING DAMP CONDITIONS

Damp conditions can cause serious problems if allowed to persist in the home, even leading to structural decay, so it is essential to deal with damp as soon as it becomes obvious. The first task is to recognize the type of damp you are faced with: it could be condensation, caused by moisture inside the home, or penetrating or rising damp from outside. In some cases, finding a remedy is relatively straightforward; in others, solving the problem can be complex and costly, and may require the involvement of professionals. If damp conditions are not corrected, they may lead to wet rot or dry rot in structural wooden framing. Both can be a major problem if not tackled quickly, since they weaken the wood with potentially disastrous consequences.

DAMP

This can ruin decorations, destroy floorcoverings, damage walls and plaster, and cause woodwork to rot, so it is important not only to treat the symptoms, but also to track down the causes. These might be rain coming in through the roof or walls, condensation, moisture being absorbed from the ground, or a combination of any of these.

PENETRATING DAMP

This is caused by moisture getting in from the outside, often because of wear and tear to the structure of your home, but it may also affect solid walls that are subjected to strong driving rain. The first sign of penetrating damp appears after a heavy downpour and can occur almost anywhere, although it may be some distance from the actual leak; mould often forms directly behind where the problem lies. Pay particular attention to rainwater systems, which are common causes of penetrating damp.

RISING DAMP

This is caused by water soaking up through floors and walls, and is usually confined to a 1m (3ft) band above ground level. It is a constant problem, even during dry spells.

The main areas to check for rising damp are the damp-proof course (DPC) around the foot of walls, and damp-proof membrane (DPM) in the ground floor. Older properties were often built without either, which can lead to widespread rising damp. If existing

ABOVE: A patch of mould on the inner face of an external wall is usually the first sign of penetrating damp.

ABOVE: Gaps between masonry and woodwork around windows will let in rain, causing patches of damp to occur.

materials have broken down or structural movement has caused defects, there may be isolated, but spreading, patches of damp where water is penetrating. A DPC that is less than 150mm (6in) above ground level will allow rain to splash above it and penetrate the wall, which may cause damp patches at skirting (baseboard) level. If a DPC has been bridged, there will be evidence of damp just above skirting level. A wall cavity filled with rubble may also allow damp to penetrate.

DEALING WITH DAMP

Once the cause of penetrating damp has been traced and repaired, the problem will be eradicated. When the damp patches have dried out, it may be necessary to replaster those areas and make good any decorations.

Dealing with a DPC that has been bridged is quite straightforward. If the ground level is the cause, digging a 150mm (6in) trench along the house wall, then filling it with gravel will allow rainwater to drain away rapidly. When you suspect that debris in the cavity is the cause, removing a few bricks will give access to remove it.

The remedy for rising damp caused by a non-existent or defective DPC or DPM is not so easy; the only solution is to install a replacement or make repairs.

DAMP-PROOFING METHODS

Laying a new damp-proof membrane involves digging up and re-laying the floor slab, which is the most effective method of damp-proofing a concrete floor. However, a floor can also be damp-proofed by applying several coats of moisture-curing urethane, but it is essential that any leaky patches are sealed first with a hydraulic cement.

A third option is to apply two coats of rubberized bitumen emulsion to the old surface, then cover this with a cement/sand screed, which will raise the level of the floor by about 50mm (2in).

Whichever method you choose, the DPM material should be taken up the adjoining walls to meet the DPC, if there is one. The problem of damp floors caused by rising ground-water levels, which typically affects basements, is more serious and requires structural waterproofing or "tanking". This is certainly a job for the professionals.

ABOVE: A damp-proof course should be clear of soil, debris or plants growing up walls, otherwise moisture can bypass it.

INSTALLING A DAMP-PROOF COURSE

There are many ways of installing a damp-proof course, ranging from physical DPCs that are cut into the brickwork to chemical slurries, which are pumped into a series of drilled holes.

In theory, it is possible to do the job yourself, but dealing with rising damp is rarely simple; it is worth seeking the advice of professionals. If there is a mortgage on your home, the lender may require a guarantee of workmanship, which rules out tackling the job yourself. The standard of workmanship is as important as the system used, so choosing a reputable company that offers an insurance-backed guarantee is essential, and often compulsory.

If you do choose to go ahead yourself, you should be able to hire the necessary equipment to install a chemical DPC, and the same company may supply the chemical too.

After installing a DPC, walls and floors can take up to a month for each 25mm (1in) to dry out, while old plaster may be heavily contaminated with salts from rising damp, which will continue to absorb moisture from the air. Delay replastering for as long as possible to allow the walls to dry out.

1 A chemical damp-proof course is injected into a line of holes drilled in the wall about 115mm (4½in) apart.

2 Once injected into the drilled holes, the chemicals overlap to form a continuous impermeable barrier.

3 When the fluid is dry, the drilled holes are filled with mortar and then a rendered surface can be painted.

WATERPROOFING WALLS

The external walls of modern brick houses are built with a cavity between the inner and outer leaves of the wall that effectively prevents damp from reaching the inner leaf. Unless the cavity becomes bridged in some way, there should be no problems with penetrating damp. However, older properties are likely to have been built with solid walls and it is possible that, over time, the masonry may become porous, allowing damp to penetrate to the inside.

Penetrating damp in solid walls is difficult to cure, and one solution, albeit rather drastic, is to build false walls inside, complete with vapour barriers, effectively creating cavity walls. However, this solution is expensive, and it will reduce the size of rooms considerably.

Less expensive is to treat the outer faces of the walls with a water-repellent coating. This will prevent rainwater from soaking into the walls and reaching the interior.

The first job is to clean the walls and make good any structural defects. Wash them down and treat them with a fungicide to kill off any mould. Check the condition of the mortar joints and repoint any that are soft and crumbling; fill cracks in the joints or bricks with mortar or an exterior-grade filler.

When the walls have dried, brush on the water-repellent liquid, following the manufacturer's instructions; you may need to apply more than one coat.

1 Brush, clean, and remove any fungal growth from the wall. Fill any surface cracks so that the surface is sound.

2 Apply the water seal by brush, working from the bottom up, coating the whole wall. If necessary, apply a second coat.

CONDENSATION

When warm, moist air reaches a cold surface, such as a wall exposed to icy winter winds or ceramic tiles, the result is condensation. It is most likely to occur in bathrooms and kitchens where the main activities are bathing, washing and cooking.

Controlling condensation requires a fine balance between good ventilation and adequate heating, but while the modern home is warm, it is also well insulated and draughtproofed, so the level of ventilation is often poor. The key to success is to provide sufficient ventilation, without allowing expensive heat to escape.

Ventilation can be provided by a variety of passive and active means. Passive ventilation may be achieved by opening windows and/or fitting airbricks and simple vents. Active ventilation relies on powered extractor fans.

CONDENSATION OR DAMP?

If you are not sure if a moisture problem is due to condensation or damp, lay a piece of aluminium foil over the patch, seal the edges with adhesive tape and leave it for 48 hours. Condensation will cause beads of moisture to appear on the surface of the foil; penetrating or rising damp will produce beads of moisture underneath the foil.

ABOVE: Water vapour from everyday activities, such as cooking, can cause condensation.

ABOVE: Poor ventilation will make condensation problems worse.

COPING WITH CONDENSATION

Steam from cooking can be removed by a fully vented cooker hood, but where a great deal of steam is produced, when you take a shower for example, the best way to remove it from the room is with an extractor fan.

To be quick and efficient, the fan must be sited properly and it should be the correct size for the room. In a kitchen, a fan must be capable of ten to 15 air changes per hour, and in bathrooms six to eight air changes per hour, which should be increased to 15 to 20 air changes for a power shower. Simply multiply the volume of the room by the number of air changes required and look for a fan that offers the same cubic metre/foot capacity per hour (m³/hr or ft³/hr).

An extractor fan should be installed as high as possible on the wall, and as far as possible from the main source

of ventilation; usually diagonally opposite the main door is ideal.

More widespread condensation can be alleviated with an electric dehumidifier, which draws air from the room, passes it over cold coils to condense it, then collects the drips of water. The dry air is then drawn over heated coils and released back into the room as heat.

RIGHT: A cooker hood removes steam from cooking at source. Beware, however, since some cooker hoods merely recirculate the air, filtering out the particles from cooking, but not the moisture. For this, you must have an extractor hood. Remember, too, that kettles produce steam, as do other forms of cooking that may not be in range of a cooker hood. Consequently, it may be worth adding a window vent or even an additional extractor fan.

DRY ROT

The fungus that causes dry rot loves moist, humid conditions and has a taste for resins and silicones in untreated wood. However, the grey strands are fine enough to penetrate masonry, which means that it can spread rapidly from room to room.

Untreated dry rot will destroy floors, doors and skirtings (baseboards), and infect plaster and ceilings. Initially, it manifests itself as a brownish-red dust, but within days the spores will have developed into a fungus that looks like a mushroom growing upside-down, and it also gives off a distinctive musty smell. This is the final stage of germination, by which time the fungus will be producing millions of spores to infect surrounding areas.

Dealing with dry rot is a job that should be entrusted to a specialist, as it may recur if not treated properly. Make sure you choose a reputable company that offers an insurance-backed guarantee.

PREVENTATIVE ACTION

• Make sure that a damp-proof course (DPC) has not been bridged, by looking for tell-tale signs of damp on walls above skirtings (baseboards).

• Dry rot will not flourish in well-ventilated areas, so make sure there is good ventilation in roofs and under suspended wooden floors. If necessary, fit air vents or extractor fans in soffits and gable end walls.

ABOVE: An example of severe dry rot on a destroyed wooden floor.

ABOVE: A sporophore, or dry rot fungus, on a structural roof timber. Immediate action is necessary as soon as the fungus is spotted to minimize its spread through wooden structures.

ABOVE: Inspect your loft (attic) space and check for the first signs of dry rot. Ensure there is good ventilation in the loft and under the floors to help prevent the conditions in which dry rot can flourish.

WET ROT

This thrives on wet wood and frequently appears where wood is close to the ground or near leaking plumbing, and in woodwork where the protective paint coating has broken down. Skirtings (baseboards) may also be affected where a damp-proof course is defective.

Wet rot can be due to a number of species of fungus, but the most common consist of brown or black strands that appear on the surface, causing the wood to crack and eventually disintegrate. Affected wood tends to look darker than healthy wood and feels spongy.

Once the cause of the damp conditions that have led to the problem is eliminated, wet rot fungus will die. Treat small areas, such as window frames, with proprietary wood hardener solution and insert preservative tablets into holes drilled into the wood to stop any recurrence. Where damage is extensive, the wood should be cut out and replaced.

REPAIRING WET ROT

1 Chisel out all the rotten wood, making sure only sound wood is left.

2 Brush the sound wood with hardener and leave to dry as recommended.

3 To fit wood preservative sticks, drill holes of the correct size in the sound wood. Push the preservative sticks into the drilled holes and below the surface.

4 Fill the damaged area with exterior wood filler. Leave to dry before sanding. Then apply a good paint finish.

INDEX

The publisher would like to thank
the following for supplying pictures:
D.I.Y. Photo Library 8bl, 58t, br;
Simon J. Gilham 57, 61; HSS Hire
Tools 54b, 58bl; Rentokil 54tl, 62t,
bl, br; Thompson's (Ronseal Ltd.,
Thorncliff Park, Chapeltown, Sheffield
S35 2YP, England; tel. (0114) 246
7171; website www.ronseal.co.uk)
1tl, 5bm, 54tr, 59bl, br.

RADICAL CURIOSITY

RADICAL CURIOSITY

QUESTIONING COMMONLY HELD BELIEFS TO IMAGINE FLOURISHING FUTURES

SETH GOLDENBERG

CROWN
NEW YORK

Published in the United States by Crown, an imprint of Random House, a division of Penguin Random House LLC, New York.

CROWN and the Crown colophon are registered trademarks of Penguin Random House LLC.

Library of Congress Cataloging-in-Publication Data
Names: Goldenberg, Seth, author.
Title: Radical curiosity / Seth Goldenberg.
Description: First edition. | New York : Crown, [2022] | Includes bibliographical references.
Identifiers: LCCN 2022000921 (print) | LCCN 2022000922 (ebook) | ISBN 9780593138175 (hardcover) | ISBN 9780593138182 (ebook)
Subjects: LCSH: Curiosity. | Problem solving. | Creative thinking.
Classification: LCC BF323.C8 G65 2022 (print) | LCC BF323.C8 (ebook) | DDC 155.2—dc23/eng/20220308
LC record available at https://lccn.loc.gov/2022000921
LC ebook record available at https://lccn.loc.gov/2022000922

PRINTED IN THE UNITED STATES OF AMERICA ON ACID-FREE PAPER

crownpublishing.com

1st Printing

First Edition

Book design by Sarah Rabinovich, Daria Nikolaeva, Shaylin Wallace, and Tamara Grusin
Photo credits: p. 98: MPI/Stringer via Getty Images; p. 100: image courtesy of the Library of Congress; p. 103: (top) photo by Lukas Meier on Unsplash, (middle) photo by Terence Burke on Unsplash, (bottom) photo by History in HD on Unsplash

This book is dedicated to my family, partners in living a life filled with curiosity. For Liz Newton, who has shown me support beyond measure and embraced blending our private and public selves in a multi-decade salon, and who has committed to making imagination the single most important value of our home—a beautiful principle that has led to Eli's cohesive empathy and Lucy's zest for aliveness. This book is for you: Eli and Lucy. Inspired by Hannah Arendt's notion that *deciding whether we love our children enough not to expel them from our world and leave them to their own devices . . . but to prepare them in advance for the task of renewing a common world;* it is my sincere hope that this book helps you prepare for the task ahead.

CONTENTS

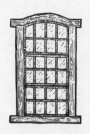

FRAMING

Curiosity Is
an Endangered
Species

On October 4, 2021, the tenth anniversary of Steve Jobs's passing, Jony Ive penned a moving op-ed in *The Wall Street Journal* commemorating his friend. As Apple's chief design officer, Ive enjoyed a special relationship with Jobs: an intimate collaboration rooted in mutual admiration of the creative process. He revealed what he believed to be his defining characteristic: *curiosity*.

> *He was without doubt the most inquisitive human I have ever met. His insatiable curiosity was not limited or distracted by his knowledge or expertise, nor was it casual or passive. It was ferocious, energetic and restless. His curiosity was practiced with intention and rigor. Many of us have an innate predisposition to be curious. I believe that after a traditional education, or working in an environment with many people, curiosity is a decision requiring intent and discipline.*

Ive elegantly articulates a portrait of Steve Jobs embodying what it means to live an intentional, rigorous life of curiosity. Such a life is characterized by an insatiable desire to interrogate the unknown. Ive continued:

> *In larger groups our conversations gravitate towards the tangible, the measurable. It is more comfortable, far easier and more socially acceptable talking about what is known. Being curious and exploring tentative ideas were far more important to Steve than being socially acceptable. Our curiosity begs that we learn. And for Steve, wanting to learn was far more important than wanting to be right.*

Society is deeply uncomfortable with curiosity as a way of living, leading, and doing daily business. Yet, ironically, curiosity is the fuel to transformative leadership and value creation.

Our modern world has been inadvertently designed to eradicate curiosity. And at a time when every sector of business and social system comprising society is facing existential challenges, the potential extinction of curiosity is an emergency. We need questions now more than ever.

Society has trained itself to move swiftly toward solutions. So fast, that too often we leap straight into answers before knowing the questions. We skate on the surface, misdiagnosing problems, assuming that every nail needs the same hammer. We are seduced by quick fixes, which somehow reassure us that we've done something, anything. The fact that a transaction has occurred becomes more important than whether the transaction yields positive impact. These transactions have become the heartbeat of a marketplace that values doing more than thinking. We've designed an economy that rewards the mere swing of the hammer. Even if we miss.

The Croatian Austrian philosopher Ivan Illich described this phenomenon fifty years ago in his book *Deschooling Society*. In it he proposes that we have conflated the act of doing with the outcome itself:

> *They school [students and citizens] to confuse process and substance. Once these become blurred, a new logic is assumed: the more treatment there is, the better are the results; or, escalation leads to success. The pupil is thereby "schooled" to confuse teaching with learning, grade advancement with education, a diploma with competence, and fluency with the ability to say something new. His imagination is "schooled" to accept service in place of value. Medical treatment is mistaken for health care, social work for the improvement of community life, police protection for safety, military poise for national security, the rat race for productive work.*

These insights are even more relevant today than when they were articulated half a century ago. Today, it may not merely be that we confuse process with substance; rather, our failure to question our processes or interrogate our actions may be symptomatic of a more significant concern: Curiosity is an endangered species.

The extinction of curiosity stifles our imaginations, paralyzing our ability to author better futures.

Without a robust culture of curiosity, imagination is rendered impotent, and all we're doing is surviving the day, administering transactions, on autopilot, surrendering our agency, and perpetuating an ineffective status quo. We become managers of the end state of a problem-solution continuum. Our roles become reduced to administrators of predetermined solutions rather than interrogators of the unknown. Consuming the choices that others have made for us, relinquishing our right to be the author of our own story. We assert agency over our future only when we challenge what is known.

Challenging what was regarded as wisdom by those before us forces us to develop a deep appreciation of existing knowledge while simultaneously revealing potential gaps or faults in the prevailing thinking. The identification of these faults and the creation of novel bridges to traverse those gaps is the invention of new knowledge. We contribute to the story of the future by updating the collective wisdom enshrined in previous chapters. The combination of inquiry and invention is the culture of curiosity that has become endangered, on the verge of extinction. And this costs us dearly, both as individuals and as a society.

We live within constraints we cannot see, rejoicing in outcomes we believe we have greater influence over than we really do. We fail to realize that we have drifted far downstream from the origin of inquiry, limiting the potential impact we aspire to create.

In fact, we've come to embrace this limited domain with great pride. In casual conversation, we hear platitudes like "Ideas are a dime a dozen." A "bias for action" or a reputation for being an "action-oriented leader" is worn like a badge of honor. These are all indications of how society has come to devalue questioning and overvalue doing.

Over the course of the twentieth century, knowledge has become hyper segregated, specialized, industrialized, and routinized. Success came to be associated with production, turning the process of thinking into a transactional activity, valuable only insofar as it enabled the production of commodified answers.

Leadership came to mean managing a vast inventory of predetermined solutions that could be deployed toward repeated, recognizable problems. Problem-solving has become reduced to a form of administration that involves merely choosing from a portfolio of prescriptions. **Operationalizing solutions is now more important than authoring new wisdom.** It is telling that the graduate-level business degree is called a master's in business *administration*. The problem is that administering blueprint solutions from past challenges naively underestimates the complexity of today's world. And it leaves us ill-equipped to address today's challenges. Many that we've never seen before or that return us to essential human-condition issues that have evaded us for centuries.

As the world has become more complex, singular-solution frameworks no longer suffice. Today's challenges require interdisciplinary approaches, diverse perspectives, and the ability to remix existing knowledge into new cocktails fit for the occasion. As activist poet Audre Lorde reminds us:

There is no such thing as a single-issue struggle, because we do not live single-issue lives.

The types of problems we face can no longer be satisfied with familiar answers; they demand the original thinking that begins with asking essential questions. The blueprints of the past are artifacts of the thinking that created the very problems we seek to confront. We need to discard these outdated models that no longer serve us.

When curiosity is translated into an inquiry-based methodology it has the power to transform the way we live. We have amazing tools at our fingertips. But the crises of our time are not commercial, technological, or scientific; they are fundamentally humanistic. We need an inquiry into the assumptions and the inherited design of the modern human experience. How will we live, learn, work, play, and sustain ourselves in the twenty-first century?

When did we surrender our claim on original thinking? When did we become disinterested in generating new knowledge? Can we pull curiosity back from the brink of extinction?

I believe that we can. But to save curiosity from extinction will require that we adopt an appetite for not just questioning but *radical* questioning.

The word "radical" was borrowed in the fourteenth century from the Latin *radicalis,* meaning "root." Radical questioning is necessary because it is the roots, the essential foundations, of today's problems that need to be excavated and interrogated. The more fundamental the question, the more fertile the ground for imagining. We spend too much time on the surface, scurrying like frantic mice from one transaction to the next and avoiding the deeper questions. We need to bravely embrace the inquiries that have the potential to reorient, rehabilitate, and regenerate the complex challenges that we are confronted with. Our contemporary moment is ripe with opportunities to reimagine our world. Today we are witnessing existential disruptions to legacy narratives that shape our society. The inherited stories, social codes, and historical models about everything from gender to social justice to money to our relationship with the natural world are being challenged.

We are living during *in-between times*. Between models of how we see ourselves, what we believe in, and how we agree to realize these values in practice. In politics, the term *interregnum* is defined as a period between two successive regimes, a lapse or pause in a series. Often viewed as a period juxtaposed between two different ideologies, this kind of interregnum is quite palpable, marked by milestones of changes in governance seen more clearly in the hindsight of history. Today, we are living in a more abstract—but no less significant—type of interregnum: one that is *cultural*, rather than political.

Society is stitched together through a shared code for what we believe and how those beliefs translate to the way we live. In the same way that the operating system of our computers dictates the basic functions it performs, culture is a kind of operating system that dictates how society functions. A set of rules, normative behaviors, and collectively accepted values encoded through millions of micro-agreements that keep the system running.

A cultural interregnum is a transition between fundamentally different sets of values catalyzing an evolution in shared frameworks of the human experience. During a cultural interregnum, ideas from the past decline, as we question the legacy narratives and, in turn, the norms, beliefs, and mindsets that we inherited from preceding generations. Simultaneously, we witness meaningful and diverse experimentation with new and emerging ideas that challenge some of our most deeply held core beliefs about ourselves, about business, about culture, and indeed about what it means to be human. In business, we often refer to this as disruptive innovation. But these disruptive innovations may be better understood as radically curious entrepreneurs contributing their part to a cultural operating system upgrade within a time of cultural interregnum.

"Legacy narratives" have a stronghold over the public imagination. They carry entrenched traditions and associated messages that reinforce the narrative, power structures, and signals anchoring our self-identities. By contrast, "challenger narratives" are newborn ideas that are still learning to crawl. Their journey into the public imagination is slower and rockier, but they will eventually replace legacy narratives as the predominant reality. This dynamic creates friction between prevailing ideas, and like a race with many cars, at different moments each idea has a moment in the lead.

The cultural interregnum is the messy middle space in which both legacy narratives and challenger narratives exist simultaneously. Friction, uncertainty, and growing pains are felt because so many facets of society are changing—but not at the same rate.

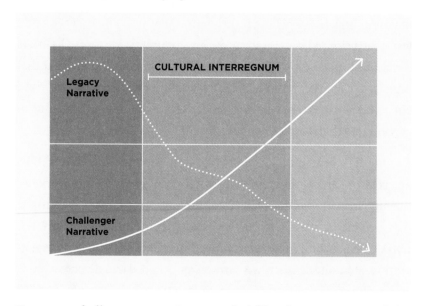

To many, challenger narratives can feel like they came out of the blue, when in fact seeds of these new beliefs have likely been germinating for some time. The speed at which they can scale, however, is a testament to the power of movements—and of those who challenge the social systems that are no longer relevant to enough of us. Too often, legacy narratives serve only a small group of people who possess power or, at their most destructive, actively disempower certain groups, populations, or ways of being in the world. When social systems fail to truly serve vast numbers of people and communities, that is when we see challenger narratives begin to emerge.

Certainly, we are seeing this today. Movements such as Black Lives Matter advocate for a new narrative on race. The transgender equality movement advocates for a new narrative on gender identity. Greta Thunberg's Fridays for Future movement advocates for a new narrative on climate. These movements are the messy processes that deconstruct legacy narratives and rebuild them anew. These examples also demonstrate that for a challenger narrative to truly take hold, the new ideas must gain awareness in the public sphere. The more widespread the awareness, the stronger the challenger narrative becomes.

Radical Curiosity questions commonly held beliefs to imagine flourishing futures. To be radically curious is to challenge the narratives inherited from the past and author new stories that reflect who we are and what we value today. It is to recognize when our collective wisdom, like any outdated technology, needs an operating system upgrade.

FIVE PILLARS OF RADICAL CURIOSITY

Radical Curiosity is a leadership practice: one that can be applied in our own lives, in the businesses and organizations where we work, and in the communities and institutions that sustain public life. It's a practice that creates the conditions for resilient value creation across sectors and domains.

LEARNING BY QUESTIONING
Radical Curiosity requires that we approach the world critically, rather than passively. It compels us to question the ways in which

power operates, often invisibly, rather than accepting the power structures that the world has presented to us. Radical Curiosity empowers us to challenge inherited realities and seek new ways to engage people through dialogue. Radical Curiosity is fueled by awe—rather than fear—of the unknown. In these ways, Radical Curiosity begins with asking better questions. **Radical Curiosity is the greatest expression of what it means to be a teacher and a learner, for whom living is synonymous with discovering new knowledge.**

CHALLENGING COMMONLY HELD BELIEFS

Radical Curiosity calibrates the evolving story of the human experience. It demands challenging the assumptions of our wisdom, rather than accepting tradition and convention as unquestionable. This is an act of philosophy, a love of knowledge. Often commonly held beliefs are so common that they are camouflaged. Identifying a commonly held belief, peeling back the assumptions it is built upon, and restlessly seeking interventions and leverage points for greater impact is the life cycle of a challenger. People who are Radically Curious are ferociously hungry in their pursuit of knowledge, not as a fixed resource but as an ongoing process. **Radical Curiosity is the greatest expression of what it means to be a philosopher: an engaged thinker dedicated to the reconstruction of new knowledge.**

RIGOROUS IMAGINING

Radical Curiosity catalyzes the invention of new realities. World-building begins with ideas. Ideas are expressions of our imaginations. We have underinvested in imagination, reduced it to a mere paint by numbers. We take the profound power of conjuring new expressions, interpretations, and constructed worlds for granted. Imagining is a rigorous discipline. Imagination is our greatest national resource, one that drives value creation across the sciences, the humanities, the arts, and business. All compelling entrepreneurial ventures, transformative social movements, and technological breakthroughs begin with an inspired sense of possibility. **Radical Curiosity is the greatest expression of what it means to be an artist and a designer: being willing to leverage the full range of our senses to author new worlds.**

FLOURISHING LIVING SYSTEMS

Radical Curiosity requires a wider definition of well-being. In an interdependent world, there can be no well-being without justice. Ethics are a key indicator of a population's health. Racism and inequity are public health issues. Do no harm is no longer enough. The moment calls for not merely a sustainable future but a regenerative future in which living systems, human and nonhuman, are flourishing. A sustained state is not an acceptable aim. Thriving ecological systems are essential to human survival. To improve our broken social systems, we must be stewards of a moral marketplace in which value is derived from our values. **Radical Curiosity is the greatest expression of what it means to be an activist, an environmentalist, and an economist. It is a practice that must be permitted to permeate our institutions, our behaviors, and our metrics.**

OPTIMISTIC FUTURES

Radical Curiosity is built upon an optimism that the extraordinary is possible. Optimism is a political disposition and a design sensibility. The future is not a single stream, defined by a single author or limited linear dichotomies. The future is plural. Many diverse possibilities are entangled by the complexity of interconnected conditions. Radical Curiosity is what allows us to experience the joy and the wonder of bringing absurd impossibilities to fruition. These are radical acts of optimism. We can aspire to achieve the moonshots, design the social utopias, adopt the ideals, and pursue those audacious visions that enable us to create resilient value for people and the planet. **Radical Curiosity is the greatest expression of what it means to be an entrepreneur, a futurist, and a leader: willing to raise the bar of our ambitions and expectations. It is an antidote to the apathy that leaves us content with how things are and emboldens us to ask what they might become.**

FIRST PRINCIPLES

The concept of "first principles" can be traced back to Aristotle, who defined a first principle as "the first basis from which a thing is known." A first principle is an essential assumption about an idea, a problem, or a situation: an integer that cannot be deconstructed any further. As building blocks of knowledge, they are the equivalent of a prime number in mathematics or an element in a periodic table.

Deconstructing ideas to get to their root, their fundamental core, is a practice that is quite familiar to design thinkers. Typically, first-principles thinking is applied to innovation, often in conjunction with mathematics, engineering, and systems design. Elon Musk, one of the most innovative minds of our generation, speaks frequently about his respect for first-principles thinking. He offers:

I think people's thinking process is too bound by convention or analogy to prior experiences. It's rare that people try to think of something on a first principles basis. They'll say, "We'll do that because it's always been done that way." Or they'll not do it because "Well, nobody's ever done that, so it must not be good." But that's just a ridiculous way to think. You have to build up the reasoning from the ground up—"from the first principles" is the phrase that's used in physics. You look at the fundamentals and construct your reasoning from that, and then you see if you have a conclusion that works or doesn't work, and it may or may not be different from what people have done in the past.

Elon Musk's appreciation for this kind of thinking is not an anomaly or outlier. Across a diverse range of industries and cultures, some of our most celebrated icons have a long tradition of breaking things down to their elements and recombining them in new ways to unlock more value. It is the premise of everything from molecular gastronomy, an innovative method of cooking that breaks ingredients down to their essential physical and chemical components, to jazz, which at its origins broke down classical musical structures to enable spontaneity and improvisation.

Radical Curiosity begins with first-principles thinking. It requires breaking down ideas, assumptions, and narratives to their most essential components and then reconstructing them anew. Practitioners of Radical Curiosity deconstruct tradition into building blocks that can be bent, manipulated, and remixed into new combinations. Due to the remixing of the best elements across diverse domains it can become difficult to classify these interdisciplinary blended practices. Pioneers build new lexicons, at first unrecognizable to audiences, and as they codify and mature their practices, they become new genres. Consider jazz, which literally deconstructed sounds, borrowed from diverse genres of music, and recombined them to build an altogether new vocabulary. There is no greater deconstruction and reconstruction than the creative instincts of Miles Davis. His Radical Curiosity was recognized in his *New York Times* obituary:

> *Mr. Davis never settled into one style; every few years he created a new lineup and format for his groups. . . . Mr. Davis came of age in the bebop era; many successive styles—cool jazz, hard-bop, modal jazz, jazz-rock, jazz-funk—were sparked or ratified by his example. Throughout his career he was grounded in the blues, but he also drew on pop, flamenco, classical music, rock, Arab music and Indian music.*

Miles Davis deconstructed genres of music to create a new kind of sound. Elon Musk deconstructs the laws of physics to build a new kind of car battery. José Andrés deconstructs food to create a molecular gastronomy. For the Radically Curious, this ambiguity is not a complication to be avoided or managed; it is where the value lies.

What if we applied this essential questioning process to the most challenging social systems issues of our time? What if we understood the opportunity that "radical" represents as not only the process of inquiry but also the permission to shift the very *subject* of the inquiry? Could Radical Curiosity enable us to take on the most essential questions that have challenged us for centuries?

All around us, traditions are being upended and legacy narratives are being rewritten by challenger narratives. Many of our beliefs, stories, and social structures remain outdated. We can do more if we ask more of ourselves. To ask more of ourselves is to embrace Radical Curiosity as a way of being, and to invite more imagination into our lives. It's time to ask the uncomfortable questions. The deep, essential questions. The quietly intimate questions. The questions that get at the roots of the matter. The questions that catalyze new knowledge, rather than merely facilitate the transfer of existing knowledge. Only by relentlessly questioning our past and present can we begin to imagine and build a flourishing future. That practice of inquiry is what I have built my life upon—and it is also what this book is built upon.

This book identifies seven themes central to the practice of Radical Curiosity, each one revolving around a narrative that is going through significant transformation. How we think about learning, cohesion, time, youth, aliveness, nature, and value is being upended. The legacy frameworks that have defined these core human conditions are giving way to new, emerging narratives. This book is a collection of essays delivered as observations, questions, personal stories, cultural critiques, and case studies meant to reveal a philosophy of Radical Curiosity.

The book is structured as thirty micro-chapters—what I call modules—that can be read individually as stand-alone essays, or contiguously from start to finish. Whether consumed in bite-sized portions or as a full meal, this book is meant to impart and inspire a new way of thinking. The insights, reflections, and questions found in these modules stem from a lifetime of challenging commonly held beliefs and more than twenty years collaborating with extraordinarily talented challengers across geographies, institutions, and sectors.

It is my sincere hope that this book nourishes your curiosity, stretches your imagination, and introduces you to bold new voices and ideas to inspire your life and work.

LEARNING

Limited Exposure to Diverse Experiences

How much can we know of the world without seeing it? How can we appreciate the many diverse ways of thinking and being in the world without experiencing them? How can we expand our worldview beyond the narrow limits of our own experience without exposure? What do we really mean by diversity?

The more we know, the more we realize we don't know. Learning and humility are kissing cousins. Humility is a celebration of the awareness that you are a part of something much greater than yourself. Holding this form of humility as a present sensibility calibrates an engagement with the world as interconnected. Through humility, we see ourselves in relationship to other forces. An ecology of relationships. Human to human. Human to nature. Living systems, constantly in motion.

Learned humility comes from living. From the front-row seat. From being exposed to the awe-inspiring vastness and complexity of experiencing the world, of experiencing ourselves. There is no shortcut. There are no CliffsNotes that can accurately translate the phenomenon of humility. Humility isn't taught in a tenth-grade textbook. To truly digest learned humility, to let it shower over us, requires lived knowledge. There is a vast difference between informational knowledge and experiential knowledge. Experiential knowledge is a multisensory witnessing rather than a Scantron-tested commodification of information. As the legendary Maya Angelou says:

I've learned that people will forget what you said, people will forget what you did, but people will never forget how you made them feel.

Experiences are profound instructors. Exposure exponentially increases our comprehension of the forces at play in the world, increases the lexicon available to us for what the world can become, and increases our capacity to imagine how we may inhabit that world.

Living through the language of experiential knowledge gives us the confidence to not fear the opacity of the unknown. Exposing ourselves to diverse environments, situations, and untrained arenas converts the unknown from friction to adventure, welcoming the invitation for us to be changed along the way. By extending our geographic radius, we extend the radius of our worldview. With every mile we travel, we overturn our assumptions and question the false constraints holding us back. These are the seeds of transformative learning. The real world is a better classroom than the artificial environment we have come to call classroom.

Over the past fifty years, advances in engineering and technology have afforded us extraordinary capacity to extend our personal radius. To travel, both literally and metaphorically. Yet, the majority of us rarely travel far from what we know. We spend lifetimes within places, institutions, and cultures—in the real world and online—that reinforce our own worldviews, not expand them. We don't genuinely have exposure to what the rest of the world believes or practices. The world is exponentially more diverse than we know. Travel, in this context, is not about luxury. Travel as a form of exposure becomes the most significant form of learning because it is the primary source of lived knowledge.

Anthony Bourdain, tragic hero of *Parts Unknown*, said:

> *If I'm an advocate for anything, it's to move. As far as you can, as much as you can. Across the ocean, or simply across the river. Walk in someone else's shoes or at least eat their food. It's a plus for everybody.*

In 2019, 37.79 million Americans—11 percent of the total U.S. population—traveled abroad. And this statistic does not reflect how far out of their familiar comfort zone the 37.79 million traveled to. Consider this for a moment. This means that, roughly, only one out of every ten Americans left their country that year. Certainly, international travel can be expensive, so there is an economic burden to the accessibility of travel. But what is the cultural burden of 90 per-

Total U.S. population in 2019: **329.5M**

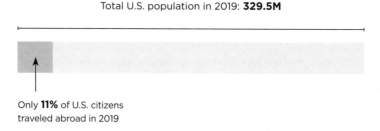

Only **11%** of U.S. citizens
traveled abroad in 2019

cent of a nation not leaving its own narrative? What might this mean to communities dangerously perpetuating echo chambers because of limited exposure to diverse experiences?

Miguel de Unamuno, the author of *Tragic Sense of Life* and a rector of the University of Salamanca, the third-oldest university still operating today, famously proposed:

Fascism is cured by reading, and racism is cured by traveling.

Unamuno didn't mean traveling to a far-flung location only to visit an all-inclusive Sandals resort. He was referring to the kind of travel that expands our radius and delivers a learned humility that can only come from seeing beyond ourselves. When we travel, when we move beyond what we know, we increase the scope of what we conceive as possible. The more time we spend in the unknown, the more we appreciate that anything is possible. Our curiosity is strengthened proportionally. Conversely, when we limit our exposure to diverse ways of being in the world, curiosity narrows.

How can we be curious about the many ways to be in the world if we are unaware of their existence? Such a paradox of awareness is elegantly described by Ursula K. Le Guin, the science fiction writer and thought leader who proposed:

> We will not know our own injustice if we cannot imagine justice. We will not be free if we do not imagine freedom. We cannot demand that anyone try to attain justice and freedom who has not had a chance to imagine them as attainable.

When I was growing up in the rural Adirondacks, my father, a lover of photography, cherished books that showed us the world. And none was more precious than his copy of *The Family of Man*, which catalogues an ambitious project curated by the prolific photographer

Edward Steichen at the Modern Museum of Art in 1955. Steichen's vision was an expression of humanism; he believed that by seeing people from around the world in their most essential elements, we could begin visualizing the universal human experience that connects us. One of the earliest forms of crowdsourcing and co-authoring, and a major artistic endeavor, the exhibition featured 503 photos from 68 countries: the work of 273 photographers. Dorothea Lange, the legendary photojournalist who documented and humanized the Great Depression, helped Steichen recruit photographers in a letter called "A Summons to Photographers All Over the World," in which she invited them to

> show Man to Man across the world. Here we hope to reveal by visual images Man's dreams and aspirations, his strength, his despair under evil. If photography can bring these things to life, this exhibition will be created in a spirit of passionate and devoted faith in Man. Nothing short of that will do.

I was a child tethered to a place I had no agency to leave, and this book offered an invitation to extend my radius of exposure. *The Family of Man* acted as a profound radius extension. One that transported me and my curiosity for the human experience beyond the limits of physical geography, through photographs that became windows and portals into unfamiliar worlds. I suspect that longing for an experience beyond ourselves is in large part what led to the record-breaking attendance of the traveling exhibition, which was viewed by more than 9 million people in thirty-seven countries over six continents. Aren't we all in search of windows that allow us to safely peer into worlds that feel fresh and new, as if we know in our hearts that there is more? Even if our feet remain anchored in place, our minds know not to respect the tidy boundaries imposed upon us.

More than sixty years later, in the great tradition of *The Family of Man*, Romanian photographer Mihaela Noroc created *The Atlas of Beauty*. At the age of twenty-seven, Noroc "decided to quit my ordinary life in Bucharest and put all my efforts and savings into travel and photography." Over the next four years she would traverse more than fifty countries, photographing women from around the world. In an interview by NPR, Noroc was asked, "We are inundated by images of beauty on social media and in advertising in magazines. From your book, what can we learn about how other cultures view beauty?" Noroc offered:

> *The [other] cultures are also getting influenced by our Western way of seeing beauty. You see, in Asia and Africa, whitening products to lighten their skin. We have to start from early age with children to show them that people are very different but very beautiful in their own way.*

What's striking about *The Atlas of Beauty* is how it documents the diverse ways to interpret a central feature of the human condition: the notion of beauty. Through portraits of women from Ethiopia to Nepal to North Korea—women with lost limbs and tattooed bodies,

RADIUS OF EXPOSURE

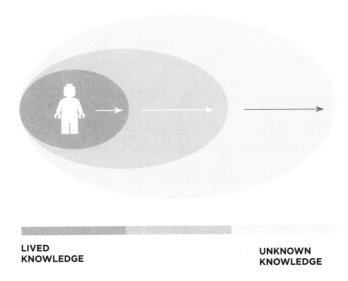

LIVED
KNOWLEDGE

UNKNOWN
KNOWLEDGE

dressed in everything from military uniforms to ceremonial garb—we see how vast the definition of beauty is. In seeing such an expanse, we are reminded of how small our own interpretation may be. How limiting our personal stories can be without the travel of our imaginations to see the stories of others.

Chimamanda Ngozi Adichie, the Nigerian writer and 2008 recipient of a MacArthur Foundation "genius grant," offers a poignant observation about the flattening of the world in her aptly titled landmark TED Talk "Dangers of a Single Story":

I recently spoke at a university where a student told me it was such a shame that Nigerian men were physical abusers like the father character in my novel. I told him that I had recently read a novel called American Psycho, *and that it was a shame that young Americans were serial murderers.*

We know so little of each other. And too often, we don't know what we don't know. Our exposure to the many ways of being in our world is more limited than we realize, which forms a relevant undercurrent to the diversity, equity, and inclusion issues playing out in corporate, governmental, and political landscapes today.

Business leaders have recently prioritized DEI, making it a masthead of strategic plans and organizational redesign. Certainly, we want more diverse and inclusive companies. And we want an economy that is more accessible and equitable and that breaks economic barriers. But why do we seek diversity in the first place? Are we engaging with the essential questions as to why? Pairing the actions that roll out corporate policies with the intellectual inquiry as to what the meaning of these practices is? Have we, as leaders and organizations, slowed down to unpack and articulate a deeper context for the desire for diversity? Are we compelled by social justice to right historical wrongs? Are we compelled to rebuild communities and organizations of trust to not alienate one another? But, as Bayo Akomolafe, the Nigerian thought leader, would propose, are we also ready to acknowledge that the way we respond to the crisis is often part of the crisis?

Have we systematically institutionalized the danger Adichie spoke about: the danger of a single story? We, too often, live within a monocultural narrative that has shrunk our radius of exposure, limiting our capacity to identify, embrace, and translate diverse knowledge.

Without an appetite for curiosity, we fail to capture our greatest engine of value creation: the extraordinary and infinite wisdom of the human experience. Wisdom is perhaps the most critical and untapped source of innovation. What we need most is not new patents, more sophisticated artificial intelligence, or deeper-pocketed venture capital committees. What we do need is to deeply listen to the wisdom beyond our familiar world in order to welcome a more holistic, comprehensive, and unfamiliar collection of voices often written out of popular Western canons.

The late Chief Dan George, who was a leader of the Tsleil-Waututh Nation, is one such voice. In his 1972 essay "Brotherhood and Understanding," he wrote:

I know that my white brother does many things well, but I wonder if he has ever really learned how to love. Perhaps he loves the things that are his own but has never learned to love the things outside and beyond him.

We must learn to love the things outside and beyond ourselves. This is a learned humility that comes only from exposure. The distance we travel expands our worldview. Exposing ourselves to new experiences diversifies our lived knowledge, leading to the retiring of assumptions and the birthing of new beliefs. We must remake learning as an activity of exposure to the infinitely diverse worlds that exist so we may not reside in the danger of a single story. Diversity is not merely a corporate policy, it is a prerequisite to surviving the twenty-first century.

2

Education Is Too Big to Fail, but Maybe It Should

Compulsory education is a policy that requires school attendance by law. But what is education for? The purpose of education has held different narratives throughout history. Is it preparing young people to join the contemporary conversation the world is engaged in? Or merely to join the workforce as skilled laborers? Why and how might we learn throughout our lives, long past the period of the compulsory? Why sit in a classroom at all?

The concept of *too big to fail* became a part of the popular lexicon during the 2008 financial crisis, commonly referred to as the Great Recession. It is a theory in banking and finance that proposes that certain corporations are so large and so interconnected that their failure would be disastrous to the greater economic system. Even with billions in federal bailout resources to stabilize the interdependent systems, the damage was exponential. According to the U.S. Bureau of Labor Statistics, the United States shed more than 8.7 million jobs as a result of the Great Recession, and according to the U.S. Department of the Treasury, American households lost roughly $19 trillion of net worth. In hindsight, *too big to fail* lost support from leading economists. The average American was upended by an underregulated, unethical, and at times illegal manipulation of finance tools and metrics to boost short-term profitability.

But *too big to fail* as a framework for leadership and decision-making has implications far beyond economic theory. A governance system that accepts and advocates for *too big to fail* is prioritizing stability over ethics, the few over the many, the bliss of ignorance over the hard work of rebuilding stronger systems. How frequently do we embrace Band-Aids, temporary treatment, and other inadequate solutions in lieu of doing the real work of addressing the core foundational flaws of our social systems? Do we know how to redesign our social systems? An overwhelming task indeed, but how long will we kick the proverbial can down the road, accepting inefficiencies, errors, underperformance, or even harm?

Might we consider that social systems other than banking have achieved a *too big to fail* status? Education is such a system. No longer effective or thriving, it is *too big to fail*—but maybe it should. Let us understand the education system as an industry. The United States spends more than $2 trillion annually on K–12, higher education, and professional development combined. A business so large that it exceeds the combined GDPs of Switzerland, Saudi Arabia, and the Netherlands. If the American education system was a country, it would be the sixteenth-largest GDP in the world, larger than 150+ other countries globally.

For such a large economy, it is oddly unsure of its purpose—even in conflict with itself. As is the case with so many of our inherited legacies, we participate in this enormous social system yet remain unfamiliar with its history, naive to the conflicting values at play, and disengaged from the cultural battle for its future.

When educators debate the purpose of education, a consistent dichotomy is on display. Is the purpose of education to *prepare a workforce* (that is, the production economy is the primary narrative), or is the purpose of education to *nurture critical thinking* (the participation in advancing society is the primary narrative)? It is as though a student can identify with either the story of capitalism or that of civic enlightenment, but never both. The dichotomy reveals a giant gap between the value of thinking and the value of skilled labor in a production-oriented economy. There are countless signals telling us that work in the form of labor is serious, while thinking is frivolous. The enterprise of thinking exists outside the economy. As though work is responsible and thinking is irresponsible. The education system today masquerades as "higher learning," but in reality it is largely vocational training.

Education is a pipeline for young people to enter the economy, rather than their lives or the conversation the world is engaged in.

In large part this is because education, like most social systems, is slow to adapt, iterate, and evolve to be relevant for changing times. The glacial pace of change of the education system cannot match the agility of the real world, where a single moment can rewrite and reorganize its foundations. During a cultural interregnum it can feel like it takes a painfully long time for social systems to catch up with the broader values of the times, often running decades of delay. This lag of slow motion, often followed by a slingshot acceleration, can cause confusion. The lag holds conflicting messages, simultaneously crossing declining legacy narratives and rising challenger narratives.

Consider, for example, the disconnect between formal institutions of education and the frictionless integration of learning that is present in our daily contemporary lives. Enhanced by private-sector investment in the digital and experience economies, we now live in a world in which Apple has democratized advanced creative authorship tools, Nike has enabled a new generation of health advocates with personal dashboards to see our bodies, Google has compressed the world's libraries of information and a real-time responsive atlas of global geography, and Netflix has ignited an edutainment renaissance by diversifying storytelling, documentaries, and global cultural content that extend our radius of exposure in ways our parents never dreamed of.

Why do we sit in a classroom at all? Why do we remove ourselves from the extraordinarily rich experience tapestries of living to place ourselves in artificial containers of instruction?

To make sense of these in-between times, it is critical to look back in history. In 2017, the website Inside Higher Ed published an essay titled "11 Lessons from the History of Higher Education," in which we are reminded:

During the nineteenth century, an older form of pedagogy, emphasizing recitation and memorization (and corporal punishment and shaming) gave way to an approach centered squarely on lectures. Around the same time, the faculty role evolved, as the faculty role became increasingly specialized, professionalized, and departmentalized. A particular mindset also overtook the academy—a set of attitudes well-suited to the Industrial era. It involved a "mass production," "one-size-fits-all" paradigm, which assumed that all students should acquire the same information at the same pace, and a "transmission" model of instruction, in which a content expert delivered a body of information to passive students. This was accompanied by an increasing reliance on standardized tests and a sink-or-swim mentality in which the role of grading was to rank students.

Why is it that in the third decade of the twenty-first century we still largely adhere to nineteenth-century pedagogy? Why does it take so long for our education system to catch up to contemporary models of living? While the routinization, memorization, and hyper specialization of knowledge may have served its purpose in the past, today's landscape requires a new relationship with learning based upon a fundamentally different view of the nature of knowledge. The mass production of education is further critiqued by the Brazilian education activist Paulo Freire, who describes it as a "banking model": a method in which the teacher has the knowledge, and thus power, and their role is to deposit knowledge into students, who are like empty vessels or savings accounts. In the worst of these conditions, knowledge is wielded as a tool of power through which education systems can actively oppress entire populations, preventing the awareness of their own agency in their lives.

Curiosity cannot be cultivated inside cultures that treat knowledge exclusively as a static object in which engagement with thinking is positioned as the banking of information. Human beings are not savings accounts, they are originators of value creation—one of the key attributes of curiosity.

Consider the overt factory overtones of schooling in America. The vast majority of public schools have been built as brick temples to industrial-age ideals. They are factories for learning synchronized through intervals or class periods resembling shifts on an assembly line. Architecturally and culturally, they even exhibit features reminiscent of coerced labor or imprisonment—students are punished if they are not in their place when their shift begins or if they leave the building before the final bell at the end of the day.

The irony of this emphasis on production is that it is contradictory to the origins of the notion of school. The word "school" derives from the Greek *scholē,* originally meaning "leisure."

We tend to have fleeting, goldfish-like memories when it comes to our history, our origins. Often our histories are too painful to confront. Or we are so absorbed in living our own lives we can only see an arm's-length distance outside our radius of exposure. Yet our present experience is anchored by legacy narratives. Our past is a silent investment partner in our future. Our ability to contribute to the next emergent chapter in our story is dependent on our ability to distinguish between resilient wisdom and situational practices that are no longer relevant. More frequently than we are willing to acknowledge, commonly held beliefs are born from conditions specific to their time. The conditions that give rise to those beliefs evolve more quickly than the beliefs themselves. Commonly held beliefs can cast long shadows over those situational conditions that no longer exist. Radical Curiosity turns a lens of critical inquiry toward these conditions to examine the governing constraints that remain unquestioned.

Applying this inquiry to education returns us to the provocative, lesser-known tradition of school as leisure. It might be more accurate to articulate the dichotomy in the purpose of education as more akin to the notions of "labor" and "leisure." Looking back in history, we can see a series of role reversals in which labor and leisure vie for the primary position in the educational establishment, shifts triggered by changes in the world beyond the walls of the classroom.

Livia Gershon breaks this pattern down in her essay "The Rise and Fall of 'Education for Leisure,'" where she reminds us of the significant role that the factor of time has played in the evolution of education:

> *Back in the early decades of the 20th century, industrialization and the work of labor unions pushed working hours down fast. By the 1930s, we'd gone from the 12-hour days and six-day weeks common in 19th-century factories to an average 35-hour workweek. As the numbers of hours people worked declined, a flurry of essays and books by academics*

and educators took on the problem of "education for leisure." Public schools, they argued, must provide students with the mental skills and cultural knowledge to make the most of their growing hours off the clock. Success could make every man and woman like a citizen of ancient Greece, honing bodies and minds with sport, philosophy, and art, while machines took on the slaves' role.

This may seem like a fantasy, a kind of utopian ideal. And, of course, it is. But one worth considering as viable if not probable. Technological advances continually increase our capacity to do more with less labor, a byproduct of the abundance that the production economy has yielded. In the present day, the rapid advancements in machine learning and artificial intelligence have become overwhelming. The arrival of the extraordinary capacity of our production economy and its impact on the future of labor is what Andrew Yang, a 2020 U.S. presidential candidate, calls "The Great Displacement." In his book *The War on Normal People*, he details how the automation of tasks resulted in the elimination of millions of jobs. These foundational observations led him to become one of the most prominent advocates for a universal basic income (UBI), which became a central platform of his presidential bid. Universal basic income is an experimental government policy that offers all citizens monthly payments without the exchange of work. This is intended as a means to curb poverty, level the playing field, and ultimately allow for a more efficient distribution of public resources through less costly uses of antiquated government programs.

In 2017, prior to Yang announcing his presidential bid, he and I shared a private breakfast in Pawtucket, Rhode Island—which, in a bit of irony, is landmarked as the birthplace of the American industrial revolution. We discussed his presentation of UBI as a timely new governance framework that, when properly understood within the context of changes to labor, may have found its moment as a logical choice for the American public.

UBI has stirred quite the controversy. Although piloted in other countries around the world, it undermines some of the very premises of the American labor-versus-leisure dichotomy. We've all heard the outcry: "What will happen if we give away free money? Won't people just sit on the couch all day?" Underpinning these kinds of questions are two essential assumptions: (1) that money, a vehicle we use to exchange value, is intrinsically linked to labor, and to separate the two would be like reversing gravity, and (2) that leisure is something lacking in value. But despite its stigma, leisure in fact has great cultural and social value. It is leisure time that is best suited for critical thinking, and for the kind of wandering through which new ideas and epiphanies can emerge. Leisure is idle, open time in which our minds are freed to engage in improvisational experimentation and to stretch what we know.

The separation of labor and leisure is central to the economic inequity and class struggle in America. The education system simultaneously holds both experiences, predominantly divided along class lines: the wealthy participate in leisure and the poor participate in labor.

The wealthy, feeling economically secure if not socially entitled, are less concerned with the need to work to gain the resources for living. This affords them the luxury of leisure time with which to work on themselves, to be occupied with the "honing" of bodies and minds. The poor, feeling less secure about being able to meet their most essential needs, are concerned with education as the direct acquisition of skills and credentials to compete for employment that ensures their cost of survival. In other words, they embrace education as a means to position themselves for labor.

What results is a national education system that deepens the economic class divide and makes curiosity available to those who have position, wealth, and the luxury of time without the burden of labor.

Curiosity is most associated with leisure because we have allowed the production economy to reinforce a separation of labor and leisure when in fact they are intrinsically intertwined. We have unintentionally delivered a devastating blow to the incredible promise of curiosity by making it a luxury good.

In part, this is what makes UBI difficult to embrace and scale. Disparity across economic classes is tiered and layered so clearly, like sedimentary rock, that a device that treats everyone equally is at odds with the legacy of the American identity.

The irony is that America so deeply espouses democracy, an idea based on equality, as a kind of modern religion, yet so many of the commonly held beliefs we hold dear are the origin points of inequity. The confusion over the very purpose of education as an activity of labor or leisure is perhaps one of the single most powerful catalysts of inequity in America.

How do we make sense of the role of leisure and its connection to curiosity? How can education cut across the typical boundaries that separate classes? How can we view the opportunities that leisure provides as complementary to labor? Livia Gershon locates a valuable illustration when she highlights a speech delivered in 1912 by Frank Gaylord Hubbard, the chairman of the Modern Language Association of America. The MLA, founded in 1883, is a membership organization of academic scholars, professors, and educators advancing a learning society:

> *"Would it not be well for us sometimes to turn from the glories of material achievement and contemplate the burdensome nightmare of labor with which the modern world is obsessed, the worthlessness, the evil, the futility of much of it, the price that is paid for it in human life and happiness?" Hubbard asks his audience. ". . . this desire for leisure is a wor-*

thy and noble desire; in it is involved the striving for higher things, the longing for fuller and richer experience, the rising to higher levels of living. ". . . many of us, I am sure, chose our profession, not primarily because we wished to teach, but because teaching would secure for us leisure to study and investigate," he says. . . . Leisure, by this account, isn't simply free time, but freedom to do interesting things, whether or not they pay. In this account, education is for helping to figure out what those things are.

This expansion of the notion of leisure as the freedom to be an active and accountable agent of change in the world is an empowering redefinition. This is precisely why leisure and curiosity are fundamentally linked. The relationship between education and freedom is a sacred one. But the idea of freedom and how it plays out in the context of education can be deceptive. While the popular narrative would have us believe that education brings freedom through upward economic mobility, leaping across the sedimented layers of inequity is more of a myth than an evidence-based promise.

The American Dream can equate freedom with the growth of economic wealth above all else. But flourishing futures are not best measured by economic growth. Rather, a flourishing future is found in the balance of personal and collective cultural growth. A balance that integrates how we harness our personal abilities to better society with cooperative efforts to be constantly iterating new and relevant models that will allow communities to thrive. Thriving takes both labor and leisure. It takes curiosity. An education system that segregates labor and leisure and that removes curiosity from our essential needs drives and sustains inequity and must be challenged.

Intentional leisure is not the absence of labor but the presence of purpose—the freedom to practice active rest that heals as an exploration that cultivates meaning. When we blend education and vacation as an integrated lifestyle it generates exponential value.

3

Unlearning as a Form of Activism

How can we frame the fundamental difference between "educating" and "learning"? Is what we refer to as "education" a legacy narrative built upon antiquated structures? Are we so blind to when life is our teacher that we can only recognize learning when it has been packaged, credentialed, and offered as currency? What if we defined "learning" as any experience that helped us realize how to live meaningful lives and contribute to a better world?

Freedom can be found in our ability to reject the expectations and roles we are born into. When we no longer accept the world the way it is handed to us, when we raise our conscious awareness of the underpinnings that shape it, we become better able to constructively contribute to reshaping it anew.

bell hooks was one of the most significant voices in the activist movements across feminism, anti-racism, and education. Deeply influenced by her friendship with Paulo Freire, her work merges *pedagogy*, a philosophy of teaching, and *politics*, a set of values. Her blend of teaching and social justice has significantly shaped the American classroom. In her book *Teaching to Transgress: Education as the Practice of Freedom*, she argues that teaching students to "transgress" against racial, sexual, and class boundaries to achieve the gift of freedom is the teacher's most important goal:

> *The academy is not paradise. But learning is a place where paradise can be created. The classroom, with all its limitations, remains a location of possibility. In that field of possibility we have the opportunity to labor for freedom, to demand of ourselves and our comrades, an openness of mind and heart that allows us to face reality even as we collectively imagine ways to move beyond boundaries, to transgress. This is education as the practice of freedom.*

bell hooks was born in 1952 in Kentucky, where she would later return as the Distinguished Professor in Residence of Appalachian Studies at Berea College, and where she carried the same torch for liberation that inspired Freire's landmark book *Pedagogy of the Oppressed*. For hooks and Freire, the classroom is a mirror of the world. So, when the world struggles with sexism, racism, and the many types of prejudice shaping social life, our education system struggles with them as well. The space for learning can be one of oppression, or one of liberation. As Freire wrote in *Pedagogy of the Oppressed*:

> *The more radical the person is, the more fully he or she enters into reality so that, knowing it better, he or she can transform it. This individual is not afraid to confront, to listen, to see the world unveiled. This person is not afraid to meet the people or to enter into a dialogue with them. This person does not consider himself or herself the proprietor of history or of all people, or the liberator of the oppressed; but he or she does commit himself or herself, within history, to fight at their side.*

The work of dissecting, dismantling, and rebuilding the practice of education is ever-present today, half a century after *Pedagogy of the Oppressed* was published. Whether adult learning through professional employment, the landscape of higher education, or the early learning of K–12, these segments of the lifelong learning system are facing some of the most significant redesigns in history. Signals of the upheaval within the education system have been emerging for years, but arguably the most profound catalyst was the arrival of COVID-19, which created a global paralysis of education—an existential crisis.

The pandemic revealed the fractures, biases, and inadequacies of our social systems. Education was not immune. At the same time, the murder of George Floyd and the Black Lives Matter protests of 2020 pulled back the veil on issues we are apprehensive to confront. But, perhaps for the first time, there was nowhere to hide. The inequities embedded in our health, economic, education, and policing structures forced us to see that institutionalized racism is a systemic issue. The issues and opportunities that hooks and Freire articulated are now active in communities across the country.

A variety of emerging strategies and models are beginning to challenge the traditional educational system through learning practices that embody a Radical Curiosity mindset. A growing movement for "unschooling" or "unlearning" (terms that complement the language Ivan Illich uses in *Deschooling Society*) is taking hold in some communities. Next City, a nonprofit established to inspire greater economic, environmental, and social justice in cities, produced a report, "Is Unschooling the Way to Decolonize Education?," that unpacked this movement amid the pandemic and the rise of the Black Lives Matter response to racism in the summer of 2020. As the pandemic brought the ways kids are learning (or not) into sharp focus, Next City looked at self-directed education, which respects each student's passions, encourages self-sufficiency, and turns the city into a classroom:

Beyond the inequities of digital access, the U.S. public education system has been failing children for decades. Systemic racism and colonialism is baked into the standard curriculum, and the biases of majority white-administered schools are on display, whether those biases are unconscious, supported by district-approved textbooks or enshrined in law. . . . [T]oday it [mindfulness] powers a quiet revolution playing out in the backyards and front stoops of American life during this time of civil transformation. As more and more people across the nation call for an end to institutionalized racism, the realization is that for equity to take root, every level of our society needs to change. . . . [People] around the world have already embraced a potential solution: self-directed education (SDE). SDE is an umbrella term for different types of education—often determined by the self-chosen activities and interests of the young person. Unschooling is one type, as are democratic schools such as Sudbury schools and Agile Learning Centers (ALCs) (many have sliding scales for tuition), and the intentional learning community. Within unschooling, there are home-based methods as well as travel-based—learning through cultures and language.

The unschooling model seeks to challenge many of the implied narratives left unquestioned in educational design. It is more than technique; it is a lifestyle, and deeply rooted in identity. The report continues:

"For so many in Black culture, the way that we identify success and validation is through how much we produce or perform, and that goes back to enslavement, [when] our safety relied on how much we produced," says Akilah Richards, the co-founder of Raising Free People and board member of the Alliance for Self-Directed Education. . . . To look at children solely as their capacity to produce and perform in school perpetuates that imprint, she explains. What if we don't focus on classroom performance, or on obtaining degrees, but on what each person's brilliance is? "I see that as a form of collective liberation," Richards says. . . . "I see it as healing work. . . . What it means to be together

and own ourselves. It's recognizing how we oppress others. It is communal and non-hierarchical. It's about ancient collaborative ways of being, that have nothing to do with being rich and white."

As a compass of values, unschooling seeks to acknowledge the burdened history imprinted on the education system. Informed by the courage to confront this imprinting, the unschooling movement is just one example of how to transcend institutionalized education by stepping beyond its walls.

Learning has come to mean the acquisition of new skills. Unlearning requires the skill of stepping outside of existing mental models and embracing new mental models. Metacognition is the most important skill of the twenty-first century.

With this in mind, we need to consider the fundamental difference between "education" and "learning." Similar to the labor-versus-leisure dichotomy, this contrast illustrates a critical pedagogical difference. Where do the power structures and agency of learning reside? Who has power: the learner, or the educator and the institutions that deliver education services? Let's frame this dichotomy as the formality of educating versus the experience of active living as the means for learning.

Is what we refer to as "education" likely a legacy narrative built upon antiquated structures and no longer the best expression of either the original intent of education or the potential of its future? Ivan Illich proposed that

> *school prepares for the alienating institutionalization of life by teaching the need to be taught. Once this lesson is learned, people lose their incentive to grow in independence; they no longer find relatedness attractive, and close themselves off to the surprises which life offers when it is not predetermined by institutional definition.*

	LEARNING IN THE 20TH CENTURY	LEARNING IN THE 21ST CENTURY
BASED ON:	Knowledge as a noun	Inquiry as a verb
VIEWS INSTRUCTORS AS:	Subject matter experts	Guides to experiences
OUTCOME:	Informed skilled workers	Engaged civic participants
CREATIVITY:	Deprioritized	Professionalized
MANAGEMENT:	Control the known	Cultivate the uncertainty

Are we so numb to when life is our teacher that we can only recognize learning when it has been tagged, packaged, evaluated, and offered as currency? This strained relationship between the formality of educating and the experience of active living may be best expressed by Einstein when he said:

The only thing that interferes with my learning is my education.

Even the question "Can curiosity be taught?" is embedded with old ideas about the practice of teaching. Teaching has been too closely associated with the transmission of knowledge as an object, the exchange of information from someone who knows to someone who seeks to know. When knowledge is treated as an object, it is like a destination to be reached. As though it has a linear and finite end point to be achieved. The failure of the question "Can curiosity be taught?" is that it assumes curiosity has a completion point, when in fact curiosity is a never-ending pursuit tied to the fundamental desire to quench the thirst of the human condition. As Paulo Freire put it in *Pedagogy of the Oppressed*:

For apart from inquiry, apart from the praxis, individuals cannot be truly human. Knowledge emerges only through invention and re-invention, through the restless, impatient, continuing, hopeful inquiry human beings pursue in the world, with the world, and with each other.

DO WE NEED TEACHERS?

What is a teacher when curiosity is the language and medium we seek to master? What if we thought of curiosity as an ability rather than a skill to be acquired? Knowledge can no longer be thought of as a destination, a fixed point, or a static state. Curiosity is a verb for living rather than a noun to hold. In this conception of learning we may not seek instructors of knowledge as much as guides to experiences. We may not need the traditional formats of teaching. We need the confidence of self-directed learning to gain wisdom that comes only from the front-row seat of living.

As Ivan Illich clearly declares in *Deschooling Society*:

> *Most learning is not the result of instruction. It is rather the result of unhampered participation in a meaningful setting. Most people learn best by being "with it."*

A similar framing comes from the prolific architect, systems thinker, and futurist Buckminster Fuller, who said:

> *I'm not a genius. I'm just a tremendous bundle of experience.*

What if learning was any time, space, or experience that helped us realize how to live meaningful lives that contribute to a better world? To be citizens of a great society?

In the wake of COVID-19, many have asked how best and safely to send kids back to school. Some of those Radically Curious voices are also asking: *Why* send them back to school? The suspension of schooling as usual opened the door for a moment of reflection, re-consideration, and redesign. Ashley McCall, a third-grade bilingual language teacher at Cesar E. Chávez Multicultural Academic Center, on the southwest side of Chicago, poses some powerful questions that get at the heart of the purpose of education and the connection between learning and living in these times:

> *What if we put our money, time and energy into what we say matters most? What if this school year celebrated imagination? In* We Got This, *Cornelius Minor reminds us that "education should function to change outcomes for whole communities." What if we designed a school year that sought to radically shift how communities imagine, problem solve, heal, and connect? . . . What if we recognized that life—our day-to-day circumstances and our response to them—is curricula? It's the curricula students need, especially now as our country reckons with its identity. What if we remembered that reading, writing, social studies, mathematics, and science are built into our understanding of and re-sponse to events every day?*

McCall seeks a kind of education that does not break apart living and learning, labor and leisure. Twenty-first-century reality does not allow for such tidy compartmentalization. What if we made *life* the curriculum? she posits. What if we understood that education should not merely catch up to the times and reflect the diversity of our com-munities, but rather function to change the outcomes of entire com-munities? These questions would be potent during normal times. But during times of crisis, they seem to be nearly the only questions worthy of being asked.

Activism is defined as efforts to promote, impede, direct, or inter-vene in social, political, economic, or environmental reform with the desire to change society for a perceived greater good. Our image of an activist as a protester holding a sign in a march has significant roots in the American story of the twentieth century. But it no longer represents all the ways in which activism has morphed in the twenty-first century, taking on many tasks of cultural work. In a cultural interregnum, we are all activists—stakeholders in our own future, working to advance society toward a greater good.

Learning is a political act because all learning consciously or unconsciously impacts our ability to contribute to a more—or less—moral world.

What if we re-embraced activism as the intentional acts carried out by each generation to guide us from legacy narratives to new challenger narratives? And what if learning was how we developed a literacy for imagining it anew for each generation?

Our current education systems leave little room for the courage of imagination. Creativity is deprioritized. This was the central theme of Sir Ken Robinson's opus TED Talk, one of the most viewed of all time. In it, he says:

> I don't mean to say that being wrong is the same thing as being creative. What we do know is, if you're not prepared to be wrong, you'll never come up with anything original. . . . And by the time they get to be adults, most kids have lost that capacity. They have become frightened of being wrong. And we run our companies like this. We stigmatize mistakes. And we're now running national education systems where mistakes are the worst thing you can make. And the result is that we are educating people out of their creative capacities. Picasso once said this, he said that all children are born artists. The problem is to remain an artist as we grow up. I believe this passionately, that we don't grow into creativity, we grow out of it. Or rather, we get educated out of it.

We get educated out of our creativity. We unlearn our willingness to take risks and be wrong. Robinson goes on in his talk to define creativity as "the process of having original ideas that have value." Our education system is educating people out of having original ideas that have value. Let that notion sink in for a moment.

Our contemporary system seeks to control the unknowns and celebrates the certainty of the known. It has organically evolved to become a purveyor of the knowledge object, rather than a means to facilitate the delight of not knowing. The theoretical physicist and 1965 Nobel Prize winner Richard Feynman said:

I don't have to know an answer. I don't feel frightened not knowing things, by being lost in a mysterious universe without any purpose.

Years ago, before Sir Ken Robinson passed away, I had the distinct pleasure of partnering with him to deliver a keynote address to nearly five hundred employees from across American Express. I was the lead curator of a conference that centered on the theme "Change by Design." As we prepared in the weeks before the event, he and I spoke about the intersection of business and creativity—about how most useful skills in business today are not the technical ones that will be outdated in a blink, but the languages of adaptability, navigation of uncertainty, and resilient value creation. To incorporate these ideas and others into the programming, we produced an extraordinary dinner. We took over the Renzo Piano–designed Modern Wing of the Art Institute of Chicago and gave the guests a private docent-led tour of a contemporary art retrospective drawn from the museum's collection, followed by dinner in the main hall of the museum, during which each of them was gifted an original micro-painting by Bruce Price, an abstract expressionist painter.

The most powerful feedback we received from this event was from a participant who wrote me several weeks later. He said he had never owned an original piece of art before, and now he had one on display in his home. He added that he had never even been to an art museum before but that the gathering had inspired him to visit a museum upon returning to Texas, where he lived. Creativity had entered his life at a moment when he least expected it. And, he promised, it was there to stay.

Learning through curiosity can reveal people to themselves. But formal education largely remains a vocational enterprise in which, Sir Ken argues, we are being steered away from the things we love "on the grounds that you would never get a job doing that." Love has been rationalized out of the system of education, but it is central to the deeply personal and intimate experience of learning. It was Hannah Arendt who said:

> *Education is the point at which we decide whether we love the world enough to assume responsibility for it and by the same token save it from the ruin which, except for renewal, except for the coming of the new and young, would be inevitable. And education, too, is where we decide whether we love our children enough not to expel them from our world and leave them to their own devices, not to strike from their hands their chance of undertaking something new, something unforeseen by us, but to prepare them in advance for the task of renewing a common world.*

Love and curiosity are dance partners, and learning is the musical score. Love is an expression of the empathy required to challenge the core beliefs of a learner, or even of a whole community. Love is a foundation of the emotional intelligences, once thought of as "soft skills," that are quickly becoming the hard skills relevant for the challenges ahead.

In 2014, in Vancouver, Canada, His Holiness the Dalai Lama held a conversation at the John Oliver School calling for "an education of the heart." He said:

Here in the 21st century, the problems and violence we see around us are not only man-made, but made by educated people. This shows that our existing education systems lack moral principles. How can we introduce moral principles? We can't expect the government to do it, nor the UN. Religion may be of some help, but will not reach all 7 billion human beings alive today. The only way is through education. However, at present most education is focused on material things, not on the importance of inner values. This is what we need to change.

If education is a practice of freedom, it comes with great moral responsibility. Unschooling, deschooling, self-directed learning, an education of the heart, enlivening a system of moral principles—these are all expressions of the same activism. If we are to take on the task of renewing the world, we need to care so deeply about the world and about the future that we are willing to unlearn many of the mental models and ideologies that have been directly or indirectly taught to us. To do this requires Radical Curiosity.

The only thing we know for certain is that uncertainty is here to stay. And if uncertainty is here to stay, we will need new kinds of intelligences to guide our learning and our living. This is vital if we are to discover new ways to create value. What we learn and how we learn are tied to why we learn.

Curiosity cannot be taught. It is neither a fact to be retained nor a skill to be mastered. But it can be harnessed. It can be practiced. It can be modeled. It can even be developed, cultivated, and coaxed out of us. Curiosity is innately in all of us. We don't need to teach it to one another any more than we need to teach each other how to breathe. But we must protect our curiosity so that it is no longer educated out of us. Freedom is a civic tool, not an economic currency.

Curiosity is an endangered species, and if we do not protect it, we may extinguish it as a human desire. The best way to teach curiosity is to throw ourselves at living. To make life our classroom, and our tremendous bundles of experiences our curriculum.

4

Stories as Regenerative Catalysts

Why are stories so powerful? How can we sharpen our ability to discern what motivations are behind the authorship of stories that surround us? How can we imagine new stories fit for the contemporary condition? How can we identify the moments in which narratives are being upended?

Walkabouts are calibration devices, compasses for mapping new, emergent narratives. One of life's rarest pleasures is taking a walk with a true storyteller, a cartographer of possibility. The most memorable walk I ever took was with Maurice Sendak, legendary author of *Where the Wild Things Are*. We spent one glorious day together in the woods of Connecticut. I hung on every word uttered by the narrator of my childhood bedtime stories, relished every minute we sat in his studio, a storyteller's kingdom full of plush character puppets and decades of imagination. Our encounter was near the end of his life. He was an affable curmudgeon, a refreshing truth-teller who inadvertently imbued a sense of both irony and hope in every sentence. Sendak was a masterful storyteller in part because the structures beneath his stories are subtle and open to interpretation; their magic depends on how the reader's imagination completes the narrative. Great books, like life, are participatory exercises in which you cannot sit passively on the sidelines.

In an interview from 2009, celebrating the film adaptation of *Where the Wild Things Are,* Mr. Sendak joined screenwriter Dave Eggers and director Spike Jonze for an interview that put his signature humor and intensity on display:

> **Interviewer:** What do you say to parents who think the *Wild Things* film may be too scary?
> **Sendak:** I would tell them to go to hell. That's a question I will not tolerate.
> **Interviewer:** Because kids can handle it?
> **Sendak:** If they can't handle it, go home. Or wet your pants. Do whatever you like. But it's not a question that can be answered.

Sendak understood that stories can be scary. He believed that we should all—kids and adults alike—experience stories that deliver encounters with all the emotions available to us; that scary stories are how we become prepared for any eventuality. Indeed, this is the very reason we need stories. We don't do well with uncertainty, and so we seek out stories to help our minds synthesize patterns to make sense of a nonsensical world. Stories hold us in place, anchoring us in a world that is ever changing. Stories are a calm anchor amid the storm of uncertainty. And in uncertain in-between times, the stories we tell ourselves are powerful frameworks that help us work out who we are in the present moment and what we value. They lure us into becoming our aspirational selves.

And stories are everywhere, even when they are not explicitly there. Embedded narratives are coded into the objects, behaviors, policies, and assumptions that our shared world is built upon. If we are to regain agency in our personal lives, to give ourselves agency as proactive narrators of our own story, we need to become more curious about how powerfully stories shape us and the common agreements that construct contemporary society.

Stories can be catalysts for generative value. Jonathan Gottschall, author of *The Storytelling Animal*, which explores the pervasiveness of stories in the human experience, helps us understand story as the air we breathe:

> In the same way that plankton isn't aware that it's tumbling through salt water, we humans aren't aware that we are constantly moving through story—from novels, to films, to religious myths, to dreams and fantasies, to jokes, pro wrestling, and children's make believe. . . . The human mind is addicted to stories. We make them up all [the] time, and we can easily be taken in by them. Once we latch on to a story (be it a religious narrative or a conspiracy theory) it's hard to give it up. So we need to be wary of the power of story.

It's not that we should be wary of stories themselves; rather, we should be wary of losing ourselves inside them. We need to acknowledge how stories can become tidal waves that overpower us and swallow us whole. We can become the characters that others assign to us, unwittingly performing a role that constrains our self-aware choices. Without knowing it, we can become captive to untrue stories, stories that are not in our best interests, stories whose time has come to be put to rest, stories that undermine or harm us. We tell ourselves stories that become such deeply rooted mythologies that we think them to be unquestionable truths and forget they are only stories authored by others before us. The American Dream, for example, is a powerful story of economic mobility, reinforcing a capitalist narrative that if you just work hard, pull yourself up by your bootstraps, wealth will come. We now have evidence this is rarely the case.

Surviving the twenty-first century requires the ability to discern which stories are true and which are really forms of selling or marketing. We then have to author new stories fit for the contemporary condition.

Our susceptibility to destructive stories is concerning, considering that stories act as vehicles "binding society together by reinforcing a set of common values and strengthening the ties of common culture," as Gottschall describes it. Story, Gottschall notes, "homogenizes us; it makes us one."

Yet we are responsible for interrogating the stories that surround us. Questioning the narratives that reinforce a set of common values asks us to assess whether the stories we live by represent our contemporary values. We are living in a messy time.

If we believe that stories aid in binding society together, then perhaps it feels like we're unraveling precisely because we are transitioning from one narrative to another on multiple subjects simultaneously.

The legacy narratives of our past are being upended, and new ones are beginning to emerge, showing themselves in both subtle and obvious ways. Some of these shifts are clearly intentional; others are more haphazard confluences of circumstance. But both are enormously consequential, and their patterns form a kind of language we need to speak. The Radically Curious leader is intrinsically multilingual, looking beyond the literal language of traditional books to read culture as a set of stories.

Developing this cultural literacy requires that we (1) be honest about naming legacy narratives, (2) listen deeply in order to identify upending indicators, and (3) begin to imagine and articulate emerging narratives.

NAMING LEGACY NARRATIVES

The act of bravely naming a legacy narrative strips away the assumptions of inherited common knowledge and challenges their validity. Honest naming is a kind of ethical responsibility. We have a moral duty not to simply accept a harmful narrative, even if it comes cloaked in positive associations as a result of tradition, efforts by the powerful to preserve that power, or ignorance. We must not cave in to peer pressure from dead people. This naming has been the power of social movements such as Black Lives Matter, #MeToo, and the fight against climate change. As Rebecca Solnit writes in *Call Them by Their True Names*:

> I think of the act of naming as diagnosis. Though not all diagnosed diseases are curable, once you know what you're facing, you're far better equipped to know what you can do about it. To name something truly is to lay bare what may be brutal or corrupt—or important or possible—and key to the work of changing the world is changing the story. . . . One of the folktale archetypes, according to the Aarne-Thompson classification of these stories, tells of how "a mysterious or threatening helper is defeated when the hero or heroine discovers his name." In the deep past, people knew names had power. Some still do. Calling things by their true names cuts through the lies that excuse, buffer, muddle, disguise, avoid, or encourage inaction, indifference, obliviousness. It's not all there is to changing the world, but it's a key step.

Through symbolism and language, we can begin to disempower and deflect toxic narratives that have gone unquestioned for too long.

IDENTIFYING UPENDING INDICATORS

Before we can embrace and articulate emerging narratives, we need to be able to identify the indicators signaling that a narrative is being upended. This is the most difficult skill of all. Our shared stories are evolving all the time, but an upending indicator is a specific event, behavior, or pattern revealing that society is transitioning from a legacy narrative to a challenger narrative. When our collective values get upended, we can see this expressed in the stories we share and the cultural agreements we live by. We are living during in-between times, witnessing upending indicators across multiple essential human experiences.

GENDER

While modern Western civilization has perpetuated a narrative of gender based on the dichotomy of male and female, today our classification of gender is far from binary. In a recent study, half of Gen Z (and 56 percent of millennials) believe the gender binary is out of date. Furthermore, Facebook now offers at least fifty-eight gender identities that users can specify. As this narrative is being revisited, society is also revisiting Indigenous wisdom, which has long embraced gender fluidity. Prior to European colonization, more than 150 Native American tribes acknowledged a third gender; today, a growing number of tribes are recognizing not three but five genders.

When the world's largest social media platform, with nearly 3 billion participants, creates fifty-eight categories to identify gender, it's difficult to imagine a more explicit upending indicator.

SEXUALITY

Over the past century, societies have struggled to imagine narratives beyond heterosexuality, and only recently have many come to acknowledge and accept homosexuality. But today, additional diverse sexual identities are becoming commonplace. In fact, in a recent Gallup Poll, the total number of Americans who identified in the broad category of LGBT increased by 2.1 percentage points from 2012 to 2020—an increase of nearly 7 million Americans.

But the data is just one indicator that the narrative about sexuality is being upended. This sexual revolution is also playing out on the public stage, bringing the conversation into the mainstream. Singer Miley Cyrus, who began her career as a child star playing Hannah Montana on the Disney Channel and grew up to shed her wholesome image by popularizing twerking (a dance that would have been considered lewd or even pornographic inside of a previous legacy narrative), rocked the Twitterverse when she announced that she had begun seeing a woman, after having been engaged to a man. She then came out publicly as queer, and eventually pansexual, declaring, "I am literally open to every single thing."

Even the Catholic Church, an institution that has condemned homosexuality for millennia, is relaxing its conservative stance, thanks to its progressive leader, Pope Francis, who says that "having sex and eating good food is 'simply divine,'" according to a *HuffPost* article, and who has praised "human, simple, moral pleasure" while criticizing the church's "overzealous morality."

When powerful brands ranging from Miley Cyrus to the Catholic Church endorse, express, or embody new values that contrast with previous narratives, they become (consciously or not) upending indicators.

WORK

While the business world has long given lip service to the "workplace of the future," COVID-19 has ushered in a truly fundamental shift in how we work. Today, the very idea of the industrial-era workplace is being upended. The narrative that work must take place synchronously, from nine to five, in an office is giving way to a Zoom-everything world of remote work. Dozens of companies are adopting indefinite hybrid or full work-from-home policies as the future of the office is put to the test. Meanwhile, exhausted and burnt-out workers are rising up against the inequities in the labor system and leaving the workforce in record numbers. In 2020, the hospitality sector struggled to find employees willing to work for two to three times minimum wage, and similar hiring challenges are being felt in industries ranging from healthcare to manufacturing to retail. As a result of what has been dubbed "the Great Resignation," experts predicted that we could see a national attrition rate of 30 percent in 2021. Facing a labor shortage of this magnitude, employers have had no choice but to respond. Bumble, the company behind an online dating app popular with millennials, and which made headlines with one of the biggest IPOs of 2021, gave all 700+ staff a simultaneous paid week off, essentially shutting down for that week, because it sensed everyone was facing burnout. Meanwhile, companies like the Wall Street giant Goldman Sachs have issued policies such as the "Saturday Rule," meant to discourage employees from working on weekends. As GE's former chief human resources officer Raghu Krishnamoorthy argues, people are not looking just to resign; they are looking for a reset. To him, a reset is a fundamental reconfiguration of one's life, a change in one's life schema. It is a sign of how profoundly the pandemic has affected each of us. Even *The Wall Street Journal* published a piece claiming that "working fewer hours can make a country more productive."

When businesses rewrite policies that have millions of dollars' worth of implications, they are purging legacy narratives that are no longer aligned with their customers' or employees' values, and reorganizing around emerging ones. Policy changes with such significant economic impact are clear upending indicators.

RACISM

In the spring of 2020, during the first part of the COVID-19 pandemic, George Floyd was murdered by a police officer in an encounter triggered by a counterfeit $20 bill. The following month, the national narrative around race shifted. Four thousand seven hundred protests were organized across the United States, drawing a total of more than 20 million protesters—an explosion of civic engagement on issues of race that *The New York Times* said may be "the largest movement in U.S. history." Derek Chauvin, the officer who kneeled on Floyd's neck for eight minutes and forty-six seconds, would later receive a guilty verdict for second-degree murder, third-degree murder, and second-degree manslaughter, and be sentenced to twenty-two and a half years in prison. Meanwhile, the New York State Assembly passed the Eric Garner Anti-Chokehold Act, which strengthens the punishments for police officers who engage in similar conduct. Even as the daily protests have concluded, a new battlefield in the fight against racial injustice has emerged in companies and social institutions across America as communities grapple with how to rethink, reengage, and rewrite their relationship to the work of anti-racism.

This work is a project of story. What narratives we tell and how we teach them can be indicators just as powerful as mass action or legislative reform. The adoption of critical race theory (or what is often misinterpreted as critical race theory) in school curricula, for example, is driving tension in communities ill-equipped for such a sudden and drastic reorientation of their narrative. The theory argues that "historical patterns of racism are ingrained in law and other modern institutions, and that the legacies of slavery, segregation and Jim Crow still create an uneven playing field for Black people and other people of color. The idea is that racism is not a matter of individual bigotry but is systemic in America." Such a narrative may be difficult to accept, but it is one we need to welcome as the story of race in America is being upended.

Twenty million people protesting across two hundred cities indicates that a narrative is shifting. In fact, a response on this scale is perhaps the most visceral expression of an upending indicator, which is why we associate change with movements. Mass participation is often a sign that a shift in narrative resonates with many people who believe that the old narrative has outlived its timeliness.

CLIMATE

While historically, religiously, and industrially humans have long imposed their "dominion over the Earth," we must urgently adopt a new story. One that sees the climate narrative not as a fringe story endorsed by tree huggers but as a narrative of existential consequence. That such a shift is now occurring may be due in part to the fact that the story is now so tangible that it cannot be ignored. Even the global investment firm Goldman Sachs, with $2.14 trillion under management, is doing major studies on climate, recognizing that the economic and business implications are vast. Christiana Figueres, former climate chief for the United Nations who led the negotiations for the Paris Agreement, has gone as far as to call for civil disobedience to force institutions to respond to the climate crisis.

In the summer of 2021, "fire clouds" sparked 710,117 lightning strikes in western Canada in fifteen hours, a rate so high that it bewildered meteorologists. The visual is so arresting that it would lead anyone to believe in apocalyptic narratives. And yet the frightening narrative on climate has yet to be integrated into the heartbeat of the public sphere. According to a recent report published by Yale University, a large portion of our citizenry is unaware there's scientific consensus on climate change, with just 13 percent of Americans "able to correctly identify that more than 90 percent of all climate scientists have concluded that climate change is real." It's hard not to attribute this mass delusion at least in part to lawmakers like Alabama congressman Mo Brooks, who attempted to spin an alternative story during a hearing held by the House Committee on Science, Space, and Technology, proposing that it is rocks falling into oceans, not climate change, that is causing seas to rise.

Our conceptualization of the narrative of climate is upended on the daily, and indicators are everywhere. But our current chaos can also be understood as a time between stories. A time in which much of the social friction, conflict, and colliding ideas can become an implicit inquiry in which society is asking: What narrative is in line with the values of our times? If social cohesion comes from the collective adoption of a narrative, our current state of incoherence is directly linked to the very public and messy process by which we are rewriting our story.

IMAGINING AND ARTICULATING EMERGING NARRATIVES

Society is experiencing the stretch marks of a rebirth, disrupting its own legacy narrative and delivering a new challenger narrative. Often these disruptions are in the form of critique. This is a key feature of the naming stage: identifying and disempowering the legacies that need to be retired. However, the work of dismantling narratives requires a second stage. It is not enough to raise awareness and launch an assault upon legacy narratives. To successfully dissolve them, we need to articulate what a healthier alternative may look like. Activism can take the form of a protest against the current state of affairs, without articulating alternatives. Protest is a form of naming, in the Rebecca Solnit sense of diagnosis. We need to be able to assess when something is wrong, identify it, and organize to undermine the power of a legacy narrative. But to author more beautiful futures, we must imagine and express what a fundamentally different possibility might be. As the award-winning poet and author Ocean Vuong described with stunning clarity:

We often tell our students, "The future is in your hands." But I think the future is actually in your mouth. You have to articulate the world you want to live in first.

Critique is needed, but inventing something better is a more advanced tool for expediting change. This is also the point at which stories have their most generative power. Each of us is a powerful stakeholder in the stories we are living within. And we can all unlock the power of stories as regenerative forces for building a better world.

The sociologist Eric Klinenberg writes on the topic of stories as social infrastructure that determines whether "human connection and relationships are fostered" in *Palaces for the People: How Social Infrastructure Can Help Fight Inequality, Polarization, and the Decline of Civic Life.* The title of Klinenberg's book comes from Andrew Carnegie, who, despite being a capitalist perpetuator of inequity, was also an immigrant who believed in the United States as a place of possibility, and funded more than 1,700 libraries nationwide, calling them "palaces for the people." For Klinenberg, libraries are the physical manifestation of the concept of social infrastructure:

> *After all, the root of the word "library," liber, means both "book" and "free." Libraries stand for and exemplify something that needs defending: the public institutions that—even in an age of atomization and inequality—serve as bedrocks of civil society. Libraries are the kinds of places where ordinary people with different backgrounds, passions, and interests can take part in a living democratic culture. They are the kinds of places where the public, private, and philanthropic sectors can work together to reach for something higher than the bottom line.*

It cannot be lost on Klinenberg that libraries are only physical manifestations of social infrastructure because they are the custodians of the human story. Vast collections of wisdom, information, and imagination that hold the collected narratives that we've written and rewritten for centuries.

If libraries are tangible manifestations of social infrastructure, then stories are intangible forms of social infrastructure, acting as shared sheet music to guide the orchestration of society. Can we translate and apply Klinenberg's notion of social infrastructure to embrace stories as regenerative catalysts of a healthy society?

As Alain de Botton reminds us in his contribution to the edited collection *A Velocity of Being,* books provide a deeply personal kind of social cohesion. One that strengthens the social capital of relating to others:

> *We wouldn't need books quite so much if everyone around us understood us well. But they don't. Even those who love us get us wrong. They tell us who we are but miss things out. They claim to know what we need, but forget to ask us properly first. They can't understand what we feel—and sometimes, we're unable to tell them, because we don't really understand it ourselves. That's where books come in. They explain us to ourselves and to others, and make us feel less strange, less isolated and less alone.*

When the uncertainty is too much to bear, we turn to storytelling to try to imagine and articulate emerging narratives that give us hope.

Civilizations heal through the creative cultural practice of creating new language. Of working out stories, immortalizing them, sharing them in the artifacts we call books. And of carefully archiving and caring for those artifacts in libraries, cataloguing each time we gave birth to a new story. As Toni Morrison once said:

This is precisely the time when artists go to work. There is no time for despair, no place for self-pity, no need for silence, no room for fear. We speak, we write, we do language. That is how civilizations heal.

Birthing new stories can be scary. The wild things can gnash their terrible teeth, roar their terrible roars. But as Sendak understood, scary stories can also be thrilling. Imagining and articulating possibilities is how all flourishing futures begin. Stories are the origination point of world-building.

Therefore I embraced the scary, thrilling, life-affirming moment of proposing marriage to my wife, a lover of books, at a bookstore. Where better to imagine and articulate a future we both wanted to build together than within a palace of stories? It is also why today, nearly two decades later, that future includes the launch of our own bookstore: a place where new, emerging narratives can be shared, amplified, and celebrated. We learn through the language of stories—narratives that have the power to regenerate worlds.

COHESION

The Decline of Participation in Public Life

After so many have fought for—and won—the right to participate in the democratic process, why is participation in a state of decline? How can we compel government to evolve along with the values and needs of its citizenry? What new designs could be introduced to bring a culture of curiosity to government?

Few forms of curiosity are more powerful than conversation. An exchange of ideas is how we explore new possibilities. Conversations, when they are at their best, are unscripted vehicles for discovery. At scale, they create the symphony of discourse.

Discourse lies at the very center of public life. Historically, this was true even in the literal sense, with conversational inquiry taking place out in the open, in the town square, the civic commons—

shared spaces where every citizen would be welcome to participate. But our contemporary world has privatized much of public life. We retreat into our homes, onto our screens, and into our echo chambers. Immersing ourselves in information mediated by algorithms. Always connected, yet rarely connecting with one another. The result is we are less and less practiced in the craft of conversation, our ability to hear one another, to be present for and have our minds changed by others.

Discourse requires participation in order to ensure that the full scope of inquiry is represented. The more diverse the conversation, the more profound the discoveries.

Participation is a prerequisite for the democratic conversation. It is also a key indicator of the health of the public sphere. To determine the quality of our discourse, we can look at who is participating and how meaningful that engagement is.

The most fundamental form of participation in our democracy is, of course, voting. Unfortunately, in America, our marks in this area are not high. While the 2016 Trump-Clinton U.S. presidential election raised a myriad of questions about the popular vote, the Electoral College, and the accuracy of polling, a more critical indicator for understanding the state of civic engagement may be found in the participation, or lack thereof, of voters themselves. While approximately a quarter of America voted for Hillary Clinton and a quarter of America voted for Donald Trump, more than 40 percent of eligible American voters didn't vote at all. With only 55.7 percent of the voting-age population participating in the presidential election that year, voter turnout percentages in the United States were behind those in thirty other countries, including Slovakia, Lithuania, the Czech Republic, Colombia, and Mexico.

In 2020, driven by a pandemic that catalyzed the most existential crisis in the lives of many voters, turnout spiked to 66.3 percent of the voting-age population. But this still means that 90 million people of voting age did not participate.

More indicative still is the trajectory voter participation is taking: decline. According to the U.S. Census Bureau, in 1876, a record high of 81.8 percent of the voting-eligible population turned out to vote. Imagine this.

The past 150 years have been a time of extraordinary civic progress, during which the political process has become ostensibly more inclusive. Women won the right to vote in 1920. The Voting Rights Act was passed in 1965. Since the mid-aughts, social media has provided each citizen with a platform on which to publicly engage in conversation or debate. Today anyone can participate in their own forms of personal punditry through these supposedly "democratized" outlets for digitized discourse.

Yet at the same time, the percentage of the national population who participated in selecting our national leader, in shaping our national story, has declined by more than 25 percent. While America maintains democracy as a cornerstone of its values, it is difficult to reconcile the gap between our stated values and our behavior. *We fight for the right to engage in inclusive discourse, but then we fail to truly exercise it.* The situation has become so dire, we are marketing to ourselves, enlisting celebrity spokespeople, and attempting to reach young would-be voters via a popular video-game streaming service. Should we really have to work so tirelessly to convince ourselves to participate in our own future?

The limited participation in public life is a form of civic decay. The strongest discourse is a diverse ecology of voices. Sameness, at its best, is boring. At its worst, sameness produces a kind of homogenization of public life that can have dire consequences. It is only through the discomfort of being introduced to truly new ideas, less familiar to us, that we might be stretched toward diverse ways of being in the world. Consider the state of voting as a symptom of the decline of curiosity.

Participation is everything—and the failure of government to be relevant is not luring people to get in the game.

It's widely believed that the oldest government in human history was established 6,000 years ago by the Sumerians in Mesopotamia, in what is now modern-day Iraq. Looking back at history, in a kind of first-principles investigation into the founding of government, may help ground an inquiry into the present challenges of disengagement. Why and how did we begin to govern ourselves in the first place? And what can we learn from the earliest models of human organizing?

There are four theories on the origins of government. Taken together, they can provide a useful framework to understand the contemporary moment of disconnect.

1. FORCE THEORY conceives the origin of government to be an act of violence or taken by force.

2. EVOLUTIONARY THEORY views the origin of government as iterative, evolving over time from the core unit of the family.

3. DIVINE RIGHT THEORY asserts that God created government through the birth of a royal line of rulers, and it is the birthright of this royal line to govern.

4. SOCIAL CONTRACT THEORY refers to an agreement by people to give their power to a government, which then has the responsibility to promote the well-being of its citizens.

Today, much of the world practices a form of governance built upon social contract theory, the foundations of which were established by the French philosopher Jean-Jacques Rousseau in *Discourse on the*

Origin and Basis of Inequality Among Men, published in 1755, and *On the Social Contract*, published in 1762. Under the social contract, governments are given power and expected to champion prosperity through policies, programs, and prioritization of shared resources. But what happens when a government does not live up to this responsibility? When prosperity is achieved not for all its citizens but only for a smaller segment, those with power? Or when the very definition of well-being and prosperity evolves faster than the model of government? How does a government adapt to the shifting needs of its people?

A government is a system for organizing a community in accordance with the values of its people. Diverse cultures catalyze diverse models for governing, each with its own frameworks for making decisions, caring for a community, and responding to the will of its citizens.

Just as the private sector can be disrupted through innovation that renders a business irrelevant, a similar disruption can easily occur when government and the values of its people fall out of sync. Americans look to our GDP as a report card on the performance of government. But how might we evaluate government's performance on its moral charge, found in a government's original social contract to actively care for the well-being of its society? What questions do we need to ask to conduct a kind of effectiveness audit that goes deeper than mere economic transactions?

In democratic governments we are accustomed to believing that voting our representatives into and out of office is the way to demand updates to our governance. But what if that model itself needs an upgrade? Do we believe that the two-party system is the best expression of the diverse civic discourse to represent 330 million citizens? That a donkey and an elephant are the only options for a nation made up of nearly 20,000 incorporated towns and cities? It is estimated that the average adult makes more than 35,000 decisions per day. So

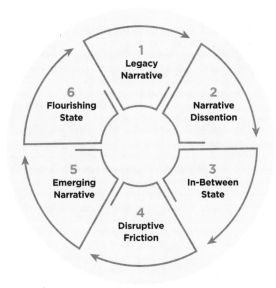

just imagine how many decisions are made during the tenure of a president or congressional leader. Beyond changing the actors in the model, how could we change the model itself?

It was Winston Churchill who famously said:

Democracy is the worst form of government, except for all the others.

The problem is that a statement like this positions democracy as a static object. Either we choose democracy or we choose another option. And other options are bad indeed. But a government is not a binary choice, like selecting a banana or an apple to have with a meal. Institutions, ideas, and commonly held belief systems are dynamic, living things. Constantly in motion and collectively being worked upon. Nor should the social contract be static. To remain relevant in changing times, such a contract requires amendments. It should exist in a constant state of redesign. We learn about the "Elastic Clause" of our Constitution, literally enabling Congress to make new laws, foreseeing the need to adapt and evolve the original framework. But how willing are we to utilize it? We have such reverence for our founding fathers that we may view their work as a more sacred gospel than they did. John Adams wrote in 1814:

> I do not say that democracy has been more pernicious on the whole, and in the long run, than monarchy or aristocracy. Democracy has never been and never can be so durable as aristocracy or monarchy; but while it lasts, it is more bloody than either. . . . Remember, democracy never lasts long. It soon wastes, exhausts, and murders itself. There never was a democracy yet that did not commit suicide.

Our nation has changed dramatically since then, in ways that would have been quite beyond the imagination of our founding fathers. Yet our Constitution has been amended only twenty-seven times since 1789—on average, approximately once every eight and a half years. Contrast this with Wikipedia, where two edits are made every second.

Even our founding fathers accounted for the likelihood of social change by including the Elastic Clause in the Constitution.

At its core, social contract theory equates power with the will of the public—unlike force theory, which equates power with violence, and divine right theory, which equates power with monarchs. The agreement, as a form of governance, is only activated when its participants deem it meaningful. Rousseau warned of the criticality of meaning for a citizen more than 265 years ago, when he wrote:

As soon as any man says of the affairs of the State "What does it matter to me?" the State may be given up for lost.

This warning is becoming particularly relevant in today's climate. Rousseau is saying that the moment a citizen questions whether government is relevant to their life, the value proposition of government has ceased to exist for that person. And citizens experience their government as relevant only when it reflects how they see themselves. Conversely, when a citizenry does not recognize the character of their government as aligned with the values of the community it is meant to serve, it's time to ask questions.

When we do not see ourselves in government, we experience alienation. The social contract is in breach, rendered null and void, not explicitly but implicitly through a sense of indifference and disengagement among the very participants whose well-being is intertwined with that contract. When this happens, what is viewed as either apathy or rebellion by those in power is actually a new challenger narrative being imagined, born, and tested by those who feel disenfranchised by a government whose interests and values remain anchored in an outdated construct that has exceeded its utility.

Black Lives Matter, for example, is not simply activism for a single group. It is a declaration by citizens, pre-enrolled in a social contract, who feel that the contract is not working for all of us. Worse, it is actively working against some of us. If we are to believe in the integrity of the social contract, we are bound to constantly ask the question: Is our government, which has accepted the responsibility to promote the well-being of *all* its citizens, fulfilling that promise in the way our resources are distributed, the way our policies are enacted, and the way our practices are expressed?

Our civic responsibility to ask these essential questions is particularly heightened when global society is going through a cultural interregnum—when we are in the midst of a fundamental redesign of the human experience, in which notions of gender, ownership, borders, the role of police, the moral implications of interdependent public health, pay equity, data privacy, and so on are being reimagined. Times of transformation require ever greater scrutiny of what kind of government is relevant to communities so essentially redefining themselves. Such times call upon citizens to be Radically Curious, an altogether more mature expression of democracy.

One measure of the social contract is trust. Without it, a social agreement is rendered irrelevant. In 2018, the Pew Research Center conducted a study engaging more than 10,600 respondents on the relationship between trust and civic life. The findings are a wake-up call:

> *Two-thirds of adults think other Americans have little or no confidence in the federal government. Majorities believe the public's confidence in the U.S. government and in each other is shrinking, and most believe a shortage of trust in government and in other citizens makes it harder to solve some of the nation's key problems. . . . Many people no longer think the federal government can actually be a force for good or change in their lives. This kind of apathy and disengagement will lead to an even worse and less representative government.*

WITHOUT TRUST OUR SOCIAL CONTRACT IS IRRELEVANT

A social contract is fueled by trust and successful outcomes. When trust or outcomes cannot be found, such agreements may become irrelevant. To build trust we need to ask questions. To be interested in one another. We will need to wrestle down the dogmas that are irrelevant or symptoms of legacies that no longer reflect the issues at hand. Is the problem a Democratic or Republican one? Is the issue blue states versus red states? Did the Russians swing the election, or was there a problem with the accuracy of mail-in voting? It seems easier to occupy ourselves with such surface-level symptoms that are better understood as downstream expressions of the underlying causes.

Can we imagine a better government? Young people, who are less committed to false dichotomies, seem to believe in such a possibility. A 2013 report from the Roosevelt Institute called "Government by and for Millennials" claimed:

We're less interested in big government vs. small government than we are in better government—making our democratic systems more inclusive and more responsive.

New generations of citizens are less entrenched in histories they didn't live through. Digital natives have witnessed the agility, the adaptivity, and the promise of innovation; they were born into a world where iterative improvement is the norm. We need to be willing to demand this innovation from our government, as we do from our restaurants, our airlines, our cellphone carriers. Incremental change will not do. If we are to reclaim our government and our democracy as an exercise worthy of our participation, then we need to reinvest in the currency of our social contract, the trust found in social capital. It is the very thing that, as Nicholas Kristof points out, the Trump-era government pulled apart:

> I'm a great believer in community, in the idea that what makes countries strong is "social capital"—the web of relationships, beliefs, trust, decency and identity that make a society work. Trump has taken this social fabric and acted as the Great Unraveler.... Trump has been a corrosive acid on America's social capital. He has cost us trust. He has dissolved our connectivity.

The good news is that questions have healing powers. The prevailing view is that activists are supposed to fight for answers, solutions, and specific goals or demands. But true activism means asking questions.

It requires us to engage, to be in the conversation, to show up and struggle with the pursuit of better. Curiosity has the opposite effect of what Kristof described as Trump's "corrosive acid." It has the magical powers of rebuilding and reconnecting. Inquiry, when done honestly, builds bridges within communities.

Questions are the purest expression of inclusive participation in public life and fuel meaningful cohesion.

6

We Don't Talk Anymore

Is dialogue a lost art? Why does discourse elude us? Why are we so polarized? How can we engage in a civil exchange of ideas in a culturally segregated world? How can we learn to embrace difference as an opportunity?

The greatest threat to curiosity is the extinction of dialogue.

In 2016, the pop song "We Don't Talk Anymore" was released by Charlie Puth featuring Selena Gomez. The song hit the *Billboard* top ten list in more than twenty countries, including the United States, Lebanon, Serbia, Czech Republic, Hungary, and Romania. The accompanying YouTube video has been viewed 2.5 billion times and ranks in the top thirty videos ever uploaded to the video-sharing site. Quite a feat, considering that 5 billion different videos are watched daily. The song memorializes the pain of heartbreak, a decoupling of lovers. But it also played as an anthem to millions who identify with it. A soft, high-pitched, pained voice repeats a chorus representing our times: the division among us. The fragmentation of a society that is at once more hyperconnected than ever, yet more isolated and lonely. "We Don't Talk Anymore" symbolizes something deeper than gossip about a relationship status. We are surrendering our language, our tools, and our spaces for benevolence—watching the extinction of dialogue occur, like a slow-motion train wreck.

The situation is more severe than just not talking anymore. It's not simply that we have disconnected from the conversation. We no longer have honest, earnest, constructive exchanges in civil society. We have normalized divisiveness. We too easily conflate disconnection and divisiveness, though they are distinctly different conditions of a continuum of discourse. Disconnection is a passive state: The plug has been pulled on being engaged, interestedness has been severed. But divisiveness is an active undermining of one another, a proactive gaslighting making its victims question their sanity, seeking to position the gaslighter as the source of the solution. A manipulation intended to establish an unhealthy dependency. The damage to the integrity of clarity is significant, and divisiveness has been normalized for so long it blends in with the other furniture. The result is spinning us out of control.

We are losing our ability to converse, to exchange ideas, to find common ground, to live in dialogue and find cooperative ways to move forward. Divisiveness vaporizes the appetite for inquiry. It undermines the hunger for exploration, shutting the door before the pleasure and joy of conversation can even begin. And conversation is, truly, a pleasure. There is even new evidence emerging that our brain waves might synchronize as people interact and cooperate on certain tasks. But we are shutting so many doors. Fewer and fewer of us may have the opportunity to experience the phenomenon of brain wave synchronization. We're isolated and on a hair trigger, ready for conflict, and it's causing America to be more polarized than ever. Consider some of the evidence:

1. ANGER AT A POLITICAL SYSTEM OF ELITE INSIDERS AND POWERLESS OUTSIDERS. A 2019 poll conducted by NBC News and *The Wall Street Journal* found that 70 percent of Americans say they feel angry "because our political system seems to only be working for the insiders with money and power, like those on Wall Street or in Washington."

2. DIVIDES IN ATTITUDES ABOUT RACE. A 2020 study by the Pew Research Center found that "across a range of political values—around race, gender and family, immigration and religion—there are stark contrasts between voters who support Trump and those planning to vote for Biden in November." Across these indicators the distance between the parties grew between the 2016 and 2020 elections. The most remarkable statistic is that 74 percent of Clinton/Biden voters agreed that it is "a lot more difficult to be a Black person in this country than it is to be a white person," while only 9 percent of Trump voters agreed with this idea, a gap of 65 percent. A gap that grew 19 percent over those four years.

3. THE 2016 PRESIDENTIAL ELECTION WAS A STORY OF TWO AMERICAS. The outcome of the election was confusing for the average American and stirred debate among policy wonks. A paradox in which Hillary Clinton received 65,853,514 votes and Donald Trump received 62,984,828 votes, yet the Electoral College vote gave the presidency to Trump. More fascinating is that we've normalized, to a point that we barely see it anymore, how close the race was. Isn't it more remarkable that our two-party system delivered a 2 percent margin vote? We may be living in times in which there are essentially two Americas. Prompting many to predict the country is not far from a civil war and *The Philadelphia Inquirer* to run an op-ed titled "America Is Over: Let's Just Split into Different Countries."

4. DIVISIONS ACROSS TRUSTED NEWS. A study asking about the use of, trust in, and distrust of thirty different sources for political and election news revealed stark differences across party lines. While Democrats trusted twenty-two of the sources, Republicans distrusted twenty of them. Moreover, evidence suggests that the gap in the use and trust of media sources has widened. A similar study done in 2014 found Republicans had grown increasingly alienated from most of the more established sources, while Democrats' confidence in them remained stable or had strengthened.

5. MAJOR REPORT FINDS THE UNITED STATES IS AN OLIGARCHY. A new study from Princeton and Northwestern Universities called "Testing Theories of American Politics: Elites, Interest Groups, and Average Citizens" sifted through nearly 1,800 U.S. policies enacted over a twenty-year period and compared them to the expressed preferences of average Americans, affluent Americans, and large special-interest groups. Researchers concluded that the United States is dominated by its economic elite.

6. SHIFT IN POLARIZATION OVER TIME. A set of ten questions asked together on seven Pew Research Center surveys since 1994 shows that the share of Americans with ideologically consistent values has increased over time and that these political values have become more strongly associated with partisanship. These shifts are particularly pronounced among politically engaged Americans. Consider how the visualization snapshot on the next page shows the further stretching of the extremes over time, across twenty-three years.

Polarization is defined as the division into two sharply contrasting groups or sets of opinions or beliefs. Polarization and difference are not the same. When difference is embraced, it can lead to discourse and discovery. A diversity of possibilities. Do we have the patience to embrace difference as an opportunity? Difference is the orchestra of diversity.

1994

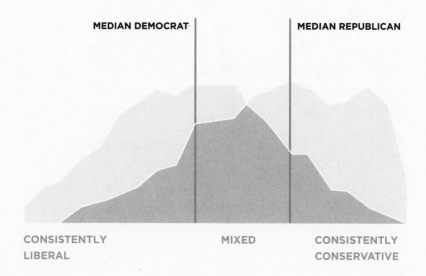

MEDIAN DEMOCRAT

MEDIAN REPUBLICAN

CONSISTENTLY
LIBERAL

MIXED

CONSISTENTLY
CONSERVATIVE

2017

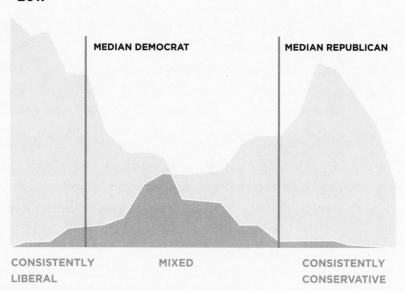

MEDIAN DEMOCRAT

MEDIAN REPUBLICAN

CONSISTENTLY
LIBERAL

MIXED

CONSISTENTLY
CONSERVATIVE

Polarization is two opposite points of a spectrum that repel each other. Two points at the ends of a continuum, entrenched and digging in to never come together. More than resistance, real polarization is the incubator for the anger associated with extremism. It's no surprise that *polaris*, the Latin root of the term "polarization," also serves as the name for the two-stage, solid-fueled, nuclear-armed, submarine-launched ballistic missile deployed by the United States from 1961 to 1996.

We've metaphorically weaponized our inability to experience a civil exchange of ideas. In 2005, on Comedy Central, Stephen Colbert's satirical persona chose a pivotal selection for the segment of his show called "The Word." With surgical timing in his delivery and an overconfident smirk, he sarcastically asserted that the word of the day was "truthiness":

> *Now, I am sure some of the word police, the "wordinistas" over at Webster's, are going to say, hey that's not a word. Well, anybody who knows me knows I am no fan of dictionaries or reference books. They're elitist, constantly telling us what is or isn't true or what did or didn't happen. . . . I don't trust books. They are all fact, no heart. And that's exactly what's pulling our country apart today. 'Cause face it, folks, we are a divided nation. Not between Democrats and Republicans, conservatives or liberals, or tops and bottoms. No! We are divided between those who think with their head and those who know with their heart.*

We are divided between those who engage with tools of knowledge and rational thinking and those who use their gut instincts and emotions to know everything. In that moment a religion of truthiness was born. Colbert brilliantly satirized that insight a full decade before the notion of "fake news" would reshape our nation. An era in which we were mad as hell and weren't going to take it anymore but couldn't remember why we were so angry and refused to utilize any wisdom to get out of such a state.

"Truthiness" articulates how satisfying it feels to make a decision that isn't supported with evidence. I want to believe what I want to believe. When I want to believe something, I will bend my thinking to support that idea, and nothing will interrupt this self-indulgent process. When we separate the tools of thinking and feeling, the result is internal polarization. This separation of rational and emotional thought processes is something we are gaining a better understanding of.

For example, in recent years, we've learned more about how emotions impact our decision-making. While we might assume that some of the many decisions we make every day are routinized, with our brain on autopilot, and for others we utilize our more rational, logical, deductive capacities, it turns out emotions are fundamentally present in all decision-making, even the most mundane daily decisions. The neuroscientist Antonio Damasio made a groundbreaking discovery. After studying people with damage in the part of the brain where emotions are generated, he found they couldn't make decisions at all:

> *They could describe what they should be doing in logical terms, yet they found it very difficult to make even simple decisions, such as what to eat. Many decisions have pros and cons on both sides—shall I have the chicken or the turkey? With no rational way to decide, these test subjects were unable to arrive at a decision. So, at the point of decision, emotions are very important for choosing. In fact, even with what we believe are logical decisions, the very point of choice is arguably always based on emotion.*

With the help of neuroscience, we see how critical our mental and emotional health is to how we comprehend, decide, and lead. As well as how susceptible we are to manipulation by external voices who may use gaslighting techniques to cloud our judgment. One of the outcomes of polarization is the creation of an emotional confusion, a kind of disorientation. Considering we need the emotional elements of our brains as partners, if not leaders, to make daily decisions, imagine how our lives might unfold when our emotions are twisted. A fog of bewilderment born from our intense need to cling to our view above all else. Polarization breeds more polarization. On a neurological level, as polarization escalates, it creates a surround sound of disorientation, and our decisions are weakened by this state. The ultimate outcome of polarization is a sustained disorientation in which our emotional comprehension loses the narrative.

On an individual level, we can probably all relate. Likely all of us have felt that Looney Tunes state of being so mad we can't even see straight, steam coming out of our ears and our face turning bright red. What we are less likely aware of is the long-term implications of the disorientation at a population scale. We think of these triggers as singular situations, not as the overall holistic state of the union of mental health for an entire population.

bell hooks, speaking at Berea College at an event celebrating Appalachian heritage in 2008, described this disorientation:

We want to know if it's possible to live on the earth, peacefully? Is it possible to sustain life? Can we embrace an ethos of sustainability that is not solely about the appropriate care of the world's resources but is also about the creation of meaning? The making of lives that we feel are worth living. Tracy Chapman sings lyrics that give expression to this yearning when she says, "I want to wake up and know where I'm going." Again, and again, as I travel around, I'm stunned by how many citizens in our nation feel lost, feel bereft of a sense of direction, feel as though they can't see where our journeys lead. That they can't know where they're going. Many folks feel no sense of place. What they know is that they have a sense of crisis of impending doom. Even the old. The elders who have lived from decade to decade and beyond say life is different in this time, way strange. That our world today is a world of too much. That this too muchness creates a wilderness of spirit. The every-

day anguish that shapes the habits of being for those of us who are lost, wandering, searching.

Living within a state of polarization is a kind of trauma. A trauma we need to diagnose. When we shut the doors to dialogue, when we eradicate conversation, when we commit to cultural segregation, we've entered an unhealthy state. One that can only be characterized by hooks's description of feeling as though we can't see where our journey leads. We hold a sense of crisis, of impending doom, and our paranoia feeds further spiraling. We've heard of writer's block. But what if our nation has a civic block? A paralysis in which we can no longer see where our national journey leads?

Umair Haque, the author of *The New Capitalist Manifesto: Building a Disruptively Better Business*, writes about this unique phenomenon—about what happens when a society stops being able to communicate—in a piece that hits close to home, "Americans Don't Know How to Talk to Each Other Anymore":

> *What does trauma do to us? It makes us hypervigilant. It makes us paranoid. We are constantly scanning the world around us, looking desperately for threats. To our existence. Annihilating threats. We always feel at risk of annihilation. We have this sense of precariousness. But isn't that how American life is? What is American life? As I often say, it's a bitter, bruising battle for existence. Americans have to get up every day and compete for things everyone else in the rich world takes for granted, because people in Europe and Canada simply give each other the basics. But Americans have to compete brutally for healthcare, medicine, a little bit of money, work, shelter, food, transport, keeping the lights on.*

We don't talk anymore. It's not simply a communication problem. It's a civic problem. At this point our polarization is breeding more polarization and our spiral has led to a kind of population-scale trauma. Our very way of life is reinforcing our extreme state of mind.

The only medicine for this mental health pandemic is dialogue. Not because a conversation directly fixes the mess. But because conversations lead to fixing the mess: slowing us down, changing our tempo, and putting us in a state of hearing each other, able to gain new insights and engage in peaceful cooperation, shrinking the distance between the two polar end points. We'd all do well to experience our brain waves synchronizing with those of another person.

7

Between Outsideness and Otherness

Where is the line between our dependence on others and our dismissal of their perspective? How interested are we in the story that is not our own? How can we see ourselves clearly without the perspective of others? What is dialogue for, if not to gain access to narratives outside our lived experiences?

Mikhail Bakhtin, the Russian philosopher, was one of the foremost thinkers on the concept of dialogue. Perhaps his most important work is *The Dialogic Imagination*. Bakhtin developed literary theory by examining the novels of Dostoevsky, analyzing the structures of the Russian author's masterful storytelling, deconstructing the plurality of voices in contrast to the monologic framework of traditional literature. Bakhtin's work brought into the study of literature the notion of polyphony—a story structure that features multiple simultaneous points of view and voices.

To Bakhtin, life is a shared event. A Rubik's cube with infinite combinations of perspectives, like a textual version of the cubist painters' view of the world. To live, he believed, is to participate in dialogue with the many voices, actors, and perspectives that constitute any narrative. In studying dialogue, Bakhtin emphasized the concept of outsideness to articulate how dialogical interactions operate. In an interview, Bakhtin said:

> In order to understand, it is immensely important for the person who understands to be located outside the object of his or her creative understanding—in time, in space, in culture. . . . Our real exterior can be seen and understood only by other people because they are located outside us in space and because they are others.

"Outsideness," in this context, is about stepping outside of ourselves to truly see the meaningful experience we are having. In fact, Bakhtin questioned whether we can see ourselves *without* the additional point of view of another perspective. He proposed that it takes another person to provide that perspective, as we cannot properly see ourselves without the mirror that another person provides. We are too immersed inside our own narrative to see ourselves clearly. A dialogue is required for the full picture to emerge.

Our own biased, first-person self-reporting must not be the only narrator of our experiences. Seeing requires the humility to depend on others more than we depend on ourselves. Outsideness is about seeing perspectives other than your own, as articulated by the popular saying "walking in someone else's shoes"—attributed to the feminist reformer and poet Mary T. Lathrap in the poem "Judge Softly," written in 1895.

Bakhtin's notion of outsideness was a foundational precursor to a variety of emotional intelligences, systems thinking, and emergence

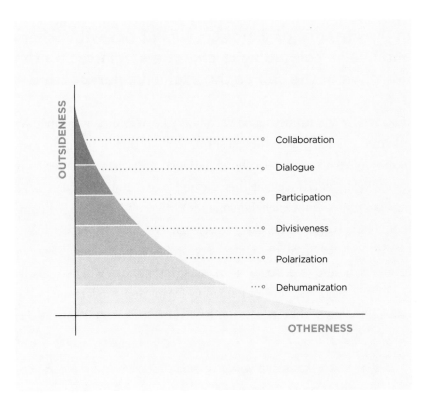

theory. But perhaps most significantly, it operates in direct conflict with the idea of otherness. If outsideness is the humility to depend on others to see ourselves, then otherness is built upon a false sense of superiority that eliminates opportunities for any greater understanding of ourselves. Whereas outsideness recenters and distributes power as shared agency with other people, otherness removes their power, divisively separates people into groups, dehumanizes, and builds walls between communities.

Otherness is bred when we are unfamiliar with one another. When we stop talking. Without dialogue, we do not see the "other" as interconnected with our understanding of ourselves. In the absence of dialogue, the beautiful integrated nature of outsideness falls away and the segregated nature of otherness sets in.

In the absence of dialogue, we cut ties with others and live in isolated echo chambers, reinforcing the narrative of the self as the exclusive perspective.

If society is not strengthened with dialogue, it will be weakened by otherness. Otherness is the parent of racism. One of the most profound voices to articulate the experience of racism in America is James Baldwin. His elegant rhetoric and rare command of language enabled him to deliver challenging ideas that undermined the commonly held beliefs of his era. On February 18, 1965, he debated William F. Buckley Jr. at the University of Cambridge. This debate, a formal structure of dialogue at its most intentional, will be remembered as a major element of Baldwin's legacy and a milestone in the understanding of the American othering of Black people. At the debate Baldwin said:

> *It is only since the Second World War that there's been a counterimage in the world, and that image had not come about through any legislation on the part of any American government, but through the fact that Africa was suddenly on the stage of the world and Africans had to be dealt with in a way they had never been dealt with before. This gave an American Negro, for the first time, a sense of himself beyond a savage or a clown. It has created, and will create, a great many conundrums.*

> *One of the great things that the white world does not know, but I think I do know, is that black people are just like everybody else. One has used the myth of Negro and the myth of color to pretend and to assume that you are dealing, essentially, with something exotic, bizarre, and practically, according to human laws, unknown. Alas, that is not true. We are also mercenaries, dictators, murderers, liars. We are human too. What is crucial here, is that unless we can manage to establish some kind of dialogue between those people whom I pretend have paid for the American dream, and those other people who have not achieved it, we will be in terrible trouble.*

Baldwin is the epitome of Radical Curiosity. His dexterity in constructing mental models with metaphor and poetic provocation helped catalyze the evolution in the American discourse. The following chillingly honest statement Baldwin made in the Buckley debate—potentially the most memorable quote from the event—pierces otherness with a personal account:

It comes as a great shock around the age of five or six or seven to discover the flag to which you have pledged allegiance, along with everybody else, has not pledged allegiance to you.

In a vote by the audience, Baldwin won the debate 540 to 160. But as Nicholas Buccola recounts in *The Fire Is upon Us*, a book that examines this historic debate in depth, the endeavor itself had failed, in one crucial way:

> Baldwin was proud of winning the Cambridge debate, but frustrated that Buckley, like so many other white Americans, had seemingly failed to understand what he was trying to say—almost like Ludwig Wittgenstein's famous proposition in Philosophical Investigations that "if a lion could speak, we could not understand him," for it would be speaking a language and of a reality alien to our own. They each had different "systems of reality," Baldwin said during the debate; they were two lions of their field who were able to spar, but unable to comprehend each other.

Can dialogue change someone's mind? How long does it take? Would we expect that each of the two voices engaged in a kind of verbal gymnastics could acquire the total life experiences and convictions that the other held prior to walking into the room? Who is dialogue even for? Is it to change your conversation partner's mind, or is it a performance for a third-party audience that bears witness either in the moment or over time? Is history our audience?

More than fifty years after the Buckley-Baldwin debate, America is still struggling with race. Still struggling with the power it awards or takes away, still walking the dangerous tightrope between outsideness and otherness. When we are at our best, we embody outsideness that sees our nation as a collective whose future is cooperatively interdependent. At our worst, we are entrenched in otherness: polarized, seething with an anger that undermines and dehumanizes.

Toni Morrison, the literary titan and Nobel laureate, is one of the major figures in the conversation on the topic of otherness. Nearly forty years after Bakhtin's death, Morrison took up his baton to critique the literary canon. Her argument moved polyphony and the dialogic to the forefront, seeking Black representation in the literary and cultural discourse. Morrison advocated for the voices, the stories, the experiences of others to be told to reclaim power stripped away by the othering of the Black perspective. As Nell Irvin Painter, the director of the Program in African American Studies at Princeton University, wrote of Morrison in *The New Republic:*

> *In her Tanner Lectures in 1988, and later in her book* Playing in the Dark, *she argued against a monochromatic literary canon that had seemed forever to be naturally and inevitably all-white but was, in fact, "studiously" so. She accused scholars of "lobotomizing" literary history and criticism in order to free them of black presence. Broadening our conception of American literature beyond the cast of lily-white men would not simply benefit nonwhite readers. Opening up would serve the interests of American mental as well as intellectual health, since the white racial ideology that purged literature of blackness was, Morrison said, "savage." She called the very concept of whiteness "an inhuman idea."*

Otherness has gone as far as erasing others from our collective narratives, from accomplishment, from being actors in the dialogue of history. In *The Origin of Others*, adapted from Morrison's Norton Lecture at Harvard University (notable in part because she was only the second Black lecturer in the history of this prestigious series), Morrison articulated perhaps one of the most explicit calls to action around otherness. As Painter writes:

> *Othering is expressed through codes of belonging as well as difference. Most commonly, pronouns convey the boundaries between "we" and "them" through the use of first- and third-person plurals. "We" belong; "they" are Other and cannot belong. Those who are "them" can be described in the negative language of disgust: black as ugly, black as polluting. Definitions of color, Morrison says, define what it means to be an American, for belonging adheres to whiteness. The possession of whiteness makes belonging possible, and to lack that possession is not to belong, to be defined as something lesser, even something not fully human. Neither possession nor lack is natural or biological. Something has to happen; a process needs to get underway.*

The codes and signals Morrison sought to make visible are part of the legacy narratives that are slowly dying out, but not without a fight. Otherness, racism, and the "inhuman idea" of whiteness are blurred into cultural signals all around us. If we are to aspire to healthy relationships with others, we need to make these invisible codes visible. Curiosity is a way of decoding these signals. Of looking, of seeing, of listening for the historical power structures governing how we relate to each other. Of consciously constructing better relationships. Of refusing to accept the world each of us is thrust into. Of being accountable for how we navigate those codes that ought to be challenged, deconstructed, defunded, and reimagined.

Codes can be explicit or implicit. Hiding in plain sight. Yet so many signals that at first glance appear benign are the remaining fossils of legacy narratives. In the summer of 2020, for example, Good Humor ice cream announced it was making a change to the widely known jingle of the ice cream truck. A soundtrack that countless Americans, myself included, associate with the arrival of joy. But as it turns out, the familiar melody piping through those speakers was "Turkey in the Straw," a song with a long racist past that dates back to the 1830s. In a piece unpacking Good Humor's announcement, NPR's Natalie Escobar writes:

> But it wasn't until the advent of traveling minstrel shows that the melody really lodged itself into American pop culture—and the tune acquired racist lyrics. In the 1830s, the minstrel performer George Washington Dixon popularized a song called "Zip C**n," set to the familiar tune and referencing a blackface character who, as Johnson wrote, was "the city-slicker counterpart to the dimwitted, rural blackface character whose name became infamous in 20th century America: Jim Crow."

Good Humor, a brand owned by Unilever—a company that has taken social impact and ethical business practices seriously—has since announced they will collaborate with the rapper, musician, and producer RZA (of the hip-hop group Wu-Tang Clan) to create a new jingle. It is a largely symbolic move given that Good Humor hasn't actually operated any trucks since 1976, but the company wanted to be "part of the solution."

We bounce through a world filled with signals from legacy narratives that are camouflaged, woven into the environment. This example illustrates the importance of excavating legacy narratives. The authorship of new narratives requires a confrontation with the old. We won't know how to improve our future if we don't find a way to assess the fractures of our past. Absent such a confrontation, our stories perpetuate identities that keep us anchored to a past that we did not speak up against.

Historical thinking, the courageous practice of confronting our past to inform our future, is a type of dialogue. We are in constant dialogue with those who have come before us. Although the protagonists of these histories have died, their stories have not. Are we aware how entrenched our present is in the stories that have unfolded before us? How interested are we in the story that is not our own? Can we understand the ways in which our present is tied up in, wrapped around, and standing on the shoulders of others? Do we care for others?

Poet and novelist Gwendolyn Brooks, the first Black person to win the Pulitzer Prize (for her work *Annie Allen* in 1950), said it best when she wrote:

We are each other's harvest; we are each other's business; we are each other's magnitude and bond.

It's that simple. We are each other's business.

8

How to Ask an Essential Question

How can we expect to arrive at the right answers if we're asking the wrong questions? Is there ever a "right question"? The frame of a question can lead to harm or to exponential value, but do we have the same discipline regarding problem-framing as we do when it comes to problem-solving? How can we begin asking more of the deeper, more fundamental questions that lead to transformation? What would it take to reinvest in a culture of inquiry-based leadership?

Curiosity is expressed by asking questions. But so much of our day is filled with tasks that go unquestioned. The speed of modern life, the convenience of socially coded behavior, and the consolidation of power have created conditions of autopilot. We are asleep at the wheel, managing the management of tasks too many of us do not understand, believe in, or participate in authoring. Often, our intentions are good. But the failure to challenge our actions is doing more harm than we realize: harm to those who may be carrying out those actions, those social actors bearing the downstream burden of unconsidered policies and ideologies.

The business world is a graveyard of unasked questions, and it is bankrupting society. To hell with good intentions. We can do better.

The culture of our production economy fills our day with lethargic transactions. Routine maintenance that displaces a sense of meaning from our work and our leaders. It's as though the business of business has become the administration of the mundane.

You know how it goes: There is a new idea circulating. A Fortune 500 company decides it wants to become a leader in the space. But no one at the company knows what the thing really is. So the team decides the first action should be to convene thought leaders in the space. But conferences take planning. So your supervisor volunteers you to be on a committee. Meetings are held, tasks are handed out, and before you know it, you are charged with coordinating the parking passes for the conference. Meanwhile, weeks have gone by, and no one has stopped to question whether the process or the tasks have produced anything useful. Instead of an inquiry into the new idea, the conversation has devolved into one about the parking committee, and we are several degrees of Kevin Bacon away from the origination of value.

Labor for the sake of laboring is the workplace equivalent of empty calories.

This happens in government too. Take the contemporary discourse on healthcare. From the moment Obamacare was passed into law in 2010 up to the 2020 election in which Democratic candidates fell over each other to explain their respective healthcare platforms,

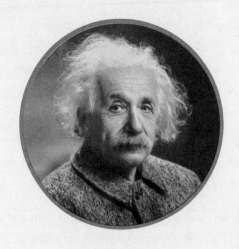

"If I had 60 minutes to solve a problem and my life depended on it, I'd spend 55 minutes determining the right question to ask. Once I had the right question, I could easily answer it in the remaining 5 minutes."

—Albert Einstein

we've been gridlocked as a nation on the wrong conversation. The healthcare discourse is not about health, it's about who pays for it.

In 2019, the United States spent $3.8 trillion on healthcare— approximately $11,582 per citizen. That is more than double the per capita spending of healthy countries like Japan, Canada, Germany, and Switzerland.

Maybe the question shouldn't be *who* pays for healthcare, but why we spend more than $3 trillion every single year on something that, overall, does not produce great outcomes. Answering this question requires defining what exactly it means to be healthy in the twenty-first century. The current state of our inquiry has abandoned Aristotle's first principles, the sacred practice of boiling things down to their most essential building blocks to allow for clarity, logic, and deductive reasoning that generate insights.

Insights—whether in organizations, in communities, or in government—begin with essential questions. Questions anchor our actions in our sense of purpose and become the building blocks of high-impact strategies. Great questions can put us on the path to resilient and exponential value creation, whereas unquestioned actions can only lead to more transactional activities. We desperately need to reinvest in the culture of inquiry-based leadership, both in our businesses and in civil society.

I believe that all value creation originates in the quality of an essential question.

Over the years I've adapted a questioning process inspired by a quote often attributed to Albert Einstein. When asked how he would approach solving a problem if he had just one hour to do it, he replied:

> *If I had 60 minutes to solve a problem and my life depended on it, I'd spend 55 minutes determining the right question to ask. Once I had the right question, I could easily answer it in the remaining 5 minutes.*

"But why, some say, the moon?
Why choose this as our goal? And they
may well ask why climb the highest
mountain? Why, 35 years ago, fly the
Atlantic? Why does Rice play Texas?

We choose to go to the moon.
We choose to go to the moon in this
decade and do the other things, not
because they are easy, but because
they are hard, because that goal will
serve to organize and measure the best
of our energies and skills, because that
challenge is one that we are willing to
accept, one we are unwilling to
postpone, and one which we intend
to win, and the others, too."

—John F. Kennedy

We need to start investing more time in understanding the problem. And if we can treat problems as questions, we can better understand what we are solving for and align on the necessary steps to get there. In Einstein's model, more than 90 percent of the problem-solving process would be spent on the activity of problem-framing: the detective work that leads to better questions, and in turn enables the most valuable insights. This is the model today's leaders must emulate in order to meet today's challenges in bold and innovative ways.

When my design studio set out to deepen our practice and method for asking great questions, we found an ideal case study in John F. Kennedy's famous "man on the moon" speech, given at the Rice University football stadium on September 12, 1962. In one of the most iconic examples of bold, visionary leadership in modern history, JFK declared:

> *We choose to go to the moon. We choose to go to the moon in this decade and do the other things, not because they are easy, but because they are hard, because that goal will serve to organize and measure the best of our energies and skills, because that challenge is one that we are willing to accept, one we are unwilling to postpone, and one which we intend to win, and the others, too.*

This is the part of the speech we remember. It is the clip we replay. But what is the question JFK is asking? What is the impact he seeks? And what actions does he propose to get there?

In my studio, we have come to deconstruct problem-framing into three elements: ***vision, vehicle***, and ***impact***.

Vision is a form of an *essential question*. When we pose our visions as questions, we are framing the problem as an opportunity ahead.

Vehicle is a form of *strategy programming*. Once vision and impact are established, we can deduce the appropriate vehicles as a set of strategic activities through which our desired outcome can be achieved.

Impact is a form of *imagining the future state*. When we describe the impact as a story, we are framing the outcome as a success narrative.

Let's apply this to JFK's vision of sending a mission to the moon. Too often we think of the vision as the moon. But the moon has simply become a shorthand symbol for a more complex vision.

JFK's vision was for an American Renaissance, for exploring new frontiers in the sciences, technology, engineering, and math. The real question JFK is asking is this: Can we reach beyond what we know and can currently accomplish to take on a meaningful task that will bring us greatness as a nation?

JFK's vehicles were numerous and comprehensive. They included dozens of strategic programs ranging from partnerships with industry to investments in NASA to extraordinary engagement in education and training. It's said that when JFK articulated the outcome of a man on the moon, we did not yet have the capacities to achieve this goal, and all of NASA simultaneously fainted. It took many years of research, tests, pilots, prototypes, failures, and experiments to build the tools and the know-how required to achieve that seemingly impossible outcome. Vehicles are the less sexy work that happens when an inspired vision and future are worth waking up in the morning for.

The impact is what happens when an abstract goal has been achieved. How will we know that we are living in the age of an American Renaissance? When every citizen can turn on their television set and see news footage of a man on the moon. That will be the tangible metric, the imagined future state playing out in real time that we will all witness. The man on the moon is not the vision; it is the outcome of success.

These are the building blocks of a cohesive strategy.

VISION	**VEHICLE**	**IMPACT**
as an Essential Question	*as Strategy Programs*	*as Imagined Future State*
Can we pioneer an American Renaissance?	Portfolio of STEM policies, investments, and partnerships.	You will see a man on the moon.

Framing a compelling essential question, imagining what achieving the desired answer to that question might look like, and distilling the vehicles to deliver on such a promise are the real work of leadership.

Over the years I've participated in framing thousands of questions with leaders and stakeholders engaged in virtually every facet of life. Philosophical questions like "What are humans for?" Social questions like "Could we unleash a pandemic of health?" And business questions like "How do we define value?" But what makes a good essential question? Essential questions embody several characteristics. Asking these deeper, more essential questions is Radical Curiosity at its best.

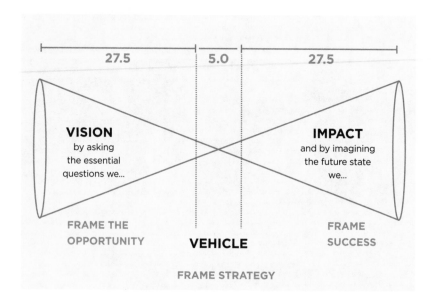

1. Essential questions invite us to revisit ideas we have taken for granted. They challenge us to reconsider what we know, to look at the familiar with fresh eyes to see something new.

2. Essential questions strip away the veneer and seek to get closer to the core motivations. They challenge us to understand *why* things happen rather than *what* things happened.

3. Essential questions allow for a wider array of contributing variables. They challenge us to consider unexpected connections in order to unlock transformative insights.

4. Essential questions focus on longer time frames, looking further out into the future. They challenge us to move beyond the present and allow for the inclusion of past and future considerations.

5. Essential questions shine a light on our biases, making them transparent. They challenge us to confront the limits of our thinking.

6. Essential questions resist the personal but embrace the empathetic. They challenge us to see the humanity of a situation but inquire into the context.

7. Essential questions contain absurdity, celebrating an inversion of expectations. They challenge us to recalibrate our assumptions through humor.

8. Essential questions are intimate. They challenge us to forge trusted social contracts with colleagues, collaborators, and partners.

9. Essential questions break disciplinary, sector, and departmental barriers. They challenge us to see holistically across the isolated, tightly managed compartments through which we've organized our lives and our organizations.

10. Essential questions empower critical thinking. They challenge the legacies of powerful ideas in the collective wisdom and originate new knowledge.

TIME

9

The Digitization of Our Self-Interests

Whom does our time belong to? Have we surrendered our voice, our free will, our capacity for original thought in exchange for easy distractions, shallow social validations, and the endless pursuit of a dopamine rush? What can we do to protect our time from the manipulation of those who seek to profit from it?

In her novel *The Dispossessed: An Ambiguous Utopia*, science fiction author Ursula K. Le Guin wrote:

If time and reason are functions of each other, if we are creatures of time, then we had better know it, and try to make the best of it. To act responsibly.

We *are* creatures of time. Time is perhaps the most precious asset in the world, as it cannot be regenerated. We can birth more people, we can generate more food, money, shelter. We can even revitalize our bodies and our health, up to a point. But we cannot create more time. And so, as Le Guin wisely advises, we better know it, try to make the best of it, and use it responsibly. However, Le Guin wrote these words in 1974, nearly two decades before the internet became mainstream. One small complication has since emerged.

We are no longer the exclusive stakeholder in our personal relationship with time. Our time is no longer our own. Time is a nonrenewable resource facing a different kind of climate crisis.

In the grand scheme of human progress, the explosion of social media is a new phenomenon. Facebook: founded in 2003. Airbnb: 2008. Uber: 2009. Instagram: 2010. Their arrival marked a new frontier for information sharing, entertainment, work, and leisure. In the early days, the overwhelming mass adoption of social media made any critique of these platforms out of the question. The social pressure to embrace and join the wave eclipsed the possibility that this new phenomenon might not be wholly positive. But more and more, it is becoming acceptable to publicly consider the (un)intended consequences of social media and the immersive nature of today's technology. Even technologists themselves, whose very livelihoods are tied to our use of technology, have begun to debate and even disavow the opportunities for manipulation a digital world presents. Architects of the social media revolution have come forward, raising questions about the detrimental effects on each of us individually as well as collectively. As neuroscientist Daniel J. Levitin explains in his book *The Organized Mind: Thinking Straight in the Age of Information Overload:*

> *Each time we dispatch an email in one way or another, we feel a sense of accomplishment, and our brain gets a dollop of reward hormones*

telling us we accomplished something. Each time we check a Twitter feed or Facebook update, we encounter something novel and feel more connected socially (in a kind of weird, impersonal cyber way) and get another dollop of reward hormones. But remember, it is the dumb, novelty-seeking portion of the brain driving the limbic system that induces this feeling of pleasure, not the planning, scheduling, higher-level thought centers in the prefrontal cortex. Make no mistake: email-, Facebook- and Twitter-checking constitute a neural addiction.

One of the most compelling TED Talks in the history of the series was delivered by Jaron Lanier, a computer scientist and pioneer in virtual reality technologies, in 2018. In it, Lanier engages the crowd in an intimate conversation that feels virtually unscripted and vulnerably honest as he offers a courageous critique of technology's hold over independent thought. Referring to a book by Norbert Wiener called *The Human Use of Human Beings,* he says that Wiener

described the potential to create a computer system that would be gathering data from people and provide feedback to those people in real time in order to put them kind of partially, statistically, in a Skinner box, in a behaviorist system, and he has this amazing line where he says, one could imagine as a thought experiment—and I'm paraphrasing, this isn't a quote—one could imagine a global computer system where everyone has devices on them all the time, and the devices are giving them feedback based on what they did, and the whole population is subject to a degree of behavior modification. And such a society would be insane, could not survive, could not face its problems. And then he says, but this is only a thought experiment, and such a future is technologically infeasible. And yet, of course, it's what we've created, and it's what we must undo if we are to survive.

The behavior modification Lanier describes, combined with the artificial pleasure Levitin calls a "neural addiction," keeps us in a kind of intoxicated state. A state that has us less intellectually aware, less in control of our own decisions, and less conscious of the hidden actors and interests choreographing those decisions, whether they be foreign actors ultimately seeking to influence elections, the seductive integration of marketing and advertising messages into what we believe is our own authentic "feed," or simply the perpetual confusion and distraction of a superficial game of "likes" and responses to things we don't actually care about. Inside this dopamine feedback loop, we lose our own voice.

How much do we *really* "like" the photo of the sandwich our friend from the eighth grade made for lunch? How sad do we *really* feel (as evidenced by our posting of a frowny face emoji) that our college roommate is moving across the country, eighteen years after our last direct encounter? The constant pressure to react and respond to the mundane is an erosion of our agency and voice. And in turn, it inhibits our critical thinking, extinguishes our curiosity, and erodes our ability to explore and create original thought. Why actively author a new idea in the world when the system is designed to reward reposting, liking, sharing, and choosing the right emoji in response to other authors? We are creating a generation of literal and figurative followers, relegating original thought to the sidelines.

Among the most formidable voices leading the charge in this discourse is Tristan Harris, once the design ethicist at Google, and now president and co-founder of the Center for Humane Technology. He framed the challenge in this way:

> *When you play with our weakness for social validation, that we cannot not pay attention when our social validation is on the line by others, in terms of likes, etc.—you get mass narcissism culture. Everyone has to be an influencer, or, do I have as many followers as my friend, I have to take that photo down, etc. Confirmation bias, that it feels good at a nervous-system level to get information that affirms our worldview and it feels bad to get information that doesn't, that way you get fake news. If you hack into our outrage, you get polarization, and if you hack into our trust, the limits of what we know, the basis of whether or not to*

trust something, you get deep fakes and bots. Sort of checkmate on your
nervous system.

Our neurological addiction, culture of narcissism, insatiable hunger for social validation, and epidemic of confirmation bias cumulatively create the perfect storm that obliterates our independent critical thinking abilities. Leading us to make more and more decisions that are objectively not in our own self-interests, but are instead reactions to the surround-sound lobbying of interests invisible to us. We have abdicated our own voice—asking fewer questions, happily satiated from the mousetrap tricks that deliver us the cheese without our having to stop and decide if we are hungry.

A wholesale rejection of technology is not a viable answer. But provocative voices like Harris and Lanier are taking up the mantle in an effort to raise our collective awareness about the risks we face. Challenging ourselves to shake our addiction to existing technologies and develop new ones that serve—rather than undermine—the human condition will require Radical Curiosity as well as radical action.

The digitization of time is a process of deconstructing and redistributing time into micro-bites (or bytes) of smaller and smaller interactions. This is in part because the digital world values the existence—the visual proof—of an interaction over the depth or quality of the interaction. Worse yet, we are mirroring these behaviors in real life. Or as we would say online: IRL. Because it takes too many bytes to type "in real life."

Jason Fried, co-founder of the web-based collaboration tool Basecamp and author of *Rework*, offers a humorous look at how the deconstruction of time is diminishing the quality of our work:

> *People go to work, and they're basically trading in their work day for a*
> *series of "work moments"—that's what happens at the office. . . . It's*
> *like the front door of the office is like a Cuisinart, and you walk in and*
> *your day is shredded to bits, because you have 15 minutes here, 30 min-*

utes there, and something else happens, you're pulled off your work . . .
then it's lunch, then you have something else to do . . . before you know
it, it's 5 P.M., and you look back on the day, and you realize that you
didn't get anything done.

We do tasks. But we don't get meaningful work accomplished. That's because people really need long stretches of uninterrupted time to do the thinking required to get something done. Fried goes on to compare the quality of deep sleep to the quality of deep work. We no longer experience full "REM cycles" of undistracted, uninterrupted time. And much like the lack of uninterrupted sleep, it is affecting our ability to reason.

Oddly, we celebrate multitasking even when we are well aware of the ample research showing that it can weaken productivity—in addition to the harm it can do to our mental health. Researchers at the University of California, Irvine, found that the typical office worker is interrupted or switches tasks every three minutes and five seconds on average, and that when this occurs, it can take twenty-three minutes and fifteen seconds to regain the same degree of focus and contextual flow prior to being disrupted. Jonathan Spira, author of *Overload! How Too Much Information Is Hazardous to Your Organization*, estimates that interruptions and information overload eat up 28 billion wasted hours a year, at a loss of almost $1 trillion to the U.S. economy.

How did this grand experiment of social media and the interconnectedness of an internet of things and the evolution of byte-sized time go so wrong? Our reverence for the illusion of being busy—a form of worship we offer to the gods of the production economy—has left us in an existential crisis, while robbing us of the ability to reason our way through it. What essential questions must we ask to help us make sense of what the point of it all is?

Can we ask ourselves why were we so drawn to the siren song of social media in the first place? Were we attracted to Facebook because we wanted to connect with community? Did we join Instagram to engage with storytelling? Did we start racking up connections on LinkedIn in pursuit of fulfilling work? Did we love Google because of our thirst for knowledge? When we ask these questions, we remind ourselves that there are in fact fundamentally human activities at the core of these technologies. After all, technologies are simply tools; it is how they are designed to be used that matters most. It's high time we redesign these tools in service of our humanity.

10

Time Travel Is Not Reserved for DeLoreans

How do we make sense of ideas, people, or organizations that are "ahead of their time"? What if we, as leaders in business, culture, government, and other change-making pursuits, could understand and harness time as a key asset?

In the iconic film *Back to the Future,* Marty McFly lives across multiple timelines. He accidentally travels to 1955 in a DeLorean, visiting his parents before they ever fell in love. His task is simple: accelerate time travel technology (which does not exist) to get back to 1985; re-create the conditions that brought his socially inept father, George McFly, and lovestruck mother, Lorraine Baines, together at the "Enchantment Under the Sea" high school dance; and, in doing so, avoid magically fading away like a reverse Polaroid picture. Whew! The climactic convergence of these circumstances peaks with an incredible performance by Michael J. Fox as Marty, who joins the band at the dance to play "Earth Angel," the requisite slow song for angsty teens of that era. But then he lets loose with a rock 'n' roll version of "Johnny B. Goode" by Chuck Berry—which would not actually be written until three years later. As the entirety of the Hilldale High student body stops dancing to gape at him in shock, Marty realizes he has overstepped his timeline, and he signs off with this quip:

I guess you guys aren't ready for that yet. But your kids are going to love it.

In a sense, the 1985 film—like the song and the performance—was ahead of its time. Despite its relatively absurd plot, *Back to the Future* and its sequels provide a useful thought experiment that pushes the limits on the notion of time. In each film in the series we are presented with a character who is first ahead of, then behind, then far ahead of, and then finally back in their rightful timeline.

But what is our rightful timeline? And how do we make sense of ideas, people, or organizations that are "ahead of their time"?

The idiom "ahead of one's time" is an interpretation of the phrase "ahead of the curve." Some sources point to the U.S. military and the technical aspects of flight as the origin of the phrase:

> *"Inherent stability of the plane—if it is being flown ahead of the power curve with level wings—will control the pitch attitude with less chance of structural damage than a pilot applying large elevator control inputs." . . . The power curve demonstrates how an aircraft's speed changes in response to changes in engine power. . . . Under this airspeed, in contradiction of common sense, it takes more thrust to decrease speed while [continuing] to fly level. An aircraft in this state is supposed by pilots to be behind the curve and it's a dangerous situation*

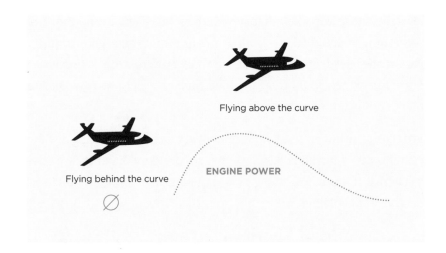

Flying above the curve

Flying behind the curve

ENGINE POWER

to be [in], nearly [at] stalling speed and with limited possibilities in case of a problem. If you're above the curve, on the other hand, you have many more choices of operation.

This engineering-based explanation offers a useful metaphor. It is dangerous to be "behind the curve." As a pilot, you have more control, more optionality in which to operate, if you stay above the curve. The power of choice is found in being ahead of the curve.

For leaders, too, being ahead of the curve is the sweet spot, the space where we are empowered with the most options for operating. Yet being ahead of the curve is undervalued and underutilized as a tool for optimizing our problem-solving processes and expanding our ways of being in the world.

What if we could understand and harness *time* as an essential currency for creating transformative impact, instead of merely relegating it to the sidelines?

I believe this lost opportunity stems from our flawed human nature. As leaders, we typically only prioritize, examine, and attempt to leverage those variables that we can control. If we cannot control something, it simply disappears from our attention, becoming just a part of the backdrop. The passage of time, by definition, is outside of our control. So we do not prioritize time as a field of play. Such a blind spot is not serving us well.

From a scientific point of view, our collective understanding of time is still quite young. Of course, we have the theory of general relativity, which illuminates how gravity impacts space-time. As one science writer explained it:

Place one clock at the top of a mountain. Place another on the beach. Eventually, you'll see that each clock tells a different time . . . because, as Einstein posited in his theory of general relativity, the gravity of a large mass, like Earth, warps the space and time around it.

This effect is called "time dilation." The size of the effect varies (on Earth it is very, very tiny), but it has massive implications for how we understand the nature of time. Maybe time is not constructed as the linear timelines assumed in many science fiction stories or the adventures of Marty McFly! Our growing understanding of time is beginning to raise questions about the commonly held belief that time is linear.

If we think about time in terms of commonly held beliefs—moving from one narrative to a new narrative, old constructs to new constructs—time dilation as a social idea could be a useful cultural framework. I would propose an expanded interpretation of time dilation as *the difference in the time it takes to encounter or absorb new thinking based on history and culture acting as centers of gravity impacting how people experience change.*

Such an expanded definition may help us consider that people exist in different personal, professional, and cultural timelines, and that an individual's "rightful timeline" speaks to his or her readiness to embrace and adopt a narrative as it unfolds. A proper reintroduction of such a concept might be called "time readiness dilation."

Scientifically, a clock on the top of a mountain and on a beach register time differently because of the effects of gravity. But replacing the scientific concepts with their correlating humanistic considerations may help us understand how it is that we all experience time so differently. A singular global event will be registered differently based on an individual's previous experiences (their history and culture), the place they occupy on the chronological scale of historical time (center of gravity), and their willingness to move toward or away from change (an alternative kind of velocity).

Consider applying this framework to the field of politics. We relentlessly poll the sentiment of the public and targeted constituents, in an attempt to predict elections or positions on key topics (though we seem to be becoming more and more unsuccessful at this). But polling is a lagging indicator and has limited utility to explain why people take up the positions they do. The position we take on an issue or event may depend less on a status of "Democrat" or "Republican" and more on where we are in our relative personal timeline. At what velocity are we prepared to encounter or absorb new ideas? Could a theory of "time readiness dilation" offer a more sophisticated analysis of the conditions, contexts, and causes that enable people to make changes in society?

What if time dilation could help us predict when people, communities, markets, or institutions were ready to adopt a new idea?

Consider applying this framework to the realm of business, and specifically to the launch of new products or services. Too often business decisions are made without strategic intelligence or data on whether or not the public, a target market, or a specific user is ready to receive that new product or service. In a business context, is it fair to say that products, services, or big ideas are ahead of their time, or is it more accurate to say that customers and clients are behind their time? How can businesses better align with the timelines of those they wish to introduce new value to?

Today, rather than a singular notion of a "rightful timeline," there exist countless personal, political, and cultural timelines, and they are not all equal. As the famed science fiction and cyberpunk author Wade Gibson said:

The future is already here—it's just not evenly distributed.

People come to embrace complex change on their own timeline, based on the gravitational pull that either slows or accelerates their acquisition of new narratives and knowledge. This timeline is often a function of economic, cultural, and geographic conditions.

If we look back in history to the many voices who were ahead of their time, we can see such readiness for transformative change in Abraham Lincoln, whose annual message to Congress, delivered one month prior to the Emancipation Proclamation in 1862, included the following remarks:

> *Is it doubted, then, that the plan I propose, if adopted, would shorten the war, and thus lessen its expenditure of money and of blood? Is it doubted that it would restore the national authority and national prosperity, and perpetuate both indefinitely? Is it doubted that we here— Congress and Executive—can secure its adoption? Will not the good*

people respond to a united, and earnest appeal from us? Can we, can they, by any other means, so certainly, or so speedily, assure these vital objects? We can succeed only by concert. It is not "can any of us imagine better?" but, "can we all do better?" The dogmas of the quiet past, are inadequate to the stormy present. The occasion is piled high with difficulty, and we must rise—with the occasion. As our case is new, so we must think anew, and act anew. We must disenthrall ourselves, and then we shall save our country.

Those who reject the "dogmas of the quiet past" will forever be ahead of their time.

Befriending
the Sounds of
Slow Time

How can we create the space for slow, wandering, idle time, designed for daydreaming? What if idleness was not the enemy, but the friend we need most?

Georgia O'Keeffe is best known for her paintings of flowers. She completed more than 200 masterworks on the subject, the products of a lifetime of study. A lifetime of slowing down, seeing a small, fragile world, and rendering it anew. Her painting *Jimson Weed/White Flower No. 1* holds the record for the most expensive painting sold by a female artist in history, at $44.4 million. Of her subject, she wisely observed:

Everyone has many associations with a flower—the idea of flowers. . . . Still—in a way—nobody sees a flower—really— it is so small—we haven't time—and to see takes time, like to have a friend takes time.

True friendships ask a lot of us. They call for long-term commitments, nurturing, and care. Like a good friendship, time is something we must work to prioritize and protect. But most of us haven't befriended time. In fact, we have entered an abusive relationship with it.

Our relationship with time is dictated by the relentless frequency of transactions that mark our daily lives, slicing our time into smaller and smaller consumable parts.

We've surrendered our very definition of time to an economic vocabulary. We ask each other, "Did you spend your time well?" as though time is a checkbook to be balanced or a kind of currency to be spent. Instead of something to be savored, we view time as something to be "managed" and "optimized." But the very concept of time management is a paradox. We do not have the capacity to manipulate time. Time manages us.

It's ironic that even as we treat time as an item on a balance sheet, we've lost the most important lesson of all: that investments in slow, quiet time pay dividends. It's the friendship that O'Keeffe cherished.

When production is the dominant idea, the urgency of these transactions privileges speed above all else, resulting in rash, short-term decisions that undermine the kind of strategic, resilient, exponential value creation that can only come from slow, deliberate, long-term creative thinking. Extended uninterrupted time is where the alchemy happens. But the relentless taskmaster of the production economy prevents us from showing what a good friendship with time could yield. A cycle we need to break free of.

At times, I believe, all of capitalism is a blunt instrument concerned more with the swing of the bat than with the precision of its aim. Time is a frequent victim of such an instrument.

According to a 2015 study conducted by Microsoft researchers in Canada, the average person generally loses their concentration after eight seconds, a drop from twelve seconds in the year 2000. Considering that the length of a goldfish's memory is documented to be about nine seconds, it may be safe to say we have become less focused than goldfish. The researchers' theory is that the internet is responsible for this drop in attention span. According to the report, "heavy multi-screeners find it difficult to filter out irrelevant stimuli—they're more easily distracted." Constantly filling our time with distracted busyness is hampering our ability to think deeply, weakening our resolve to be present, and tempting us with the immediacy of fleeting sensations at the expense of a fuller, more meaningful life.

Our resistance to slow time and our addiction to accelerated, frenetic time is deeply rooted in capitalistic influence. The phrase "time is money" originated in an essay by Benjamin Franklin in 1748 that was meant to illustrate the monetary cost of laziness and idleness:

Remember that Time is Money. He that can earn Ten Shillings a Day by his Labour, and goes abroad, or sits idle one half of that Day, tho' he spends but Sixpence during his Diversion or Idleness, ought not to reckon That the only Expence; he has really spent or thrown away Five Shillings besides.

In the capitalist narrative, idle time is a diversion equivalent to throwing money away. But more than 270 years after Benjamin Franklin's declaration, even he would be surprised by how severely entangled time and money have become, thanks to the marketplaces our contemporary digital world has constructed—marketplaces that draw upon and monetize our time. In her book *How to Do Nothing: Resisting the Attention Economy*, Jenny Odell offers a lexicon for a society struggling to makes sense of such an addiction and loss of intentional control over our time. She advocates:

> *In a situation where every waking moment has become the time in which we make our living, and when we submit even our leisure for numerical evaluation via likes on Facebook and Instagram, constantly checking on its performance like one checks a stock, monitoring the ongoing development of our personal brand, time becomes an economic resource that we can no longer justify spending on "nothing."*

Odell's book was published less than a year prior to the arrival of the coronavirus pandemic, but her wisdom about slowing down and rethinking our relationship with time took on new meaning as the whole world paused. Two months into the pandemic, the Harvard Graduate School of Design held its first-ever virtual commencement and selected her as the guest speaker. During her speech Odell addressed her own relationship with the timeline of her professional career:

> *I want to come back to that word "career." As a verb "to career" means to move at full speed. It's etymologically related to the word "car." And yet, in my experience, many people who feel fulfilled in what they do would not see their trajectory that way. Certainly I would not. What I have done and what I enjoy doing feels closer to a walk that starts and stops. One with no destination where I often got lost or waylaid by something interesting.*

The meandering path Odell describes is an accurate reflection of how so many creatives, entrepreneurs, and knowledge workers experience the nonlinear trajectory of contemporary life and work. To embrace a slower path can feel counterintuitive, as the pressures on our time have grown exponentially. But there is increasing evidence that the meandering, idle time that Odell speaks of creates ideal conditions for breakthrough thinking. As Emma Seppälä, the science director of Stanford University's Center for Compassion and Altruism Research and Education, writes:

> *I found that the biggest breakthrough ideas often come from relaxation. History shows that many famous inventors have come up with novel ideas while letting their minds wander. . . . Simply put, creativity happens when your mind is unfocused, daydreaming or idle. . . . The idea is to balance linear thinking—which requires intense focus—with creative thinking, which is born out of idleness. Switching between the two modes seems to be the optimal way to do good, inventive work.*

How might we protect this valuable wandering, idle time, designed for daydreaming? We need slow time to provide a space for curiosity to flourish. New ways to drown out the ever-present noise with precious quiet.

Neuroscientist Daniel Levitin, in his book *The Organized Mind*, points out that ambient noise has become nearly inescapable. Americans now consume five times as much information as we did twenty-five years prior—Levitin estimates that we process roughly 100,000 words every day outside of work.

Quieting this noise may be the most powerful factor in enabling our curiosity to thrive.

Think about it: When, in your waking hours, are you ever in an environment without noise? Do you ever go stretches of time without any demands on your attention, in which you are called upon to simply be present and listen? How often are you truly present with yourself, your thoughts, your ideas? When have you experienced a silence that finally enabled you to hear everything you had previously missed?

The power of silence has long been a subject of artistic inquiry. In 1952, John Cage, the conceptual artist known as the co-inventor of the Fluxus movement, staged what he would later call his most important work: 4'33". In it, a pianist walks onstage, sits at the piano, and for four minutes and thirty-three seconds makes no sound. No music. Not a single note. What emerges through that silence are the sounds we typically drown out. The wind, the rain, people uncomfortably shifting in their seats, the buzzing of a light, and, eventually, our own thoughts. 4'33" is an act that invites us to reclaim listening.

An experiment conducted in 2014 by Timothy Wilson, a social psychologist at the University of Virginia, reveals just how uncomfortable people are with the quiet of their own thoughts. Hundreds of community members were invited to take part in "thinking periods" in which they put away their phones and other belongings and settled into sparsely furnished rooms. After a series of exercises, they were given a choice: They could sit alone and think quietly for fifteen minutes or receive an electric shock. Astonishingly, 67 percent of the men and 25 percent of the women chose to inflict the shock on themselves in order to avoid a mere fifteen minutes of silence.

But it turns out that silence might be the soundtrack we need.

And that's just what a new field of acoustic ecologists, sound trackers, deep listeners, and recording musicians are up to. There is an emerging genre of champions who are befriending the sound of slow time.

Some important voices who are carving out the field include:

- **Pauline Oliveros,** *an accordion player and founder of the practice of Deep Listening. Oliveros was a trailblazer, carving new frontiers as a publicly gay feminist musician in the 1970s. She performed onstage until her eighties. Her work as a performance artist, teacher, and sound actionist pushed the boundaries of listening for silence and enabling the whole body to listen. Today, Rensselaer Polytechnic Institute is home to the Center for Deep Listening, driven by her teachings. Her wisdom included: "Take a walk at night. Walk so silently that the bottoms of your feet become ears."*

- **Gordon Hempton,** *a self-described "sound tracker" who has traversed the world in pursuit of the planet's last pristine soundscapes. He is driven by the question "Are there any places on Earth left untouched by noise pollution?" His multimedia documentary projects range from* Earth Is a Solar Powered Jukebox *to* The Ocean Is a Drum. *Perhaps his most ambitious is* One Square Inch of Silence—*an independent research initiative located in the Hoh Rain Forest of Olympic National Park. Within this 1-million-acre forest is a spot that Hempton believes is the least noise-polluted place in the lower forty-eight states. An acoustic haven, free of undesirable human-caused sound.*

- **Dr. Miriam-Rose Ungunmerr-Baumann,** *an Indigenous elder from the Australian tribe Ngangikurungkurr (the name means "deep water sounds"). Her work as an artist and educator has focused on* dadirri, *which she says is the greatest gift Aboriginal Australians can give. Dadirri is an inner, deep listening and quiet, still awareness. She translates it as similar to what we may call "contemplation." It is something that she describes as the way her culture learns—not by asking questions but by listening and being comfortable in silence.*

- **Gibi ASMR,** *a YouTuber, cosplayer, and Twitch streamer who is considered one of the most popular performers of autonomous sensory meridian response, or ASMR. This growing phenomenon* *can be best described as the experience of tingling sensations, micro-euphoria, or kinesthetic pleasure derived from listening to unexpected ordinary sounds of daily life like paper tearing or inti-mate targeted whispering voices. With a background in theater, communications, and film from Northwestern University, she has become what* The New York Times Magazine *called "the Lebron James of touching stuff." ASMR itself gained mainstream notoriety during the 2019 Super Bowl when Anheuser-Busch broadcast an ASMR-themed commercial for its Michelob Ultra Pure Gold beer, where Zoë Kravitz uses ASMR techniques including whispering and tapping on a bottle.*

These practices are part of a larger framework of rethinking our rela-tionship with time, excavating the power of listening, and challeng-ing some of the commonly held beliefs about the conditions under which our best work can unfold. Certainly a pertinent inquiry as we all seek new models for living, working, and flourishing in the Great Reset catalyzed by the pandemic.

There are a variety of movements centered on the concept of "slow" and its benefits, from the slow food movement to the slow reading movement to slow cities. A through-line linking them is the protec-tion of time to enable diversified value outcomes. Capturing time like the emerging idea in urban planning of the fifteen-minute city radius, creating moments like quiet activated alleys between streets, making smarter choices by seeing and connecting patterns. These are the skills of people who work with sound as their profession. Mu-sicians may be the entrepreneurs to convert slow time into real value.

As Panos Panay, senior vice president for global strategy and innova-tion at the Berklee College of Music, and R. Michael Hendrix, a part-ner and global design director at IDEO, propose in their book, *Two Beats Ahead: What Musical Minds Teach Us About Innovation:*

As musicians, we believe that there is something instructive here for our work as entrepreneurs and business leaders. Musicians know how to create moments that break patterns, fill gaps, capture our attention, and inspire not only because of skills they have developed at a keyboard or a microphone, but because they have honed their ability to listen. . . . A musician understands that listening to the world, drawing ideas and inspiration from outside yourself, is only the first part of innovation. It also requires listening to yourself for points of resonance between the world and your own vision and values.

Listening is a business imperative. Only recently has the world of business begun to truly embrace empathy as a leadership practice. But one key piece of the puzzle is too often overlooked: Empathy requires curiosity. We must be curious enough to care about others, but we must also be curious about ourselves. And to truly know ourselves, we must be willing to listen to ourselves.

In today's noisy world, it's all too easy to mute the rich diversity of silences to the point that we are even uncomfortable with our own thoughts. But as Jenny Odell reminds us, these times of complexity require the space for thought that is bred in the slow sounds of silence. She proposes:

On a collective level, the stakes are higher. We know that we live in complex times that demand complex thoughts and conversations—and those, in turn, demand the very time and space that is nowhere to be found. The convenience of limitless connectivity has neatly paved over the nuances of in-person conversation, cutting away so much information and context in the process. In an endless cycle where communication is stunted and time is money, there are few moments to slip away and fewer ways to find each other.

Counterintuitively, we need to slow down in order to speed up. We urgently want to get to the destination of our personal and professional goals, but ironically we might need to take the long way to actually get there. Too frequently the fast solutions we choose lead to errors, flawed assumptions, or missed opportunities—in the end requiring costly rework. Listening to slow time reveals new soundscapes that provide much-needed clarity and uncover the new paths that ultimately realize our goals for fewer resources and less time.

In today's hyperconnected world, we need more contemplative conversations with ourselves, just as much as we need intimate dialogues with each other. We need the quiet solitude that makes space for the deeper, more curious thinking: a space where idleness and slow time are not the enemies, but the friends we need most.

Afrofuturist Time: Ms. President 2036

How might we see historical events as harbingers of possible futures? In what ways can we collapse the past, present, and future to time-travel toward better possibilities? Are artists and creatives world-builders, uniquely positioned to prototype the future? Might it be that the present moment is possible only because some of them have challenged legacy narratives?

It's 2008, during the Democratic National Convention. I was backstage at the Ellie Caulkins Opera House in Denver, Colorado, awaiting showtime for *Terra Nova*, a new large-scale performance by the experimental composer, multimedia artist, and musician DJ Spooky. But *Terra Nova* was no ordinary opera. Instead, it was a multimedia performance—inspired by DJ Spooky's fieldwork in Antarctica—that remixed the images and sounds of ice shifting, melting, moving, and shattering: a symphony for climate change awareness. And it was featured as part of a citywide festival I founded, curated, and produced for the Democratic National Convention called Dialog:City.

The eight installations that constituted Dialog:City were commissioned by John Hickenlooper, a geologist turned brewpub owner/entrepreneur turned mayor of Denver. His vision for the event hinged on an essential question: The city of Denver will be hosting a historic dialogue. This moment is a milestone, launching the first African American nominee of a major political party. Considering all that the Obama "Hope Campaign" represents, how can we engage citizens in this milestone civic conversation?

Normally, ordinary citizens can't attend the actual political convention; that is a privilege reserved for the states' official delegates. But here in Denver, democracy was for everyone. Dialog:City created alternative spaces for civic conversations to spill out into every neighborhood across the city: A utopian experiment in service to the hope Obama campaigned upon. Pulling the future into the present.

Terra Nova offered us a glimpse into the dismal future of our ailing planet. A sensory argument for climate change awareness. A composite of time that existed in the now while simultaneously looking through the lens of the past to project the future. Moments like these are rare and special, offering a window into possible futures, into what could become. Every now and then, we can witness the future being prototyped. I call these experiences *The Present Future*.

Often it is artists, designers, musicians, poets, and cultural entrepreneurs who illuminate The Present Future. As the British writer and artist Wyndham Lewis said:

The artist is always engaged in writing a detailed history of the future because he is the only person aware of the nature of the present.

The Present Future is particularly pronounced in Afrofuturism, a cultural aesthetic, philosophy, and social movement that evaluates the past to create better future conditions for the present generation of Black people. As Essence Harden, a contributing curator to the exhibition *Mothership: Voyage into Afrofuturism* at the Oakland Museum of California, puts it:

What Afrofuturism is attempting is to collapse time so that the past and the future are very much about the present.

The term "Afrofuturism" is attributed to cultural critic Mark Dery, but its earliest roots date back to W. E. B. Du Bois, who laid the foundation for the Afrofuturist school of thought in his short story "The Comet." In a powerful piece published in *Wired* magazine, "How Afrofuturism Can Help the World Mend," C. Brandon Ogbunu inquires:

> *Why do we care about what the Afrofuturist has to say? And why would we suspect that their answers would differ from that of an average futurist? It is because the Black experience is defined by a historical struggle for existence, the right to live, to be considered a person, to be afforded basic rights, in pursuit of (political, social, economic) equality. Because of this, the Afrofuturist can see the parts of the present and future that reside in the status quo's blind spots. . . . Futurists ask what tomorrow's hoverboards and flying cars are made of. Afrofuturists ask who will build them?*

ADRIENNE MAREE BROWN

KEHINDE WILEY

ARTHUR JAFA

OKWUI ENWEZOR

RHIANNON GIDDENS

W. E. B. DU BOIS

JANELLE MONÁE

THEASTER GATES

KIMBERLY DREW

A new genre of contemporary creatives who compress past, present, and future are reinterpreting Afrofuturism.

Creatives live on a tightrope that crosses the present and the future simultaneously.

Creatives are in the business of creating. The act of creating is itself a time-travel activity. It requires an artist to time-travel into the future and reverse-engineer the steps needed to realize it. This idea is reflected in the colloquialism "The best way to predict the future is to create it."

Some of the best laboratories for prototyping the future are those theaters in which artists thrive: museums, concert halls, festivals, and public spaces. This is how Dialog:City converted neighborhoods, karaoke bars, alleyways, empty storefronts, and sidewalks into sites of discourse. And it's also the reason that I traveled to Denver in the first place. To help build a contemporary art museum that would provide artists with a bigger stage on which to experiment with The Present Future.

Museums are platforms for world-building. Playgrounds for The Present Future. They open visitors' imaginations by holding histories and future promises as cultural artifacts. This is in part why the museum architect, whose role it is to design these spaces, has risen to prominence. Historically, the process of selecting a museum architect has been not unlike that of electing a president. Museums nominate a slate of candidates, who campaign to win the majority of the votes of board members and donors. The Museum of Contemporary Art (MCA) Denver inverted that tradition, making the process extraordinarily public, democratic, and community-led. As *The New York Times* described this progressive approach in an article titled "A Museum Rises, but Not the Usual Way":

> But rather than cleaving to the usual protocol—asking architects to make their presentations behind closed doors—Ms. Payton took the process public, requiring each architect to give a lecture to the community. . . . The architects were grilled by two more selection committees—

one comprising architecture students from the University of Colorado at Denver, and the other of high school students from P.S. 1, an alternative public school.

The architect selected through this unique process was David Adjaye, the son of a Ghanaian diplomat. Born in Tanzania, Adjaye lived in Egypt, Yemen, and Lebanon before moving to Britain, where his firm is now based, and his work is a reflection of this global mindset. The building itself does not have a front door (a symbolic gesture of accessibility to the public), it achieved LEED Gold certification (making it the nation's first LEED-certified contemporary art museum and a pioneering example of sustainability), and it has a rooftop designed for community gatherings that quickly became the place to be on a Friday night. Denver set up an Afrofuturist architectural experiment, and not only did it work, it soared. The selection of an emerging African architect to spearhead an Afrofuturist architectural experiment convinced my wife and me to move halfway across the country so that I could accept the museum's offer to come on board as deputy director.

The inaugural exhibition of MCA Denver, curated by executive director Cydney Payton, was called *Star Power: Museum as Body Electric.* A love letter to Walt Whitman's poem "I Sing the Body Electric" from *Leaves of Grass,* the exhibition featured artists such as Mexican animator Carlos Amorales, Maori traditional carver Rangi Kipa, British painter Chris Ofili, and Canadian installation artist David Altmejd.

Of the featured artists, Kenyan artist Wangechi Mutu stood out. Her work consistently uses collage and mixed media to stitch together creatures who borrow from diverse cultural traditions but are anchored in African identity and narratives. In an astounding body of work spanning three decades, she has developed a language that challenges colonialist, racist, and sexist worldviews. As Carrie Mae Weems—the recipient of a MacArthur "genius grant," winner of the Harvard University W. E. B. Du Bois Medal, artist, and friend of Mutu's—described Mutu's work:

She creates whole new mythologies for her vivid, ever-expanding artistic domain, inventing radical cosmological creatures that can be seductive, monstrous, secretive, triumphant, and all-powerful, as if mating folklore with sci-fi cyborgian fantasy. Mutu has often been linked with Afrofuturism—the cultural movement that welds the iconography and history of the Black diaspora with advanced technology to evoke alternate futures and embolden an awakening consciousness.

Out of textile patterns, fashion, and historical references, she builds new alternative worlds. Voices like Wangechi Mutu and David Adjaye belong to a multidecade process of deconstructing legacy narratives and creating spaces in which new and diverse voices can flourish. Theirs is a vision for a more inclusive future made possible by challengers who paved the way before them. And few have done more to enable these emerging narratives in the arts than the Nigerian art historian and curator Okwui Enwezor, whose string of projects has included launching *Nka: Journal of Contemporary African Art* from his Brooklyn apartment ("Nka" is an Igbo word that means "to make, to create"; it is also the Basaa word for "discourse"); becoming the first non-European artistic director of Documenta in Germany, one of the largest arts events in the world; curating *The Rise and Fall of Apartheid: Photography and the Bureaucracy of Everyday Life* for the International Center for Photography; and becoming the first African-born curator in the Venice Biennale's 120-year history. His Biennale show, titled *All the World's Futures*, envisioned new ways of living in a time beyond our current moment. It was presented at the Arena, an auditorium designed by the architect David Adjaye.

Enwezor's legacy of addressing colonial histories and surfacing the voices of the invisible to create a better world for humanity reflects the very principles David Adjaye himself has come to practice. Two architects of time. One an architect of theaters for world-building, one an architect of spaces for civic discourse.

Adjaye brought his commitment to The Present Future to the next level as the architect of the National Museum of African American History and Culture. Located on the National Mall at the heart of our nation's capital, its very presence reminds us of the need to mend a broken national narrative. When President Obama spoke at the museum's opening ceremony in 2016, he invoked the same Walt Whitman who inspired the inaugural exhibition at MCA Denver, *Star Power: Museum as Body Electric*. With the suffering and pain of the African American story inescapably present in the backdrop, he reassured us by saying:

We are large, Walt Whitman told us, containing multitudes. We are large containing multitudes, full of contradictions. That's America. That's what makes us go. That's what makes us extraordinary.

Afrofuturists are optimists who refuse to allow the atrocities of the past to shatter their faith in what the future may bring. Dreaming, in the Afrofuturist paradigm, is not fantasy, but a form of activism. Obama thanked Congressman John Lewis, the civil rights icon who spent fifteen years fighting to make the museum a reality. In his own speech that day, Lewis declared:

> *There were some who said it couldn't happen, who said "you can't do it," but we did it. . . . This place is more than a building. It is a dream come true.*

This is why museums are stages for world-building. They help us time-travel. They invite us to transcend the limits of the present moment and study our past in the spirit of hope for the future.

In 2018, I staged a surprise field trip for my team from Rhode Island to Washington, D.C., to visit the National Museum of African American History and Culture. It was my first time at the museum. It leveled me.

A mark of Adjaye's brilliance is that the visitor experience is designed to give you time to contemplate the collapse of time. To unpack the weight of the centuries-long legacy narrative you just compressed into hours. To acknowledge your own responsibility in shaping the emerging narrative of what comes next for this country. Etched onto the wall is Sam Cooke's lyric "A change is gonna come."

The architecture of this museum itself follows the Afrofuturist tradition of collapsing past, present, and future. As David Adjaye describes it:

> *I think about the building in three parts. There are the historical galleries, which make a kind of crypt, in an underground space. Then a second part deals with migration from the South to urban centers and the beginning of the professional classes. I wanted the journey from that crypt up into the corona to be analogous to history, as a kind of migratory process, toward the light. Then you go up to the uppermost level; I call it "Now." It's about the arts. So, this tripartite structure relates to the corona's three tiers. It's meant to suggest the link between symbolic form and the museum's content.*

A three-tiered structure housing the three tiers of the African American narrative: History. Migration. Now.

And what is *now*?

Now is January 20, 2021, on the same National Mall where President Obama delivered his message of hope at the opening of the Smithsonian National Museum of African American History and Culture. It is time for another pass of the baton. An interregnum. The transition of power from President Trump to President Biden. Just weeks after a violent insurrection and attack on the Capitol, the friction between legacy and emerging narratives is acutely palpable. The air is heavy, the excitement dampened by the sobering knowledge that this day almost didn't come to pass.

Of course, the day did happen. Democracy did prevail. And the voice of a new leader did emerge. But it wasn't who we expected. Twenty-two-year-old Amanda Gorman brought the country to its knees that day with a poem based on the events of the insurrection just fourteen days prior. As she stood on the podium and looked out onto the National Mall, her cadence, her body language, and her stirring delivery cast a spell over the crowd. She was just what America needed. She was, most certainly, what I needed.

Gorman collapsed time to heal us. She confronts a past we cannot escape and imagines futures we can only co-create. She inherits those histories. But she is also The Present Future. As she reminds us:

> *We, the successors of a country and a time where a skinny Black girl descended from slaves and raised by a single mother can dream of becoming president, only to find herself reciting for one.*

It turns out Amanda Gorman has dreamed of becoming president of the United States since she was eleven. She even has a date in mind: 2036. In an interview with *WSJ.* magazine, aptly titled "Why Poet Amanda Gorman Wants to Be President," she says:

I think to make the impossible more proximate, you have to treat it as if it's in reaching distance.

Will her dream come to pass? Only time will tell. But here is what I know for sure:

When Amanda Gorman is ready to run, I will join her campaign. She is a present future.

YOUTH

13

Innovation as a Practice of Awe

What is innovation for? In our desire for shiny new objects, have we forgotten the wonder of new ideas? How can we incubate truly awe-inspiring innovation? How do we evaluate successful innovation? What is the relationship between innovation and awe?

Innovation—as practiced today—is overrated, misunderstood, and in service to the wrong outcomes. In contemporary business, too frequently innovation has been redefined as a vehicle for economic gain. Why is innovation so closely associated with *economic* growth, when there are many types of growth—personal, intellectual—worthy of innovation? Innovation has become the language of financial accounting rather than the language of progress. Imagine if the CEO of a corporation announced, "This year we will achieve double-digit growth"—and the metric referred to the increase in knowledge, happiness, or meaning that employees experienced in a calendar year. Imagine if the president of the United States was elected on a promise of "an era of growth like America has never seen"—and that growth referred to the increase in equity, culture, and collective care of all its citizens, rather than GDP.

Innovation has historically meant the creation of new ideas—but in modern times it often seems as though the only new idea that matters is money. We've inverted the equation. Money should be a byproduct of profoundly valuable ideas, not the idea itself. When ideas are culturally relevant, they are valued by the market. Profit, then, is an outcome of ideas that are culturally valued by society. This inversion—treating money instead of ideas as the primary objective—is making us idea impotent.

The irony is that our financialization of ideas is preventing the very thing we need for valuable new ideas to emerge. Ideas with resilient, transformative, purposeful value come from changes in the way people think. If we want big, bold ideas, we need to re-engineer our minds, not engineer new products. The work ahead is not mechanical, technological, or production-based. True innovation requires us to ask the Radically Curious questions that lead to deeper insights, not greater profits. To change not the tools that we wield, but what we wield them for.

Such a task is not easy. And it requires something unexpected. It requires awe.

Psychologists Dacher Keltner and Jonathan Haidt have proposed a conceptual approach that defines the experience of awe in terms of two phenomena: (1) perceived vastness and (2) violating our understanding of the world. These concepts are distilled in a white paper by Summer Allen titled "The Science of Awe," which explains:

"Perceived vastness" can come from observing something literally phys-ically large—the Grand Canyon, for example—or from a more theo-retical perceptual sense of vastness—such as being in the presence of someone with immense prestige or being presented with a complex idea like the theory of relativity. An experience evokes a "need for accom-modation" when it violates our normal understanding of the world. When a stimulus exceeds our expectations in some way, it can provoke an attempt to change the mental structures that we use to understand the world. Accommodation . . . refers to psychologist Jean Piaget's "process of adjusting mental structures that cannot assimilate a new experience." In other words, your conception of the world needs to shift or expand in order to make sense of this new experience.

Experiences of awe shift or expand our conception of the world. To describe the experience of awe, we often say, "That was mind-blowing." We *have* blown our minds, in that an awe-inspiring ex-perience blows up a previous worldview. Then our minds can accommodate a new, reorganized view of the world.

Awe catalyzes an operating system upgrade. But not merely at a sur-face level. Awe can play with our minds in ways that challenge what we think we know to be certain. Causing our "truths" to feel uncer-tain and our core beliefs to feel unstable. Is the Earth the center of the universe, or is the Sun? Is there one God, many gods, or no God? What is the relationship between humans and the natural world? Awe tends to make us question the big stuff.

We need to become more comfortable with this sort of questioning. To be content viewing knowledge as not a static object but an activ-ity, a sustained inquiry in which the blowing of minds is a constant. The most valuable explorations are always elusive. They yield not answers but new questions, better questions, until we go deep enough to see that the process of inquiry is itself awe-inspiring. This is where the magic lies. In the space between what is known and what is unknown. That is where awe yields tremendous possibility.

Helen De Cruz wrote about the bridge between what is known and unknown in her essay "The Necessity of Awe." In it she describes the difficult human experience of innovation in terms of dismissing one narrative and harvesting a new one:

> When a scientific paradigm breaks down, scientists need to make a leap into the unknown. These are moments of revolution, as identified by Thomas Kuhn in the 1960s, when the scientists' worldview becomes untenable and the agreed-upon and accepted truths of a particular discipline are radically called into question. Beloved theories are revealed to have been built upon sand. Explanations that held up for hundreds of years are now dismissed. A particular and productive way of looking at the world turns out to be erroneous in its essentials. The great scientific revolutions—such as those instigated by Copernicus, Galileo, Newton, Lavoisier, Einstein and Wegener—are times of great uncertainty, when cool, disinterested reason alone doesn't help scientists move forward because so many of their usual assumptions about how their scientific discipline is done turn out to be flawed. So, they need to make a leap, not knowing where they will land. . . . To change the field or accept radical changes in it, you need to alter your outlook on the world. Awe can do this. It focuses attention away from yourself and makes you think outside of your usual thought patterns.

This is a useful articulation of the difficulty in breaking out of legacy narratives. De Cruz challenges us to look at what we ask of ourselves when we innovate: to accept the possibility that beloved theories have been built upon sand, that centuries-old views of the world must be dismissed. There are profound and frightening implications when innovation means the breaking and rebuilding of mental models.

Margaret J. Wheatley, in her book *Turning to One Another: Simple Conversations to Restore Hope to the Future*, asks us to consider our willingness to be challenged, to risk revealing that our personal truths have been built upon sand. She proposes:

As we work together to restore hope to the future, we need to include a new and strange ally—our willingness to be disturbed. Our willingness to have our beliefs and ideas challenged by what others think. No one person or perspective can give us the answers we need to the problems of today. Paradoxically, we can only find those answers by admitting we don't know. We have to be willing to let go of our certainty and expect ourselves to be confused for a time.

We live in perplexing times. Times in which innovation has come to mean something less profound. Our resistance to spending more time not knowing—at a time when there is so much we don't know—has left us with a kind of innovation we might not recognize.

Somewhere along the way we substituted the awe of radically new ideas with a desire for anything new. The production economy loves a shiny new object. Which perhaps explains why the buzzword "innovation," perhaps the most overused, misunderstood, and meaningless term in recent years, has become synonymous with the notion of any new transaction. As early as 2013, *Wired* magazine declared:

Like Miss America contestants wanting world peace, the term "innovation" has become the canned response of executives, politicians, and educators to the question, "What do we need to be successful?" . . . To be competitive in this changing world, we have put an emphasis on coming up with new ideas, products, and services that add value. We have called this solution, "innovation." . . . To be truly innovative, you need a combination of critical, conceptual, creative, reflective, and visionary thinking skills combined with behavioral traits such as curiosity, resilience, the ability to collaborate, and the development of both observation and communication skills. While this list can be modified, the main point is that innovation is mostly used as a slogan with no substance and should be seen as a process.

If we look back in history, there are some important clues to why the term "innovation" has evolved in the way it has. The Canadian historian Benoît Godin has researched the foundational origins of "innovation" as a practical, theoretical, legal, and business concept. One of his most significant books, *Innovation Contested: The Idea of Innovation over the Centuries*, offers a studious historical examination:

> *In the particularly entrenched religious atmosphere of sixteenth and seventeenth century Europe, doctrinal innovation was anathema. Some saw this kind of newness as an affiliation with Puritanism, or worse popery . . . in an extreme case from 1636, when an English Puritan and former royal official, Henry Burton, began publishing pamphlets advocating against church officials as innovators, levying Proverbs 24:21 as his weapon: "My Sonne, feare thou the Lord, and the King, and meddle not with them that are given to change." In turn, the pot-stirring Puritan was accused of being the true "innovator" and sentenced to a life in prison and worse—a life without ears.*

Henry Burton's invocation of Proverbs 24:21 is particularly meaningful. The final phrase, "meddle not with them that are given to change," has been reinterpreted to mean "don't associate with the rebels" or "don't get involved with the revolutionaries," suggesting that being an innovator was synonymous with being a heretic. Likely because innovators destroy beliefs that had gone unquestioned for centuries.

The fear of newness is innate. Instinctually, when we take our first steps as babies, we feel our way forward with trepidation, as though the floor may fall out from under us. As adults, newness and uncertainty produce a similar sensation: as though we are standing at the edge of a cliff. We have such charged emotional associations with the dichotomy of certainty and uncertainty. Certainty makes us feel safe. Uncertainty makes us feel like our stomach is leaping out of our body. Still, given that uncertainty is part of the human condition, you'd think we'd be better at navigating newness.

Awe can help us navigate. It builds a humility and curiosity suited for traversing the unknown. In "The Science of Awe," Summer Allen writes:

> *Studies have found that awe can create a diminished sense of self, give people the sense that they have more available time, increase feelings of connectedness, increase critical thinking and skepticism, increase positive mood, and decrease materialism. . . . Research suggests that awe diminishes a person's sense of self, shifting their focus away from their own concerns. Accordingly, perhaps the most studied psychological effect associated with awe is the "small self"—the feeling of being small relative to one's surroundings.*

It seems a life filled with awe is quite healthy. When we seek out experiences of awe, we welcome wonder into our lives. So it's not surprising that true innovators often have reputations as fantastical, as frivolous, as dreamers. Awe and wonder are the currencies of innovation labs, start-up incubators, design studios, and other places where creative work happens. Such places exist to grow ideas. Big, bold ideas don't easily fit into Excel spreadsheets. As *Fast Company* magazine described, "If Willy Wonka had microchips, his factory would have been the MIT Media Lab . . . known for creating some of the most wondrous marvels of our era—from computers you control with levitating orbs to architecture woven by silkworms."

Those big, bold ideas require patience and imagination because they are at the rare intersection of awe and extraordinary possibility. Organizations have aspired to harness this power within centers of innovation, writing the American story along the way. Think Bell Labs (born from within AT&T in 1925), Xerox PARC (founded in 1970), the MIT Media Lab (founded by Nicholas Negroponte in 1985), and Y Combinator (founded in 2005, it has launched more than 2,000 companies with a combined valuation of more than $300 billion).

A book by Jon Gertner titled *The Idea Factory: Bell Labs and the Great Age of American Innovation* chronicled this history. In his review of the book for *The New York Times,* Walter Isaacson wrote:

> *"The Idea Factory" explores one of the most critical issues of our time: What causes innovation? Why does it happen, and how might we nurture it? The lesson of Bell Labs is that most feats of sustained innovation cannot and do not occur in an iconic garage or the workshop of an ingenious inventor. They occur when people of diverse talents and mindsets and expertise are brought together, preferably in close physical proximity where they can have frequent meetings and serendipitous encounters.*

Today, nearly a century after Bell Labs was founded, everything has changed, and nothing has changed. We can live, learn, and work anywhere through virtual interactions. We've become dangerously accustomed to social distancing. But what Walter Isaacson distilled from *The Idea Factory* is that places themselves—places where diverse, talented people convene around a purpose—can be theaters for awe. More than anything, these incubators of ideas are social phenomena.

Dava Newman is bringing that awe back to the theater of wonder known as the MIT Media Lab, where she took the helm at the end of 2020. She brings a social, civic edge to the renowned innovation hub: an operating system reboot to keep it relevant in a changing world. In a letter announcing her appointment, Hashim Sarkis, dean of MIT's School of Architecture and Planning, described her as "a convener, a communicator, a futurist, a humanist and, importantly, an optimist." Newman, a previous deputy administrator of NASA during the Obama administration, is reframing the vision of the organization under this simple "three P's" approach:

> *People: That's the magic, the genius, that means our entire community. Everyone does bring a sparkle, something unique we can all learn from.*

Parity: We can focus on all types of amazing things. But of those technologies and experiences we're inventing, what will have the largest impact for society?

Play: This is a playful place. And it needs to be. Play brings out some of the best in us in terms of taking risks, trying this, trying that. It's not linear thinking. You have to give yourself time to think and be creative.

The MIT Media Lab can conjure images of curious engineering nerds in garages playing with mechanical circuitry. And it still can be, as long as it is also a place propelled by equity, participation, and risk-taking: a place where people are "stretched beyond their comfort zone to collectively imagine a better, bolder future."

In times of uncertainty, I am betting on magicians like Dava Newman to lead the way. It's time for a new era of leadership. An awe-based leadership.

We need more Radically Curious leaders like Astro Teller, the co-founder of Alphabet's moonshots division, X, who understand we need to think in questions, not answers. In a 2020 commencement address Teller advised the young graduates:

On the one hand, this is an incredibly daunting time. On the other, we have a once-in-a-century opportunity to hit the reset button, let go of conventional ways of thinking, and rebuild the world in radically better ways. This shift in perspective might feel difficult, even premature. However, the alternative—to try to claw society back towards an old normal that wasn't working that well in many ways—is far worse. And counterintuitively, those of us who are newer and fresher in our fields, like the Class of 2020, may have some of the strongest tailwinds as we search for new approaches to the world's most pressing problems. We've seen many times over the years at X that strategic naivete is actually a superpower.

Innovation can no longer mean more food delivery apps or more shiny new gadgets nobody needs. We can no longer afford to dedicate the greatest minds of a generation to convincing people to hit the "like" button. We need to hit reset and redefine innovation to take on the world's most pressing problems. I'm all in. You?

14

May We Never Grow Up

What are the special qualities of youth that we might learn from as adults? How do we shift from viewing youth as an early stage of development to embracing it as a lifelong approach to engaging with the world?

When I was a child, my highly anticipated holiday gifts from Grandma Pearl were VHS tapes of Disney animated films. *Snow White and the Seven Dwarfs, Pinocchio, Fantasia, Bambi,* and my favorite: *Peter Pan*. They were mesmerizing. Invitations to explore and invent new worlds.

The films became my entry into a love of drawing at the early age of eight. I spent hours studying the characters, translating them into sketchbooks. Learning to see. Learning to draft. Practicing breaking down the building blocks of shapes, spatial dynamics, and composition. Embracing drawing as a creative language for world-building. In the quiet space of a rural childhood, drawing was a way of wandering. Of thinking. Of imagining. Of traveling everywhere without going anywhere.

Drawing became a ritual. Like breathing. Riding a bike. A physical rhythm that would center me. An activity that I now credit as a primary source of my mental health. The associated routine, right down to the smell of a number two pencil, was a familiar comfort that represented, for me, Maya Angelou's idea of a child's relationship to home:

Home is that youthful region where a child is the only real living inhabitant. Parents, siblings, and neighbors, are mysterious apparitions, who come, go, and do strange unfathomable things in and around the child, the region's only enfranchised citizen.

Twenty years later I found myself at the Disney Imagineering offices, the research and development arm of Disney charged with the design of theme parks and attractions. Bruce Mau, the legendary designer and an early pioneer of design thinking, and I were invited to join Bruce Vaughn, then chief creative officer at Disney Imagineering, for a strategy workshop to discuss the future of EPCOT. The meeting was curated by Barb Groth, an extraordinary experience maker who found a way to bridge the worlds of the two Bruces. About a year earlier I had joined Bruce Mau's firm as the lead of the Massive Change practice. Given Mau's reputation—he has worked with Frank Gehry, Coca-Cola, and MoMA—we frequently received unusual invitations to apply design to ambitious projects. To be invited to work on EPCOT is a near-religious event for a Disney experience designer, one treated with reverence out of respect for the history and symbolism of what it represents. It's a legacy project that is wrapped up in the identity of being an Imagineer, a term that first emerged as early as the 1940s in an ad in *Time* magazine for an aluminum company that read: "*Imagineering is letting your imagination soar, and then engineering it down to earth.*" In 1966 Walt Disney filmed a twenty-five-minute short film, perhaps the world's earliest "explainer video," meant to articulate the vision for the Experimental Prototype Community of Tomorrow. In it, Disney outlined what would later become known as "The EPCOT Philosophy." He envisioned a utopian planned community. A kind of living lab in which the process of inventing and testing new ideas and finding solutions to urban systems would be exhibited.

EPCOT would always be in a state of flux, flowing, embracing change as central to its core reason for being. A key design principle that is still present with me today. Disney died before his film was shared publicly, and the full, audacious scope of EPCOT was abandoned by the company. For the millions who visit it, EPCOT is an amusement park. For Walt Disney, the man who conceived it, EPCOT was a grand experiment. Its roots are more radical than what is seen on the surface.

When Bruce and I were invited to work with the Imagineers, we were welcomed into a rare behind-the-scenes conversation that returned us to those roots. A conversation focused on a fundamental inquiry: (1) What was EPCOT originally envisioned to be? (2) What did it become? (3) How might we honor Walt Disney's original dream with a vision bold enough to change the trajectory of its future?

The evening of our Imagineering workshop, we went to a dinner that would change my life. Too often, the obligatory ritual of business dinners with clients and colleagues can slide into the mundane. However, that evening was anything but. It was the kind of shared experience that forges lifelong friendships.

Where would Imagineers take someone out to dinner? The Bazaar, naturally. A restaurant by trailblazing chef José Andrés, brought to life in a physical environment by the French industrial designer Philippe Starck. The restaurant is aptly named. The Bazaar is a multisensory adventure, a cultural theater, and a bustling marketplace all in one. The environment is like walking into a Salvador Dalí painting, heightening the disorientation.

José Andrés, originally from Spain, is a major force in bringing the avant-garde genre of molecular gastronomy to the United States. "Molecular gastronomy" has become a popular term that describes, but does not do justice to, an expanding field of experimentation in the culinary arts. The field embraces scientific techniques to deconstruct food down into primary building blocks, enabling chefs to reconstruct elements in unexpected ways that transform the experience of dining into a tour of wonder. A version of Aristotle's first-principles philosophy embodied in the culinary arts.

Our meal that evening was punctuated by signature experiences, not dishes. We started with a liquefied shrimp cocktail, served in a set of chemistry-style pipettes used to squirt the experience into your mouth. This is when you know you need to check tradition at the door.

My favorite sensory experience from that evening, and one I have enjoyed introducing others to since, are the olives in honor of Andrés's mentor, Ferran Adrià from El Bulli. The experience is presented as olives in two ways: old school and new school. The old-school way is the most fantastic green olives from Spain. Plump, juicy, well seasoned, organic delight. Juxtaposed next to those olives is the modern interpretation of olives. Each of these olives is presented on a single spoon as a liquid flavor encased in a kind of edible membrane, like a micro-balloon. It enters your mouth and bursts with a single bite that explodes rich flavor, more pronounced than its "real" pairing. Clearly choreographed as a comparison between natural and synthetic, old and new, recognizable and strange. Forcing you to ask, between giggles, *"What was that?!"*

The collision of real and surreal subverts expectations. When we experience this disorientation, we upend the certainty of what we think we know, recalibrate our minds, and stretch our imaginations to absorb and acquire new conceptions of what might be possible. This simulation, delivered by a marriage of art and science, is a heightened expression of what I call wonder.

A particular kind of wonder is best characterized by Albert Einstein:

This "wondering" appears to occur when an experience comes into conflict with a world of concepts already sufficiently fixed within us.

In the language of science fiction, "sense of wonder" is defined as "*a feeling of awakening or awe triggered by an expansion of one's awareness of what is possible or by a confrontation with the vastness of space and time.*"

Awe triggered by an expansion of what is possible. Imagine that food could deliver such a radical experience, triggering awe that expands awareness, challenging you to question what you know. Molecular gastronomy demonstrates that our commonly held beliefs can be quickly deconstructed and put back together in unrecognizable formats, challenging the certainty and safety that adults call wisdom. Adulthood is, too often, synonymous with the safety of familiar convention. We wrap ourselves in the security blanket of conventional wisdom, limiting the countless possibilities promised to us in our youth. But kids are unconstrained by a distinction between what is real and unreal. This is true too for Andrés, boundaryless in his craft, daring us to be youthful once again. Childlike in our arrival to a situation for which there is no precedent, demanding us to embrace *not knowing*.

When observed in adults, the state of childlike wonder—of awe—is often looked down upon as naivete. But why do we project such a negative lens on *not knowing*? Must everything be *known*?

In Joe Moran's review of the book *Beginners: The Joy and Transformative Power of Lifelong Learning*, by Tom Vanderbilt, he reminds us that the term "dilettante" comes from the Italian *dilettare*, which means "to delight," but the English word is generally understood to mean a frivolous dabbler. The term "amateur" is rooted in the French word for love, *amour*, yet is often used to describe someone inept, bungling, uncommitted.

That we have ascribed pejorative meaning to so much of the vocabulary related to the joy of learning is telling. Why must we be contemptuous of the sheer delight of finding what one loves about the world? How else do we determine what's worth knowing, unknowing, and remaking anew?

When something is known, it gets fixed in place. And when things are fixed in place, life can become stale. It's the wrestling with the complexity of a dynamic, ever-changing world that makes life interesting.

No wonder Peter Pan didn't want to grow up. Growing up meant missing out on the joy of discovery.

To seek greater understanding of the world, we must start with the recognition that ideas are in flux, iteratively redefining themselves all the time. Core concepts we may have been taught to think of as static are in fact constantly in motion. This is foundational to Radical Curiosity because it gives us permission to challenge traditions that others believe to be sacred.

Our experience in a world of concepts already sufficiently fixed in our adult mindset.

When we are standing in the nowness of our youth we are more agile and able to imagine with a sense of wonder.

Our lives—and the ideas that constitute them—are iterative works in progress. Humans understood this as early as the sixth century B.C., when the Greek philosopher Heraclitus insisted that change was inevitable and ever present—that we are constantly in the process of "becoming." As Heraclitus famously declared: "No man ever steps in the same river twice," meaning that everything flows, nothing stands still. Because youth is itself an in-between time, existing in the space between childhood and adulthood, it is an era of becoming.

In the mid-1800s, the French poet and essayist Charles Baudelaire wrote:

The child sees everything in a state of newness. . . . Nothing more resembles what we call inspiration than the delight with which a small child absorbs form and colour. . . . Genius is nothing more nor less than childhood recovered at will.

I love this idea. Genius is nothing more than childhood recovered at will, because a child sees the potential in everything. Artists, entrepreneurs, inventors, and innovators seek to hold on to this aspect of youth: a time in which every encounter is new, pregnant with possibility. After all, isn't this what children instinctively do, and Walt Disney spent decades trying to do—imagining and building new worlds?

For me, Peter Pan and a number two pencil were the tools for worldbuilding. For my son, games like Minecraft and Fortnite are his field of play. Games that literally simulate the act of creating, exploring, and enacting stories within new virtual worlds. The tools may have evolved over the years, but the joy of discovery is the same.

In 1966, Robert F. Kennedy delivered his most impactful speech, known as the "Day of Affirmation" address (or the "Ripple of Hope" speech), to more than 18,000 students in Cape Town, South Africa, stirring an optimistic narrative to confront apartheid and justice in both South Africa and the United States. While the address is largely remembered for how it shook up the politics around civil rights issues in the two countries, it also contains a stirring reflection on youth as a state of mind:

This world demands the qualities of youth: not a time of life but a state of mind, a temper of the will, a quality of imagination, a predominance of courage over timidity, of the appetite for adventure over the life of ease.

I long for leaders who throw timidity aside and act with the kind of courage and appetite for adventure that was alive in their youth. This isn't as implausible as it may seem.

In *Letter to My Daughter*, Maya Angelou optimistically muses that maybe most of us don't ever truly grow up. That our childhood selves are our real selves, and that even as we grow older our youthful spirit remains. She writes:

> *I am convinced that most people do not grow up. We find parking spaces and honor our credit cards. We marry and dare to have children and call that growing up. I think what we do is mostly grow old. We carry accumulation of years in our bodies and on our faces, but generally our real selves, the children inside, are still innocent and shy as magnolias. We may act sophisticated and worldly but I believe we feel safest when we go inside ourselves and find home, a place where we belong and maybe the only place we really do.*

Children are beginners at being in the world. But even as adults, we are constantly finding ourselves in situations, contexts, and cultures where we feel like a fish out of water, where we're still figuring out the rules of the game. We may do grown-up things like finding parking spaces and paying our bills. But we shouldn't equate this with growing up. The world needs our youthful courage now more than ever.

Looking back at my own childhood, maybe it wasn't a coincidence that Peter Pan was the Disney character I fell most in love with. After all, even Captain Hook knew the truth:

> *Growing up is such a barbarous business, full of inconvenience . . . and pimples.*

15

Coming to
Our Senses

How are we to absorb the fullest experience of living? Why are we so desensitized to the visual feast the world has to offer? Can curiosity heighten our senses, allowing us to receive and register more from our experiences?

When I was working with Bruce Mau, he introduced me to people in a peculiar fashion. At twenty-seven years old, I was leading client teams made up of people who were sometimes three decades older than me. They would ask me upon our first meeting, as if to tiptoe around the subject of my youth, "What's your background?" Bruce, without missing a beat, would quickly assert: "Seth has no background, he's all foreground."

A profoundly witty quip. Foreground is a space that optically is perceived as larger than the background, a stage design technique to orient readers to the space in which the action is taking place.

The perception of youthfulness is a recurring theme in my life. But my conceptualization of the idea of youth refers to how we show up to our lives, rather than a marker of chronological time. For me, youth has meant the sheer delight of finding what one loves about the world, what's worth knowing, unknowing, and remaking anew. The beginning of a lifelong adventure, full of surprises as we unfix what we thought we knew to be certain. Keeping us young, on the edge of our seats.

So it has come as a great shock to me to repeatedly hear the phrase "You're too young"—a phenomenon that reflects our collective inability to accept anomalies that do not conform to the expected timeline.

But life isn't a schedule, it's a collection of encounters.

Sometimes I imagine myself as Benjamin Button, the character from the F. Scott Fitzgerald short story, aging in reverse. Traveling *from* somewhere rather than *to* somewhere. Packing lived encounters into a nonsensical order. It's in these encounters that something original is born, or as Salman Rushdie describes, "a bit of this and a bit of that is how newness enters the world."

But this also raises questions: How does this collection of encounters change us? How present are we, how able to absorb the fullest experience of living? Can curiosity heighten our senses, allowing us to receive and register more from our lived experiences?

Curiosity calls upon all of our senses. It demands of us to be *resensitized* rather than desensitized. Our lives are filled with transactions. It's difficult to not simply check out and go through the motions. But amid the noise are meaningful signals that we can reattune to. When we embrace a Radically Curious mindset, we can deeply listen to the diverse signals being sent our way, receiving a trove of information, as though through multisensory sonar. How might we become hyperaware of and make sense of these signals?

In my chronological youth, I experienced a life-altering encounter with an Egon Schiele painting. An artist whose work is sensually expressive, and certainly ahead of his time. A protégé of Gustav Klimt, Schiele focused on portraiture, depicting dynamic, intimate, erotic, or tortured bodies: youths coming to their senses. Schiele was born in Austria in 1890, and he held an uncanny resemblance to my grandfather. The resemblance was so striking, in fact, that it led me to research my family history, and I discovered that my great-grandfather had been born in Austria and traveled through many of the same places where Schiele spent his youth.

At age sixteen, I attended one of the largest retrospective exhibitions of his work, which included more than a hundred of his drawings and paintings from the Leopold Collection in Vienna, temporarily on display at MoMA. The exhibit came at a time when my own identity as an artist was at a critical juncture—my curiosity was at its peak. I was devouring all the creative stimuli available to me. But the rural, isolated environment in which I lived then had its limits—so the visit to the big city of New York was like a lightning bolt at a time when I would have been satisfied with simple static electricity.

Schiele took my breath away and taught me how to feel with my eyes.

I'd never seen lines like his before. They didn't describe a shape objectively. Schiele's lines are the visual equivalent of Ella Fitzgerald's scat singing and Miles Davis's jazz. His gestures treat the brush, the pencil, the entire exercise of painting as improv. Crafting an image that can only come from the subject truly being seen. As a result, I felt seen by Schiele himself. It was perhaps my first sublime encounter. In aesthetics and philosophy, "the sublime" is a state beyond the possibility of calculation, measurement, or imitation. A sublime encounter exceeds our expectations, catalyzing a sense of awe that shifts our worldview. It is what Jason Silva describes as "an experience of such perceptual vastness you literally have to reconfigure your mental models of the world to assimilate it."

When we are young, we exist in a state of perpetual awe. Every new encounter exceeds our expectations, simply because we have nothing to compare it to. Schiele himself linked youthfulness to a kind of awe when he wrote:

One needs to observe and experience the world with naïve, pure eyes in order to attain a great weltanschauung.

"Weltanschauung" is a term, derived from German, that simply means a specific life philosophy or comprehensive worldview. Isn't this what we are seeking as we collect life's experiences? To develop our own view of the world?

Our daily lives are a visual feast, brimming with signals and clues. In fact, we are primarily visual creatures. The ability to see shapes, colors, textures, and symbols and then synthesize them to make complex observations and meaning is a superpower unique to humans. *More than 80 percent of the information that our brains process is visual.* And our brains process that visual content at an incredibly high speed. In fact, by one estimate, we process visual information 60,000 times faster than textual information. In other words, we were biologically designed to be visual communicators.

But this capability is too often underdeveloped. Driven into hibernation by the de-beautification of a modern world that has convinced itself of our visual illiteracy, a hibernation reinforced by a business environment full of graphs and PowerPoints that are like an assault on our visual sensibilities. Moreover, technology has exponentially increased visual production, resulting in an oversaturation of imagery, a cacophony of visual inputs. Consider photography. In the year 2017 alone, humanity shot 1.2 trillion photographs. In the contemporary moment, more photos than existed in total 150 years ago are being taken *every single moment*. No wonder we've become desensitized to the power and potential of visual culture.

We are constantly recording, reporting, sharing, and resharing—yet rarely reflecting. Moving on before we have fully experienced what we have photographed. It's as though we've been operating with one eye closed, leaving to chance what kinds of visual information we receive.

Yet as neuroscience leaps forward, we are discovering that our brains have capacities far beyond our traditional expectations. Henry Markram leads the Blue Brain Project at EPFL, a Switzerland-based technology research university, where they are spending ten years digitally scanning, mapping, and simulating all biological activity in the brain at a cellular level. By 2024 this unprecedented effort will yield the first biologically detailed simulation of more than 100 million neurons and nearly 1 trillion synapses. Historically, it's been commonly believed that there are four dimensions—length, width, depth, and time. More recently, string theory has proposed that the universe operates with ten dimensions. But the emerging research out of the Blue Brain Project reveals that our brain creates neural structures with up to eleven dimensions—abstract mathematical spaces articulated in visualizations akin to "sandcastles."

Each of us has a personal visual processing system, in other words, that is operating in more dimensions than our most theoretical model of the universe. Consider what our imaginations can construct, given our natural engineering. Talk about human potential, waiting to be unleashed.

Yet to truly *experience* the visual world requires us to go beyond brain processes and allow our hearts to make meaning of what we see.

The term "experience" has roots in the Latin word *experīrī*, which means "to put to the test." It's as though what we now casually describe as experiences are the encounters that put both our brains and hearts to the test. It is through this synthesis that curiosity truly thrives. Maturity, then, is not merely our exposure to time, but the wisdom that comes from putting our senses to the test. Artists, designers, and creatives of all stripes are particularly well tuned to the sensory world around them. After all, the artist's objective is to deliver sublime, awe-inspiring experiences.

Nearly twenty years after walking MoMA's galleries to see Schiele's work, I found myself once again at the museum to see another retrospective: the first comprehensive survey presenting the work of Olafur Eliasson, an Icelandic Danish artist who, like many contemporary artists, no longer confines his work to a single medium, such as painting or sculpture, but employs a range of techniques and mediums to create the conditions for experiences. Eliasson's exhibition, *Take Your Time,* was a series of ephemeral phenomena that made it impossible for the viewer to *not* come to their senses. In one of my favorite installations, called *Beauty,* Eliasson engineered a floor-to-ceiling curtain of fine mist that, with the help of a spotlight, created a gorgeously textured, gently undulating indoor rainbow. Visitors were invited to walk through the curtain, feeling the mist on their skin. I was so moved by the experience, I couldn't help but reach out my tongue and taste a drop of the rainbow.

Eliasson's creative practice sits squarely inside of phenomenology, a branch of philosophy that studies how we perceive and understand phenomena, and the meaning they have in our subjective experience of the world. Essentially, phenomenology is the study of how individuals create experiences. And business is catching on.

Nearly thirty years after Eliasson first premiered his rainbow installation, it seems every Fortune 500 company is building entire departments of experience designers. We are seeing companies hire their own chief experience officers and investing heavily in the "customer experience journey," while artists and designers are increasingly being welcomed into the boardroom to help companies and brands extend their customer touchpoints beyond the essential transaction. All of which can only be described as an arms race to gain a foothold in one of the fastest-growing marketplaces: the experience economy, the goal of which, as Joseph Pine and James Gilmore described in their landmark book *The Experience Economy*, is to "connect businesses with their customers and secure their loyalty through memorable experiences." While it no longer feels revolutionary, corporations are *coming to their senses.*

However, there are essential questions we need to ask about the experience economy. For one, what constitutes an experience? We cannot equate my sublime encounter with Schiele's subversive brushstrokes with my experience of the Walmart app following me into my home and using my search data in the name of loyalty and analytics. As an artist who utilizes the senses myself, I am encouraged that business is beginning to speak the language of experiences. At the same time, we must acknowledge that not all experiences are meaningful, or even welcome. To understand how experiences impact people, communities, and complex societies—for better or worse—we must ask: What is the intention driving the architect of these experiences? In service to what is this medium being wielded? What are the ethical responsibilities of experience designers? These questions begin to highlight the dichotomy between the *cultural* and *commercial* domains of the experience economy.

Experiences are *cultural* when the intent is to activate the senses in ways that stretch people beyond the limits of what they thought was

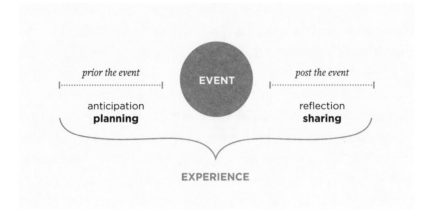

prior the event
|····················|
anticipation
planning

EVENT

post the event
|····················|
reflection
sharing

EXPERIENCE

possible, and in turn give them the opportunity to learn something new about themselves and the world around them.

Experiences are *commercial* when the intent is to activate the senses in ways that stretch the primary value of a product or a service beyond the limits of a production economy, and in turn capture new profits.

The field of experience design is in its infancy. Today, much of it is concerned with engineering commercial experiences in service of economics. But imagine if the focus were on designing cultural experiences in service of eudaimonics, the art of attaining happiness? What if designers were willing to engineer powerful, holistic, multisensory experiences to help tackle the most essential challenges of our time? What if the goal of the experience economy wasn't the monetization of experiences but the maximization of happiness?

Just as advances in neuroscience can help us better understand the connection between our senses and the meaning we make of them, there are powerful insights from psychology to help us understand the connection between experiences and happiness. In a 2014 piece for *The Atlantic,* "Buy Experiences, Not Things," writer James Hamblin codifies the work of the Cornell University psychology professor Thomas Gilovich, who has been trying to figure out exactly how and why experiential purchases make us happier than material purchases. One of his key findings is that much of the happiness derived from experiences is found in the anticipation prior to the event and in the savoring after the event, the memories and retelling of the story. Experiential purchases like trips, concerts, and movies, in other words, tend to deliver more joy than material purchases because the experience of buying anything really starts accruing before you buy it. As it matures, the experience economy may cease to be a particularly unattractive form of capitalism and become a champion for the profound design of possibility.

Artists have long understood the intrinsic value in experiences. As Ursula K. Le Guin, the provocative science fiction author, once said:

One of the functions of art is to give people the words to know their own experience. . . . Storytelling is a tool for knowing who we are and what we want.

Let's come to our senses and commit to being present: to ourselves, to each other, to all the signals we receive, to finding and enjoying the many types of value in our daily experiences. That value will not always be sublime, or sublimely obvious. But if we are open to it, we can tap into our youthful, curious nature and continue to experience the world anew. This is the wish I have for my seven-year-old daughter, Lucy. Already a tremendous bundle of experiences, Lucy has no background. She's all foreground.

16

The Joy of Conversation

Do we really think that our simplified digital communications embody the full wonder of conversation? Can they replace the sacred ritual of sharing a meal with others? Where do we go today to seek out stimulating dialogues in which to revisit unexamined assumptions and imagine a better society? Can we embrace the dinner table as a conversational theater in which trust, empathy, compromise, and new ideas emerge?

Irma Rombauer was born in St. Louis, Missouri, in the year 1877. A pivotal moment in time, as the country struggled to remake itself in the aftermath of the Civil War. The Compromise of 1877, an agreement to settle the results of the 1876 presidential election, marked the end of the Reconstruction era, as politics overrode the federal commitment to protect African Americans' rights.

Irma Rombauer, whose father immigrated to the United States from Germany, lived at a time when women were largely excluded from civic life, a source of frustration for an independent spirit whose father was active in civic affairs and whose half brother would be responsible for introducing the idea of social distancing as the St. Louis health commissioner during the 1918 flu pandemic. And yet she thrived as a hostess of formal dinners and other social gatherings that convened influential civic leaders and political associates of her husband, Edgar Rombauer, who would become Speaker of the St. Louis House of Delegates. His existing mental health challenges were exacerbated by the arrival of the Great Depression, and in 1930 he committed suicide. Left alone at fifty-two years old with little savings and no means of supporting herself, she resolved to write a book. The book she self-published in 1931 was called *The Joy of Cooking*. And today, after nine editions, it has sold more than 18 million copies and remains one of the most popular and best-known cookbooks in the United States.

A cookbook that could be mistakenly described as a collection of recipes was much more. Indeed, *The Joy of Cooking* could easily have been titled *The Joy of Conversation*.

As Irma's daughter, Marion Rombauer Becker, who co-authored key elements of *The Joy of Cooking* and created the illustrations, would later note:

> *Mother's early housekeeping days ... gave little evidence of culinary prowess. . . . Indeed, it is an open secret that Mother, to the very end of her life, regarded social intercourse as more important than food. The dinner table, in our childhood, frequently suggested a lectern rather than a buffet. What I remember better than the dishes it upheld— which, I must admit, constantly improved in quality—was the talk which went 'round it, talk which burst forth out of our richly multiple interests.*

The Joy of Cooking is less a cookbook than a collection of recipes for conviviality. Much of its charm could be found in Rombauer's conversational voice, commentary, and anecdotes; the recipes were composed as narratives, with the ingredients as characters who would be introduced as the story unfolded. This innovative approach to the cookbook genre came to be known as the "action method."

The joys of cooking have long been deeply intertwined with the joys of conversation. Food is a catalyst for what Becker called social intercourse: the dialogue through which anything meaningful begins. We relate to one another through conversation. Like a ping-pong volley, an unchoreographed dance. An improvisational sport whose exertion is not necessarily physical, but intellectual, emotional, and social. Because conversations are unscripted, they ask more of us than the routine transactions of much of our lives.

Conversations—calisthenics for the mind—call upon our ability to be present, attuned to our dance partner, and willing to refine (usually in real time) our understandings of our own ideas to better convey them to others.

Yet, sadly, conversation is a dying art form. As society steers us toward more and more time spent alone, the open nature of conversational exchange is being increasingly mediated and constrained as more and more discourse moves into the digital realm. But a digital environment is not equipped to be a theater for conversation. A conversation, by design, includes an infinite number of variations, whereas digital communication is an operation governed by rules and limits, a code made up of 1's and 0's. Let us not confuse the exchange of information with unscripted conversational exchange.

Do we really think our simplified emoji vernacular—*thumbs-up, heart, crying face, laugh out loud*—represents the full wonder of conversation? Can it replace the sacred ritual of sharing a meal with others, a conversational theater in which trust, empathy, compromise, and new ideas emerge?

The theater of a shared meal may just be the design device required to revive curiosity.

History has been written, punctuated, and revised through milestone conversations that occurred over meals. Cultural transformation is initiated, planned, and carried out at the dinner table. From political progress to activist action to the poetics of the arts, the meal is an opportunity to show that we care enough for ourselves and each other to move new narratives forward. Sharing a meal has the power to change the tenor of relationships and alter the trajectory of what could possibly come next. We break the ice by breaking bread.

In eighteenth-century France, the most significant conversations took place against the backdrop of salons: signature gatherings hosted in private homes, usually by prominent women who became known as *salonnières*. Curious guests would come to discuss the ideas of the day, everything from literature to science to politics. The salons became the epicenters of political thought, places where revolutionary documents, including the Declaration of Independence, the Virginia Declaration of Rights, and the U.S. Constitution, were dissected and discussed.

Salons were incubators for conversations that challenged legacy narratives and urgently shaped new ones. The format of the French salons ranged from informal, casual, and unstructured to more formal debates with agendas and invited guests. American diplomats like Benjamin Franklin and Thomas Jefferson were frequent visitors. Indeed, Jefferson's participation in the Paris salons from 1784 to 1789 is said to have influenced his approach to diplomacy and fueled his revolutionary spirit, leading him to eventually launch his own salon-like moment, which would alter the course of America's future.

In June 1790, after returning from France, Thomas Jefferson hosted perhaps the most significant dinner conversation in U.S. history. Alexander Hamilton and James Madison were the only guests in attendance. Over the course of a single meal, they came to an agreement dictating how the federal government would pay state debts and redistribute capital—a conversation that came to be known as the "Dinner Table Bargain." It would also become a pivotal scene in Lin-Manuel Miranda's Broadway hit *Hamilton* and the inspiration for the song "The Room Where It Happens."

Really, who doesn't want to be in the room where it happens? Whatever our motivation, we all want a seat at the dinner table. The song is a kind of anthem to the modern meme FOMO, fear of missing out. Participation is everything. Our spirits can be lifted by the simple gesture of invitation or crushed by exclusion. However, today the opportunities to be invited into conversations that matter seem few and far between.

The traditional centers of conversations have been dissolving for some time. Today we urgently need new stages for social discourse, places where cultures of conversation can be revived. Organizations whose mission is to lead inquiry.

Where do we go today to seek out those stimulating dialogues in which we can revisit unexamined assumptions and imagine a better society?

We need to design new kinds of spaces for these conversations. Not inside of government, but civic-minded. Not inside of business, but focused on wealth creation. Not inside of the philanthropic sector, but dedicated to activism. Not inside of academia, but infused with deep intellectual roots. Absurdly creative places like the Museum of Contemporary Art Denver, which, nearly a decade after I moved on from my role as deputy director, would declare its mission to "stimulate dialogue, imagine a better society, and attend to unexamined assumptions and unheard voices in our communities."

We need to invest in what sociologist Ray Oldenburg called "third places." Oldenburg defined these as spaces distinct from our home (first place) and work (second place): places where people exchange ideas and build the relationships that strengthen social capital. These are needed now more than ever. But they are not enough. A revival of recreation centers, parks, pubs, hair salons, and other places of gathering is not sufficient in itself for the complexity of the times in which we live.

We need spaces in which to ignite the revolutionary spirit of the French salons, where visitors understood their work as not merely the act of gathering but championing unheard voices, examining emerging narratives, and drawing upon their creative capacity to build new kinds of futures.

We need *Fourth Places.*

First place is home, second is work. Third places are community spaces. Fourth Places are dedicated to the future.

Fourth Places are a new, much-needed addition to the three spheres Oldenburg articulated more than three decades ago. The future is a dimension we need to pay attention to, because we are all stakeholders in it. The Fourth Place is where we reclaim *our identity as civic actors responsible for shaping the emergent future.* It is a place where we can bridge our public and private lives, manifest a sense of purpose as we do the work of imagining what comes next.

And that requires conversation. It requires curiosity. In part because we aren't so sure what should come next. As the writer Margaret J. Wheatley puts it:

> It is very difficult to give up our certainties—our positions, our beliefs, our explanations. These help define us; they lie at the heart of our personal identity. Yet I believe we will succeed in changing this world only if we can think and work together in new ways. Curiosity is what we

need. We don't have to let go of what we believe, but we do need to be curious about what someone else believes. We do need to acknowledge that their way of interpreting the world might be essential to our survival.

In the spring of 2011, along the ocean coast of southern Rhode Island, I began a radical experiment in Fourth Place living. Invoking the French salons and the Jeffersonian Dinner Table Bargain, I set out to convene a conversation about the future. A dinner party over three days that became the first of many Ideas Salons.

It was a bold act at a juncture in my life between stability and uncertainty. I had just enjoyed a series of successes—participating in the launch of the Museum of Contemporary Art Denver, curating Dialog:City in conjunction with the Democratic National Convention, and leading a series of major projects with Bruce Mau Design, including with the Oprah Winfrey Network. I was ready for the next stage of independence: launching my own company. To become an entrepreneur, without a safety net to catch me if I fell. Once I'd decided to launch my own business, I knew there was only one way to do so: host a legendary dinner party.

The inaugural Ideas Salon had a simple formula: sixty guests convened for sixty hours across six tables to articulate the challenges and opportunities in the epic decade ahead.

The location was the Ocean House in Watch Hill, Rhode Island. A bright yellow grande dame of a hotel in the style of a seaside resort, originally built in 1868. The original building, falling apart and impossible to rehabilitate, had been bulldozed in 2005, then rebuilt based on the original blueprints in 2010. The Ideas Salon was one of the very first events following the launch of the revived hotel. My team and I booked the entire hotel for three full days, and collaborated with staff to custom-design new processes and rituals to enhance the experience of visiting this historic place.

The inaugural Ideas Salon was designed to be a marathon dinner party, or what Hemingway might have dubbed a "moveable feast." It was an anti-conference. An invite-only gathering, filled with people I wanted to break bread with. I was the sponsor, breaking the bank to launch an extraordinary adventure that, quite frankly, I couldn't afford. I was taking a leap of faith. As anthropologist Margaret Mead is reputed to have said:

A small group of thoughtful, committed citizens can change the world; indeed, it's the only thing that ever has.

I had to believe that if we set the table of a Fourth Place to construct a new kind of environment in which the promise of joyful conversation would inspire people, they would rise to the occasion. And rise they did.

The guests included leading figures in the arts from the Guggenheim Museum, pioneers in artificial intelligence from Singapore to Silicon Valley, health leaders from Colombia, top experience designers from Disney Imagineering, leaders from the world of retail who would go on to lead design at Google, computer scientists from Microsoft, creatives reimagining television, global supply chain experts, Hollywood film producers, and more. There were climate change specialists rethinking sustainability, food thinkers revisiting the notion of the grocery store, Iranian artists challenging identity politics, and educators teaching leadership to Navy SEALs.

We broke bread. Seated at a single table with thirty place settings on each side, we passed dishes of food served family style, intentionally designed to force guests to bump elbows with each pass. Every detail was deliberately designed to break down the ordinary social codes, to force people to drop their guard and allow the joy of conversation to be discovered. It was like summer camp for Radically Curious adults.

When preparing for this gathering, I had the rare pleasure of meeting Maurice Sendak. The intention was to present him with a lifetime achievement award at the Ideas Salon, but he humbly refused, shunning the spotlight. Instead, I promised to deliver a message for him to the sixty guests. During my welcoming remarks, we projected one of his signature illustrations, which depicted the Wild Things dancing, howling at the moon, with Max riding on Carol's shoulders. With this image in the background, I told the guests of the history of salons and their crossover in the arts:

> *A salon is an assembly of guests in a drawing room, consisting of leaders in society. A gathering of intellectual and culturally engaged individuals, to increase knowledge through conversation. A place to imagine and plan the future with a set of creatives, primarily as an alternate arena of trust. The history of salons dates back to 1648 when it was the official art exhibition of the Académie des Beaux-Arts in Paris. It was considered the greatest annual creative event in the Western world. In 1725 it was held at the Palace of the Louvre, where it remained until 1737, when it became more public. In 1884 a group of artists formed the Société des Artistes Indépendants, creating a modern update to the historic French salon of the Académie des Beaux-Arts. Exhibitors included Chagall, de Chirico, Braque, Giacometti, Kandinsky, Miró, Modigliani, Munch, Matisse, Van Gogh, and Toulouse-Lautrec. Now, more than 350 years later, we reconvene the salon as the drawing room of the twenty-first century, to envision a flourishing future.*

And then I channeled Mr. Sendak as I conveyed his message, which, in this space full of radical thinkers and unapologetic disruptors, could not have been more apt. He'd said: "Seth, tell those Wild Things to keep rattling the cages and howl at the moon!"

At the end of the Ideas Salon, during my closing remarks, I was interrupted by one of the guests, who rushed onstage and asked me to sit in a chair in front of the audience. It turned out that my dinner guests had banded together to sculpt a papier-mâché crown, upon which everyone in attendance had written a few words of thanks. He asked that I bow my head as he officially crowned me Max, King of the Wild Things, to a standing ovation.

The Ideas Salon has become my own *Joy of Cooking*. What we are cooking is Fourth Places—civic imagination laboratories committed to the future.

ALIVENESS

17

The Flourishing State of Languishing

How can we respond when our sense of normalcy is upended without warning? Is languishing the new normal for our whole nation and for potentially large swaths of the globe? How can we pursue meaning as an antidote to the state of languishing?

The summer of 1997 grabbed hold of me like a tornado. Twisted me around. Accelerated the sunsetting of youth. Pointed me onto a path of aliveness.

At sixteen years old I joined a Canadian Jewish youth group on a six-week trip across Israel. I had been awarded a scholarship toward the costs of this cultural journey by a local philanthropist, part of a movement subsidizing Jewish youths traveling to Israel with the intent of instilling in us nationalistic pride in the Jewish state.

My trip was filled with firsts.

My first shawarma, whose purveyors could be found on every street corner. My first (and last) time trying hashish, traded openly on the street in neatly packed matchboxes. My first time being in a room with no other Americans, experiencing a potent critique of the U.S. narrative. My first time shooting an automatic weapon, a taste of military immersion meant to bring to life the reality of mandatory service for all citizens. My first time harvesting ostrich eggs, the task I was assigned while staying at a kibbutz. My first hospitalization for an undiagnosed condition. My first encounter with a terrorist bombing.

In July 1997, I left the nearly forty members of my youth group and checked into a hospital in Jerusalem, where I was told I had a severe case of gastroenteritis that was doing damage to the lining of my stomach. (After my return to the United States I would eventually have surgery to implant a dissolvable medical tool that would support and strengthen my duodenum.)

On July 30, 1997, there were two consecutive suicide bombings at the Mahane Yehuda Market in Jerusalem. Witnesses later reported that "the two men apparently maintained eye contact and were about 90 feet apart when one pulled a string inside his jacket to set off his bomb at about 1:15 P.M. The second erupted seconds later, creating a huge fireball and a shower of bodies, limbs, fruit, fish, plaster and plastic roofing panels." Sixteen people died, and 178 were injured. Hamas would claim responsibility.

The Mahane Yehuda Market is a mere handful of miles from the hospital from which I had just been released. A popular open-air market, with more than 250 vendors selling everything from dates and spices to kibbeh and baklava. It is a nexus of energy, with merchants calling out prices and quips to you as you walk through the crowded aisles. I know because I visited the market just days before the bombing.

Everything felt heavier for me after July 30. Though I hadn't witnessed the bombing, its proximity and the fact that I had missed it so narrowly shook me deeply. The disruption to my narrative of normalcy was swift and deep. Requiring me to recalibrate my worldview. In my physically weakened state, a deadly suicide bombing in the exact location in which I had been standing a mere twenty-four hours earlier catapulted me into a state of trauma.

This trauma followed me back home, casting its long shadow over my final two years of high school. I was diagnosed with PTSD, but in hindsight, I am not sure that diagnosis was correct. Psychologists find that one of the best strategies for managing emotions is to name them. But I didn't have the language to name the full range of unfamiliar emotions I was experiencing. I was not myself, though at that young age I was a long way from knowing what *myself* might mean.

But one thing was for sure: I was questioning *everything*. I began to notice juxtapositions all around me: narratives in such sharp contrast that they felt irreconcilable.

One narrative was characterized by the safety of my daily routine. Peers consumed with coming-of-age rituals, like getting their learner's permit and what the color their wished-for car might be. This was the narrative of a typical Adirondack teen.

Another narrative was characterized by thoughts of violence. Peers halfway around the world consumed with their own coming-of-age ritual of mandatory military service. This was the narrative of an Israeli teen.

I identified with both narratives, seeing myself in both.

The contrast was ever present. How could the school dance hold up as something meaningful in comparison to a suicide bombing? With my summer experiences always in the backdrop, my normal routine felt meaningless, petty, and naive. *My* new normal was to forever be on high alert. I pondered existential questions constantly. Fortunately, I managed to channel what could have otherwise become a dangerous mental health condition into a path that gave me a whole new lease on life.

Upon returning home from Israel, I began to spend a great deal of time alone. Essentially keeping social distance from my peers. To some this might have been a cause for concern, especially given my PTSD diagnosis and the commonly held belief that a healthy life requires a slew of social rituals—going to parties and joining clubs and being on sports teams. But I understood that an abundance of activities is not the same as their intended goal: deep social ties and the health benefits that come from the construction of genuine relationships with others.

I am an advocate for social capital as a form of currency. But I also believe that construct*ing* relationships is not the same as construct*ive* relationships.

So I assigned myself the task of constructing a constructive relationship with myself. To get to know myself again, now that everything I'd thought I understood had been upended.

I found myself inside of my practice as a portrait painter. Painting is typically a solitary activity, and the studio is typically a sacred space for the quiet, deep reflection found in the act of making. Painting is also an extraordinarily ritualized and rhythmed activity. The methodical gestures of stretching a canvas, preparing an easel, mixing colors, and shaping an image have a kind of meditative quality. I learned how to be alone effectively. How to slow time and focus on the flow of my energy. I viewed this not as a time of isolation but rather as a time of curation. It also served as a form of rest and recovery, of making deposits into my mental health savings account.

I would later learn that my instinctual behavior had a name: *active recovery* or *active rest*. Most frequently utilized by professional athletes, active rest means giving your body a constructive kind of break. Not stopping all activity, as with what might be called passive recovery, but knowing that there is scientific value in not going at full speed all the time.

While active rest is closely associated with physical health, it should be put into practice to strengthen our mental health as well. We need to protect different types of slow time in which we can construct and deconstruct meaningful relationships with ourselves. Space for us to respect the work of healing and rehabilitating our most critical project—the self. This will require us to break free of the inherited tradition of filling our time with transactional activities devoid of meaning. Being constantly in motion is holding us in place, keeping us in a state of languishing, preventing flourishing.

Leave it to Tyler Durden, the alter ego featured in *Fight Club* and played by Brad Pitt, to put languishing into perspective:

> [*We are*] *working jobs we hate so we can buy shit we don't need, and the things you own end up owning you. We're the middle children of history, man. No purpose or place. We have no Great War. No Great Depression. Our great war is a spiritual war. Our great depression is our lives. We've all been raised on television to believe that one day we'd all be millionaires, and movie gods, and rock stars, but we won't. We're slowly learning that fact.*

Active rest enabled me to turn my state of languishing into one of aliveness.

PUBLIC PROJECTS

The second pattern that emerged was a newfound sense of moral urgency. I counteracted a feeling of emptiness by seeking out intensely purposeful opportunity. Just as I had listened to my natural instincts to build upon my practice as a painter, I leaned into the foundational practices of my Jewish heritage: ethics, public service, and participation in civic life. While active rest was about offering care to the self, throwing myself into public projects became about offering care to others.

A handful of months later I was serving as president of the student government, as the sole student representative on the district leadership team made up entirely of adults, and was frequently presenting to the elected school board on key topics and giving public addresses about my insights stemming from traveling in Israel. In short, I became a citizen of my community. These opportunities became an education in how diverse groups of people cooperate, find agreement, navigate disagreement, and jointly plan their futures.

It's as though I was on a mission to study everything I could about better alternatives to the explosive conflict I had come across in Israel. A research inquiry asking, Isn't there another way?

I befriended my school principal to learn more about how she led an organization, got connected to the SUNY Plattsburgh painting department, got permission to attend local art talks and gallery shows, was invited to be a guest speaker for the teachers' professional development day, and was called upon to speak to the student body to calm their anxieties when we had a copycat Columbine shooter arrested at our school. My last twenty-four months in the Adirondacks were consumed by a portfolio of public projects.

Much of youth is strung together as a series of fleeting moments that deliver momentary happiness. The smallness of these moments makes them easy to mistake for insignificance. But they are building blocks of something greater.

We learn that joy without a sense of purpose is not sustainable; that without purpose, we cannot flourish.

As Corey Keyes, a professor of sociology at Emory University, offers about flourishing:

There are lots of American adults that would meet the qualifications of feeling happy, but they don't feel sense of purpose. . . . Feeling good about life is not enough.

My portfolio of public projects grounded me in a sense of purpose, and they became encounters with joy.

PANDEMIC AS POPULATION-SCALE TRAUMA

The tumultuous summers of 2020 and 2021 were eerily reminiscent of what I experienced back in the summer of 1997.

By the fall of 2021, more than 700,000 Americans had died from the coronavirus. A number so massive, it was estimated that nearly one out of every five Americans knew someone who had died of the pandemic. In my own family we grieved the passing of my grandmother Selma through tiny Zoom windows, robbing us of the opportunity to practice the traditions of grieving. The pandemic has taken a great deal from all of us. Beyond the tragedy of death, it immersed all of society in a state of trauma, grieving the loss of normalcy.

Dr. Alex Jadad, my close friend, colleague, and a leader in the field of public health, has been tracking what he calls the echo pandemic. He paints a picture of the emerging mental health tsunami—a crisis that was already brewing but has been further catalyzed by the arrival of the pandemic:

By the end of March 2020, two weeks after the start of the US national lockdown because of the COVID-19 pandemic, 78% of all antidepressant, anti-anxiety and anti-insomnia prescriptions filled were for people who had never taken them before. A month later, there were spikes of up to 1,000% in requests for support from national suicide and distress hotlines. The same month, 69% of workers described the pandemic as the most stressful time of their career, and 91% reported moderate to extreme stress when working from home, reflecting the poor preparedness levels of the corporate sector, which remained unaware that negative ideas, emotions and behaviors, such as suicide, have been shown to spread socially.

We will need to consider that the entirety of our nation is experiencing a mental health crisis. The repercussions, which are only now emerging, will rewrite the national narrative for the future of health, work, and flourishing within the new normal. To prepare to take this on, we will need to name the state that we are in. Diagnosing it is a form of having power over it.

Adam Grant, a professor at the Wharton School of the University of Pennsylvania, codified our collective experience of the pandemic with an article titled "There's a Name for the Blah You're Feeling: It's Called Languishing." As I read his analysis of languishing, I thought back to my own diagnosis some twenty-five years earlier. He writes:

It wasn't burnout—we still had energy. It wasn't depression—we didn't feel hopeless. We just felt somewhat joyless and aimless. It turns out there's a name for that: languishing. Languishing is a sense of stagnation and emptiness. . . . In psychology, we think about mental health on a spectrum from depression to flourishing. Flourishing is the peak of well-being: You have a strong sense of meaning, mastery and mattering to others. Depression is the valley of ill-being: You feel despondent, drained and worthless. Languishing is the neglected middle child of mental health. It's the void between depression and flourishing—the absence of well-being.

And just like that, an exhale. The power of naming. Of a diagnosis that feels so spot-on, it's scary. Is the whole nation, potentially large swaths of the globe, experiencing languishing? What triggers languishing? Grant refers to a popular post from the *Harvard Business Review* that described our experience as grief, saying:

Along with the loss of loved ones, we were mourning the loss of normalcy. "Grief." It gave us a familiar vocabulary to understand what had felt like an unfamiliar experience.

For me, the relevant insight here is not simply the naming of the experience with the term "grief," but that we can feel the loss of normalcy just as we feel the loss of a loved one to death. That we can grieve the loss of things that are not living, or perhaps not even tangible, like mourning the death of an idea, or of a time now long in our past.

We are deeply affected by such an interruption in what we have known our lives to be. Consider that for decades we have been planning, learning, and practicing those professions that have become woven into our identities. And suddenly, by no fault of our own and for reasons out of our control, we cannot be those people any longer. Add to this the fact that social distancing prevented many of us from connecting with loved ones for months upon months. Close family members felt more distant, friendships atrophied, and the rules of dating and of forming new relationships were thrown out the window. The norms of social etiquette, with their millions of messages and cues we've rehearsed over and over throughout our lives, were turned inside out. Worse yet, there was no warning, no training, no preparation for this upheaval and rewiring of the operating systems of our lives. Certainly, there is population-scale trauma.

The loss of normalcy has given rise to the colloquial term "the new normal" to describe the new reality inside COVID-19. But from a mental health perspective, we may not be accounting for what it does to all of us to be thrust into an alternate reality, or what it takes to recalibrate and thrive. That doesn't mean we are all clinically depressed. This is what makes "languishing" such useful language to describe the space in between state of well-being and ill-being.

But I propose that we were languishing long before the arrival of the coronavirus. In the United States we resist mental health conversations. Despite the growing evidence from diverse indicators that the United States has been facing an epidemic of mental health problems, such problems are still stigmatized, viewed as weakness. As though John Wayne himself, our national archetype for rugged individualism and stoic self-sufficiency, would roll over in his grave if we embraced mental health as an integral part of our culture.

The World Happiness Report is a landmark survey of the state of global happiness that ranks 156 countries by how happy their citizens perceive themselves to be. In 2021, the World Happiness Report focused on happiness and the community: how happiness has evolved over the past dozen years, and the technologies, social norms, conflicts, and government policies that have driven those shifts.

In 2019, prior to the pandemic, the survey asked: "Taken all together, how would you say things are these days—would you say that you are very happy, pretty happy, or not too happy?," measured on a scale of 1 to 3, with 3 being the happiest. In more than forty years, the average score has not once reached 2.3. And over that period it has declined from 2.25 to 2.16.

Jean M. Twenge, a professor of psychology at San Diego State University, offers a theory about why:

This decline in happiness and mental health seems paradoxical. By most accounts, Americans should be happier now than ever. The violent crime rate is low, as is the unemployment rate. Income per capita has steadily grown over the last few decades. This is the Easterlin paradox: As the standard of living improves, so should happiness—but it has not. . . . I suggest that Americans are less happy due to fundamental shifts in how they spend their leisure time.

Our declining mental health is costing us dearly. Not only are we failing to achieve a state of flourishing, it's as though we have accepted and made our peace with that fact, as though the social, emotional, and economic costs of fractured mental health are simply a part of the calculation of overhead.

Many are also pointing to loss of meaningful social connectedness in our communities. For example, U.S. surgeon general Vivek Murthy believes that loneliness is one of the most significant threats to our physical health. Loneliness has been estimated to shorten a person's life by fifteen years, equivalent in impact to being obese or smoking fifteen cigarettes per day. And a recent study found that a staggering 47 percent of Americans often feel alone, left out, and lacking meaningful connection with others. This is true across all age groups, from teenagers to older adults. In the United Kingdom, loneliness has become the source of such significant health challenges that a new cabinet-level position, the minister for loneliness, was established.

It's ironic that we are experiencing a pandemic of loneliness at a time in history when social media has connected us more than ever. But this irony is easily explained once we understand that loneliness is not the same as a lack of social activity. The nature of the two experiences is different. Experts now are saying that loneliness is about "the subjective perception of isolation," the absence of meaningful connection:

People can be socially isolated and not feel lonely; they simply prefer a more hermitic existence. Likewise, people can feel lonely even when surrounded by lots of people, especially if the relationships are not emotionally rewarding.

Languishing has been the hidden enemy of flourishing for decades. While thought leaders are presenting many informed hypotheses about a variety of contributing factors, including social media, I think we need to dig deeper. I agree with Professor Twenge that our leisure time needs to be reimagined. But in service to what? It's not that the good life will miraculously arrive if we simply all join bowling leagues. The critical factor to emphasize is not social connection but *meaningful* social connection, which includes staying connected with ourselves.

Active rest and public projects were my tools for preventative care during an extraordinary loss of normalcy that thrust me suddenly and without warning into a new normal I wasn't prepared for.

We have been in a declining state of happiness for forty years, and our entire world has been interrupted, causing PTSD on a population scale. Our fight against the pandemic has required increased social distancing in a culture that was already lonely. We must prepare for an era in which our collective decline in mental health may be the greatest threat to flourishing we've ever faced. It will show up quietly, not announcing itself. But it will be a crisis nonetheless.

The pursuit of meaning will be the antidote to the state of languishing we are all experiencing. Today more than ever, we need avalanches of meaning to bring us back to life.

Aliveness as a Moral Responsibility

How can we design more stages for spontaneity? For possibility? For self-actualization? Is self-actualization a luxury afforded only to the privileged and powerful? Is it our moral duty to move beyond self-actualization, in pursuit of collective actualization?

I don't drink coffee. I don't drink alcohol. But I am not without vices or guilty pleasures. One of my addictions is the singing-competition genre of television shows: *American Idol, X Factor, America's Got Talent, Britain's Got Talent.* I can't get enough.

Several years ago, a friend asked me what about these programs I was so drawn to. What about this format inspires me? It's taken me some time to construct a thoughtfully articulated response.

It's about the nervous prison guard Sam Bailey, who believed she was too old but sings the verse "The time has come for my dreams to be heard" from Beyoncé's "Listen." It's about Jahmene Douglas, the socially awkward Walmart price checker, who delivers a devastating rendition of Etta James's "At Last" that proves his soul is older than his years. It's about the overly confident Sal Valentinetti, arriving with his family entourage (including his cannoli-eating, cigar-smoking, right-out-of-*The Sopranos* cousin Big Tommy) and who tells Simon Cowell, "I want to make something of myself. I want to bring back those Dean Martin–style roasts"—and then launches into "My Way." It's about the delightful chaos of the Flakefleet Primary School choir, dozens of kids between four and seven— "some are amazing singers, some are just enthusiastic," says the choir director as they launch into a prop-filled extravaganza interpreting Queen's "Don't Stop Me Now." It's about the pure joy of Revelation Avenue, a gospel choir, hitting a cappella the heights of Katy Perry's "Roar."

But it's also about much more than any individual performer. These shows are stages for the ordinary to become extraordinary. For the democratization of talent. Theaters for voices to be heard, in an era when we so rarely listen to one another. It's a master class in defying expectations. We do a double take when Susan Boyle stuns with her golden lungs that seem to not fit her persona. A real-time lesson in dismantling previously held assumptions.

These shows are also arenas for self-actualization. A concept of self-actualization was popularized by Abraham Maslow as a part of the evolution of humanistic psychology. In 1943, Maslow published his most famous paper, "A Theory of Human Motivation." It called for a re-visioning of psychology beyond behaviorism's focus on humans' basic motivations toward food, sex, and safety. Maslow suggested that after the needs for food and safety have been satisfied, higher needs emerge in a hierarchy—love, belonging, esteem, and finally self-actualization. He defined self-actualization as

> *self-fulfillment, namely . . . the tendency for [the individual] to become actualized in what he is potentially. This tendency might be phrased as the desire to become more and more what one is, to become everything that one is capable of becoming.*

To watch these singing-competition programs is to bear witness to self-actualization. We come to know the people onstage, and find ourselves rooting for them, touched when we see them become everything they are capable of becoming. We have a front-row seat to the drama of ordinary people realizing their potential. It makes for compelling television. It makes for compelling storytelling. And it often compels everyone to cry: the performer, the family of the performer, the audience, the judges, and certainly the viewers at home. They are crying because the emotions are so intense, their body is literally overwhelmed by what Maslow called a peak experience—defined as "an altered state of consciousness characterized by euphoria, often achieved by self-actualizing individuals."

Aliveness is when we experience the highest-order version of ourselves. To realize such a heightened state requires imagination. Tears are evidence of aliveness.

Aliveness can only occur when we imagine a possible self that pierces through the mundane and becomes something extraordinary. This is the greatest gift of imagination: our ability to bridge the gap between possibility and realization. When we watch the performances on these shows, we are all moved by an encounter someone is having with the highest-order versions of themselves. In part because it is so rare and in part because it offers us hope that we too can add a little extra to our ordinary. The stage is a place where constraints fall away, enabling people to raise the stakes on themselves. Often exceeding their own fixed expectations. Delivering a peak experience, delivering aliveness.

I am not a performer. But I find myself in search of stages where remarkable things can happen. "Stage" is a metaphor for the mix of the right conditions. The term has roots in the French term *estage*, meaning "position, situation, or condition," and even further back to *ester*, meaning "to be standing." The stage is a place where one is standing inside of one's highest self.

Such a phenomenon raises a number of questions: What other kinds of stages deliver these peak experiences? What other theaters are incubators for human potential? What roles can we play on the stages offered to us? How can we design new stages in our own lives?

The most powerful stage I've had the privilege to stand on was the set of *The Oprah Winfrey Show*, at Harpo Studios in Chicago. One of the great pleasures of my life was the opportunity to work with Oprah and across several of her businesses as the long-running talk show went off the air and we prepared for the launch of the Oprah Winfrey Network. I remember the first time I walked onto the Harpo Studios stage. In preparation for our work, I had studied the history of the talk show, ferociously consuming the most profound of the 4,561 episodes—in effect, a master class on self-actualization. Her signature motto, "Live Your Best Life," captures the same aliveness found in the singing competitions: ordinary people inside of extraordinary peak experiences.

Oprah's mythology casts a long shadow. The story of her influence, her impact, and the cultural milestones she has achieved mirror the story of the nation. So, naturally, the visit to the studio was built up in my mind. It could never live up to the expectations I internalized. When we were brought onto the stage, the show was between segments. No crowds, no real set, no tour, no spectacle. It was quiet. As

I walked onto the stage, the first thing I thought, while standing inside one of my own peak experiences, was: *It's so small.*

I found the small scale beautiful. It was the first of several key lessons I learned during my time working with Oprah. The power of the show stemmed not from the physical architecture but from the social architecture. Oprah and her team, perhaps more than anyone gives them credit for, are masterful experience designers. They know how to design the social conditions for something remarkable to happen.

There is no greater case study in experience design than Oprah's famous Legends Ball, perhaps my favorite "Oprah moment." While working with her I enjoyed a discussion unpacking what made Legends Ball so special. Held in 2006 and memorialized as a documentary television special, the three-day celebration honored legends such as Maya Angelou, Shirley Caesar, Ruby Dee, Aretha Franklin, Toni Morrison, Leontyne Price, Della Reese, Alice Walker, Tina Turner, and Cicely Tyson. As part of the ceremony, the legends were greeted by "young'uns" such as Alicia Keys, Angela Bassett, Mary J. Blige, Missy Elliott, and Janet Jackson, creating an intergenerational community. An intentional design decision we can all learn from.

The entire weekend was a marathon of aliveness. But the peak experience came on the final day with an outdoor gospel musical celebration led by gospel singer BeBe Winans. Surrounded by such extraordinary talent, BeBe started to pass around the microphone. How could he not? Nothing was scripted. No one was briefed in advance. But the talent rose to the occasion. These legends poured their hearts out, embracing the language of music to produce an experience that could only be called spiritual. As Oprah herself recalled in the documentary, "I knew it, I knew it. You could not have Gladys Knight and Dionne Warwick and Patti LaBelle and Shirley Caesar, the mother of gospel music, here, you could not have all of them anywhere and not have Jesus show up. Jesus showed up and showed out!"

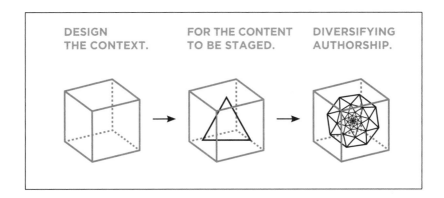

As actor Sidney Poitier, one of the guests for the gospel brunch, declared: "Spontaneity was the force, it was spectacular!" It was spontaneous in that it was unrehearsed. But it wasn't arbitrary or unplanned, either. Today, Legends Ball is a case study we use within our studio to illustrate the idea of context design for companies ranging from Apple to American Express. Spontaneous, but choreographed. Unscripted, but highly curated. If you design a stage, stack it with talent, and set the right conditions, it is impossible for magic not to happen.

The objective of context design is not to design the outcome, but to design the stage on which outcomes can unfold. This philosophy is counter to how we tend to run businesses today, where leadership is often practiced as micromanagement, overwhelmingly focused on hyperspecific actions and transactions to be executed: a practice that has become ever more prevalent as the sophisticated tools of data analytics and the study of behavioral economics enter every consumer business. But this control mindset can flatten the experience, take the aliveness out of the equation. Life is not merely a set of scripted transactions. It is the unexpected that often yields the most powerful outcomes.

From a business perspective, context design represents a shift in the fundamental objective. While design typically focuses on the creation of an object or an image steeped in classical aesthetics of beauty, design thinking values the process of problem-solving above all else. Context design takes this another step away from the confines of objecthood, making the value the very design of the game board. How a problem is framed, who the problem solvers are, and whether vital and unexpected collisions can occur through play are key questions of context design.

Today we are living in the age of platforms, where the value is in the interaction between people, the cooperation between them, thus enabling an infinite number of permutations for people to realize opportunity.

Imagine how disingenuous and how completely counterproductive it would be to try to overly choreograph the open-ended network systems of Uber, Airbnb, or Instagram. While certainly there are problematic constraints and biases embedded in the design of these systems, the very fact that those constraints and biases are currently being confronted, challenged, and changed by users and activist critics tells us how far the mindset and expectations have come. To design systems as stages, rather than design the outcome of fixed operations, is the guiding principle behind today's most impactful businesses and the philosophy behind the sharing economy, the blockchain revolution, and the cooperative agreements making up so many of our social systems.

The greatest opportunity of the twenty-first century is found in designing for possibility. To realize this, we need to stop making things and begin making opportunity. We need more stages for aliveness.

To participate in your own life is a form of self-actualization. It is a route for us all to, as Oprah would put it, live our best life.

I cannot flourish if *we* cannot flourish. If this is the case, our task is not self-actualization but collective actualization. Self-actualization is a legacy narrative of the twentieth century, one of the set of principles that shaped the dominance of the production economy. Maslow's concept of self-actualization was well suited for its time and context. But along the way, fueled by ideologies of American exceptionalism, individualism, and capitalism, its intent was corrupted and became nearly synonymous with the success of the self above all else. For me to win, someone else must lose. These ideas of individual success versus shared success are now emerging as part of the anti-racism discourse, helping to shift the mental model of the self by illustrating the cost of such outdated belief systems. The religious commitment to a survival-of-the-fittest competition reinforced everywhere we turn has led to self-actualization as a luxury afforded only to the privileged and powerful, while preventing us from even conceiving of business and cultural models for collective actualization.

The legacy narratives run deep. In her recent book *The Sum of Us: What Racism Costs Everyone and How We Can Prosper Together*, Heather McGhee addresses how zero-sum thinking is keeping all of us from collective actualization. In a review of McGhee's book, Jennifer Szalai writes:

> *This cramped mentality is another legacy of slavery, McGhee says, which really was zero sum—extractive and exploitative, like the settler colonialism that enabled it. She writes that zero-sum thinking "has always optimally benefited only the few while limiting the potential of the rest of us, and therefore the whole."*

This is a belief system founded on the fiction that a commitment to competition is the path toward wealth creation. A narrative in which survival of the fittest is the only form of actualization, in which competition is the exclusive actor. McGhee lays out the case for the opposite, arguing that systemic racism is a context design that prevents collective actualization, at the cost of self-actualization. Inclusion, in other words, is an act of wealth generation:

A new Federal Reserve Bank of San Francisco study calculated that in 2019, the country's output would have been $2.6 trillion greater if the gap between white men and everyone else were closed. And a 2020 report from analysts at Citigroup calculated that if America had adopted policies to close the Black-white economic gap 20 years ago, U.S. G.D.P. would be an estimated $16 trillion higher.

Scientists Brian Hare and Vanessa Woods, both researchers at Duke University's Center for Cognitive Neuroscience, propose in their book *Survival of the Friendliest: Understanding Our Origins and Rediscovering Our Common Humanity* that we misunderstood Darwin. The old adage of survival of the fittest may be all wrong. As a review of their book summarized:

Friendly partnerships among species and shared humanity have worked throughout centuries to ensure successful evolution. Species endure—humans, other animals and plants—they write, based on friendliness, partnership and communication. And they point to many life examples of cooperation and sociability to prove it.

In a post-pandemic world, if we are to courageously move away from legacy narratives and toward challenger narratives, we must question commonly held beliefs. Capitalism good, socialism bad: These are tenets of a belief system that Radical Curiosity demands we grow out of. It demands that we question ideas and traditions that no longer serve us—all of us.

Aliveness is our ability to love life, to show up for it and devour it as a meal. We cannot realize this by bringing harm to others. We cannot self-actualize without collective actualization. This is the great context design project of this century. It will measure the sum of us, not simply the singularity of each of us. It is our moral responsibility to be alive. Looking back to the transcendentalists for guidance, we discover these words from Henry David Thoreau:

We must learn to reawaken and keep ourselves awake. . . . Only one in a million is awake enough for effective intellectual exertion, only one in a hundred million to a poetic or divine life.

I believe in the wisdom of Thoreau, but also question his implicit elitism in considering just how many of us may feel the experience of aliveness. Must it be one in a million who are awake? Must it be one in a hundred million who will live a divine life? I am reminded of Walt Whitman's definition of a poet as a "lover of life." Can we design the context for more of us to actualize our poetic selves? Collective actualization is the promise to love life.

The Comedian
as Gladiator

**How has stand-up comedy become the modern-day arena for cu-
riosity? How do we make sense of things that break tradition? By
what criteria do we measure art that inverts genres? How do we
distinguish comedy from commentary? And should we? How can
humor be a language for curiosity?**

Comedians are today's philosophers, utilizing their unique brand of
rhetoric to help us see ourselves anew. Their practice capitalizes on
questioning by serving as a tour guide to an absurd world, asking us,
Are you seeing what I'm seeing?

Comedians use their keen powers of observational storytelling to reorient us and help us see the world in its raw and often uncomfortable form. Humor softens the tragic blow of re-meeting reality with
the veil pulled back. Wielding juxtaposition to help us realize how

profoundly bizarre our commonly held beliefs have become. The revival of stand-up has become a powerful forum to confront conflict and explore the wicked problems we face. The stand-up format is an arena for conversational battle. Proving to be more relevant than conventional vehicles for discourse and conflict resolution.

Humor is a language for curiosity.

There are three philosophical frameworks that can help us better understand humor and mine it as a source of curiosity. Emerging over the past several hundred years, and cumulatively developed by diverse voices from Kant to Kierkegaard, the three frameworks are known as superiority theory, relief theory, and incongruity theory.

1. SUPERIORITY THEORY represents the idea that we find humor in our feelings of superiority over others. Enter the clown or the slapstick genre of comedy, which invites us to laugh at the mistakes of others, the foolishness of others, or at ourselves as mirrored by others. This type of comedy expresses superiority over some target the performer has chosen, whether it be themselves, someone in the audience, a politician, or a celebrity. This is what could be called a cheap shot, as it demeans others to get a laugh. A gateway drug to bullying.

2. RELIEF THEORY represents the idea that emotions take the physical form of nervous energy and tension, and that humor is found in the release of that anxiety or pressure. Enter my wife, who suggests she laughs not because things are funny but because she is nervous. It may be the purest route to laughter—less constructed, more of a physiological response to a set of circumstances. A way in which our body is physically making sense of a set of conditions, expressed through the release of laughter.

3. INCONGRUITY THEORY represents the idea that humor is found in the perception of something incongruous—something that violates our mental pattern of expectation. Laughter is found in the space between our expectations and our experience. We find joy in the illumination of these contradictions because we find it oddly reassuring that someone else is experiencing the incongruity that we have. This type of humor uses storytelling to illustrate the vast disparity between how the world is and how the world is imagined.

It is this third framework of humor, the incongruity theory, that is most useful to better understand Radical Curiosity. Arthur Schopenhauer, an influential German philosopher writing in the early 1800s, would argue that we notice the incongruity when we experience a concept and a perception that are supposed to be the same but turn out quite differently. This serves to draw our attention to the ways in which reality doesn't conform to our expectations of it. We cannot help but laugh when we are confronted by the misalignment.

Incongruity theory serves as a popular recipe of present-day stand-up. Following the equation of the setup as a misdirect and the punch line as a surprise resolution that produces both laughter and insight. Beyond the format as a craft, comedians have become political commentators and cultural critics whose currency resides in their ability to highlight the absurd and the paradoxical in contemporary life.

For several years the only news anchor I trusted was Jon Stewart. As the host of *The Daily Show,* Stewart became the patron saint of a whole new category that blended activism and comedy. His ability to entertainingly build awareness, speak truth to power, and deliver grave insights in a joyful manner reinvented what engaged citizenship could look like.

Jon Stewart did more to advance civic discourse than any elected official has in my lifetime.

Stand-up has become the modern arena for pioneers of Radical Curiosity, providing an uninterrupted hour in which to convince you to leave behind what you thought you knew and embrace an imagined alternative. Every so often, audible gasps exit your lungs as you inhale an alternative view. As you experience such a disruption in perception, your laughter is evidence that you are reconfiguring your mental models to assimilate new insights. It's as though laughter is physiological evidence, a signal from your body, that you are changing from the inside out.

Through the format of the single-person monologue, comedians have been challenging commonly held beliefs and bringing inherited wisdom to its knees. And they've done so with such deftly skilled oratory and storytelling, such wittily timed tempo, that audiences barely realize they are witnessing a calculated injury to toxic narratives. Comedians are empathetic knights, slaying legacy narrative dragons.

One of the most powerful examples is Hannah Gadsby, the Australian comedian who exploded on the global stage with her 2017 Netflix special *Nanette*. An unwitting advocate for Radical Curiosity, she talks about stripping back a joke "to its bare essential components" (like Aristotle's first principles) and concludes that a joke is "essentially a question with a surprise." Her mastery of her craft allows her to both deploy it and stretch its boundaries to do more for her and her audience.

Gadsby brings us into her personal story of abuse and trauma, inverting topics that are traditionally treated as private into public conversations. Her medium begins to depart from stand-up and resemble a confessional, a political speech, a call to arms. *Nanette* is the penultimate incongruity theory of comedy. It is a show in which we expect to experience seventy-three minutes of escapism, and unexpectedly encounter a tour de force on issues ranging from gender to gay rights, from rape to misogyny—all found in a Pandora's box of a performance that is so utterly timely it takes your breath away.

HANNAH GADSBY **DAVE CHAPPELLE**

There is too much hysteria around gender from you gender-normals. You're the weirdos. You're a bit fucking hysterical. You're a bit weird, a bit uptight. You need to get a grip. You gender-normal. . . . Seriously, calm down, gender-normals. "No, a man in a dress, that's fucking weird!" No, it's not. You know what's weird? Pink headbands on bald babies! That's weird. I mean, seriously, would you put a bangle on a potato? No, that's organic. I paid a lot for that potato. Of course, I understand why parents do it. Clearly, they're sick and tired of their beautiful baby girl being mistaken for a boy baby because of the no-hair situation. But the thing is, I don't assume babies are boys. I assume they're angry feminists, and I treat them with respect. How about this? How about we stop separating the children into opposing teams from day one? How about we give them, I dunno, seven to ten years to consider themselves on the same side?

Nanette went on to win an Emmy Award and a Peabody Award and to be featured in international journalism and late-night shows as the piece of genius it was. Even *Wired* magazine published an article called "Seriously, We Really Need to Talk About *Nanette*" in which the author said in part:

Like you, I was stunned, overwhelmed, floored. But I gotta ask: Does this count as comedy? Or stand-up? At least two friends of mine kept calling it a "speech," which feels belittling. Others seem to prefer "one-woman show." That's closer, maybe (though—do we ever say "one-man show"?), but I still maintain it's a stand-up comedy special. In a sense it had to be called that, because the whole point is that, midway through, she completely subverts what that means. The show worked for me in many ways, but the main one might be as a kind of meta self-interrogatory anti-comedy.

In recent years the form of stand-up has been broadened, deepened, and amplified. Voices like Gadsby's have found a home and an audience thanks to the extraordinary content proliferation of digital platforms. There has been no greater investor in the stand-up genre than Netflix, and no greater champion than Lisa Nishimura. As the vice president of original documentary and comedy programming she has signed up A-listers such as Jerry Seinfeld and Chris Rock, while also supporting rising talent like Ali Wong and Hannah Gadsby. By expanding the volume of timely new content, Netflix has brought the stand-up special into the bustling center of popular culture.

In doing so, Nishimura has inhabited a role akin to the one a curator plays in the museum art world: someone who seeks out, identifies, champions, and contextualizes the work of wildly talented artists. Presenting the artists to audiences, enabling their ideas to travel through and impact culture. Nishimura invests in people and the stories that engage viewers in some space between joy and discomfort. A critical space that civil society must find the courage to visit frequently.

Often, this involves using Netflix's famous data integration abilities in novel ways.

The Netflix system has more than 2,000 "taste clusters" that measure content by tone, timbre and feeling to predict what you will want to see when you log onto the site. . . . 50 percent of its 130 million subscribers have watched a [stand-up] special in the last year, and a third of those viewers have watched three such shows.

With a slate of programs that reads like a cultural commentary on our time, it's no surprise that Nishimura has been celebrated by headlines like "Netflix's Lisa Nishimura Is One of the Most Powerful Asian Americans in Hollywood."

As a genre, stand-up comedy has taken its place beside documentary as one of the more complex, intelligent, story-based cultural catalysts in production today.

When these forms are at their best, they are mediums of activism. They present unfiltered arguments for self-awareness, transformative change, and expressions of an alternative future.

Nishimura articulates an elegant link between the sensibility of curiosity uniquely found in documentarians and comedians:

> *I find the best documentarians and comedians are hands-down some of the smartest people you'll ever meet. They're tireless with respect to their curiosity; they are endlessly observant of the world around them. And they're unsatisfied with anything surface-level, and want to understand what's the intent, what was the cause of this, what was the cause of that cause, and the deeper-rooted cause of that cause of that cause of that cause. They allow people to enter a distinct experience to help us try to better understand the world around us.*

One of Nishimura's most considerable investments in people and the dialogues they have opened has been in the (previously) reclusive Dave Chappelle. She is credited with staging his first return to stand-up in 2016, after a thirteen-year hiatus.

Chappelle goes all in, ripping the Band-Aid off the most precarious issues of American identity: race, poverty, violence, sexual identity, police brutality, money. He seems to only be content going after the radioactive topics. What makes Dave Chappelle Radically Curious is a rare trifecta: (1) his courage to use his platform to confront, challenge, and actively dismantle commonly held beliefs, (2) his deep respect for and experimentation within his medium, and (3) his desire to prototype better futures by highlighting the absurdities of life in the present.

Nina Simone famously declared:

An artist's duty is to reflect the times.

Chappelle does not disappoint. Dave Chappelle is a gladiator. He came to do battle. Cultural discursive dueling.

Twelve days after a police officer murdered George Floyd in Minneapolis, Dave Chappelle hosted a show in a cornfield in his hometown, Yellow Springs, Ohio. The piece is titled 8:46, a reference to how long the officer kneeled on Floyd's neck. Ultimately leading to his death. A number that Chappelle would repeat over and over, recontextualizing it, hovering over it to remind us just how long that amount of time really is.

In 8:46, Chappelle conjures a textbook example of incongruity theory. First, he slowly draws us in with an intimate setup of his experience of the 1994 Northridge earthquake in Southern California, a terrifying event that drove him to panic, believing he was about to die. He takes his time, walking through everything he did in a kind of sequential list—stretching the time of panic into a slow-motion accounting. His setup concludes by reminding us how many things he did, thought through, and experienced in his perceived encounter with dying in no more than thirty-five seconds. Then the unexpected punch line drops, pivoting his tone and delivering an alarmist urgency:

This man kneeled on a man's neck, for eight minutes and forty-six sec-
onds! Can you imagine that? This kid thought he was going to die. He
knew he was going to die. He called for his mother. He called for his
dead mother. I've only seen that once before in my life. My father, on his
death bed, called for his grandmother. When I watched that tape, I un-
derstood this man knew he was going to die. People watched it. People
filmed it. And for some reason, I still don't understand, all these fuckin'
police had their hands in their pockets. Who are you talking to? What
are you signifying that you can kneel on a man's neck for eight minutes
and forty-six seconds and feel like you wouldn't get the wrath of God?

And there it was. Incongruity theory of the highest order. Not so
much a one-liner, but a full shift in Chappelle's entire demeanor. A
delivery that is somewhere between a church sermon, a political
rally, and a cathartic expulsion of his own pain. We are presented
with the raw clarity of the misalignment between the fiction of how
we perceive the world (as one that is righteous and fair) and the way
it truly is (unjust and corrupt). Chappelle seems to lose himself in
this reconciliation; he raises his voice and his body to stand up for his
essential message: Are you not seeing what I am seeing? Is it not obvious that our commonly held beliefs are flawed?

8:46 is perhaps the most important conversation Chappelle has ever hosted.

Like Hannah Gadsby's *Nanette,* people weren't quite sure what to
make of it. Was it comedy? Or was it commentary? Of course, it was
both. That's the thing about the Radically Curious. They defy catego-
rization. They blend and remix languages, typologies, and genres of
cultural expressions.

A review in *The New Yorker* struggled to place the genre-bender, but
in the end perhaps understood it best of all:

"8:46" is most impactful if received as a workshop. Chappelle just about
announces it as such, periodically taking the audience's temperature

(figuratively, that is, though B-roll footage at the start of the video shows attendees lined up for "temperature checks" with a forehead thermometer). He leans into the untried nature of the performance. "The only way to figure out if this shit works," he begins, "is to do the goddamn show." He gives his audience the opportunity to watch an iconic American comedian toil to narrate a manifold event that's too immediate for disciplined humor—an event whose other side we can't yet perceive, and which may leave no room for discipline anyhow. "We'll keep this space open—this is the last stronghold for civil discourse."

In 2019 the John F. Kennedy Center for the Performing Arts awarded Dave Chappelle the Mark Twain Prize, a sort of lifetime achievement award and the highest honor for comedians offered by the U.S. government; it had been awarded to such legends as Richard Pryor, George Carlin, and Carol Burnett before him. The televised ceremony became a poignant look at the body of work Chappelle has created and the legacy of his unique influence on culture. In the Mark Twain Prize special Chappelle reflects on his experience of comedy as activism:

Everybody is mad at me for sayin' these jokes, but you understand this is the best time to say them. More now than ever we have a responsibility to speak recklessly. Otherwise, my kids may never know what reckless talk sounds like. The joys of being wrong.

The work of expressing, exploring, and experimenting with dangerous ideas is not for the faint of heart. The last stronghold of civil discourse includes the joy of being wrong. Discourse can be messy.

More than that, it ought to be. The act of confronting and challenging legacy narratives can be filled with friction—but this is how new narratives are born.

In business, a corollary can be found in the notion of "failing fast"—a practice urging iterative prototyping to drive learnings, recover those insights, and improve products and services moving forward more quickly. In theory, this kind of business leadership is to be admired. In practice, it often misses the point, as corporations have built complex safety nets to ensure nothing can ever be truly risked. In doing so, very little can be truly learned or advanced either. What business leaders often tout as "bold innovation" is often safer and much less courageous than they believe. For many businesses any interruption in normalcy *is* reckless, and thus before they begin they miss the very point of innovation. Innovation is not a tweak; it is the birth of new narratives.

But Chappelle, unlike most business leaders, is willing to bet the farm. He is willing to commit to an idea, whatever the cost. Willing to dance in dangerous territory to instigate and provoke further conversation and growth. And willing to be wrong. We can learn a great deal from Chappelle's particular form of recklessness to elicit learning.

The irony is, Chappelle is not truly reckless at all. There is greater precision to his methods than he lets on.

Later in the same special, he reflects:

This is sacred ground. Live comedy is the most incredible thing in the world to me. You're standing up there like a gladiator. That's the only time I feel like myself.

Standing on this sacred ground, looking out into the sea of an audience, is a singular experience. Simultaneously a private battle—in that you are alone onstage—yet public in that you are on display in the most exposed fashion. Unlike a debate, a formal exchange in which there is a dialogue with another actor, stand-up is essentially a conversation with yourself. A kind of extended hypothesis. Stand-up has a different texture and relationship with an audience than a typical lecture, speech, or, worse yet, the artificial and overwrought TED Talk format. As a monologue, it affords an incredible length of time to work out and push the boundaries of ideas in an intentionally provocative way.

Ironically, in the fall of 2021, Chappelle and Gadsby found themselves sparring about the controversy sparked by Netflix's clumsy handling of concerns over transphobic jokes that Chappelle peppered throughout his recent special, *The Closer*. In response to the Netflix CEO's invoking her in the company's defense of its decision not to pull Chappelle's special, Gadsby called his narrative an "emotionally stunted partial world view" in an Instagram post. In an insightful piece in *The Atlantic* titled "Dave Chappelle's Rorschach Test," Helen Lewis elaborates:

> *The negative reaction to* The Closer *has revolved largely around what he says about LGBTQ people. Chappelle has always been clear about the political argument he is making with this material: In a few short years, gay- and trans-rights activism has achieved the kind of cultural veto that Black Americans have failed to win through decades of struggle. In Chappelle's telling, no other movement has such power. The rapper DaBaby, censured for remarks about AIDS, was once involved in the fatal shooting of a Black man at a Walmart. (He was not charged in the death but was convicted of carrying a concealed weapon.) "Nothing bad happened to his career," Chappelle says. "Do you see where I'm going with this?" In the United States, he says, you can shoot and kill a Black person, "but you better not hurt a gay person's feelings."*

The friction and hurt caused by reckless talk are real. Chappelle is setting up a framework for what Lewis calls a "hierarchy of suffering." Ranking the victims of ideology, prejudice, and violent abuse within our society is a pill not easily swallowed.

The essential question may not be whether Chappelle is right or wrong but rather why a stand-up comedian such as Chappelle commands so much power over debates that have historically been hosted within the domains of civil society. Why are other forums for debate so ineffective that the gladiators of stand-up are the ones inviting and igniting millions into engaged discourse? That comedians yield significant cultural influence while 77 percent of millennials could not name the senator of their home state is itself an indicator of an upending narrative.

Whether you agree with Chappelle is less consequential than the fact that his efforts are causing us to have the conversation at all. If we listen carefully to the full seventy-two minutes, we may find that his intellectual gymnastics have converted passive entertainment into the kind of activism that invites people into Radical Curiosity. Gadsby and Chappelle are sharing the legacy narratives that created the world they live in, a world that has produced very real and extraordinarily painful lived experiences. Their ability to articulate these narratives and engage us in upending them is what creates the possibility for new narratives to emerge.

More than getting the laugh, they want to challenge commonly held beliefs by naming them out loud. Letting their stories be exercised publicly rather than held privately.

We need people like Dave Chappelle and Hannah Gadsby as gladiator guides to help us name and navigate the absurdity of the legacies still inhabiting our world.

20

Olé, Willy Wonka

How can we design spaces and conditions for human potential to flourish? Must we accept monotony as an inevitable feature of modern-day work, or can we choose to bring surprise and delight to the rituals of our jobs?

The most critical capital asset for the twenty-first-century organization is people.

No one is a bigger champion for this idea than the human capital architect of Apple, Dan Walker. He has a physical presence that could intimidate anyone. A towering six-foot-three, he is a solid oak of a man. His quiet confidence infects everyone around him. Many of us write off HR as simply the administration of payroll, benefits, and transactional hiring, reviewing résumés. But Dan has spent more than three decades radically reinventing the role of human resources as a central force for transforming organizations—bringing an element that often disappears into the background into the forefront of business and culture. His mission has been to redefine HR into what he calls "a front-line product operation . . . not a staff function." He thinks of talent itself as a product, more important than the actual product or service that is being sold, and has spent his career helping companies "fuel enterprise growth with an overabundance of extraordinary talent." That's precisely what he did as the chief talent officer of Apple during the early years of what has come to be known within the company as "the second reign of Steve Jobs."

When we first met, I sat in awe, listening to Dan's tales of building a team that would later create iTunes, anticipating Steve Jobs's growing interest in music before he even articulated it as a strategy. We built a friendship over many conversations held in his San Clemente home, where an easel board still bore the original sketch of the idea for the Genius Bar: an outcome of a series of workshops that brought one of the most successful retail operations in history to life. Talk about being in the room where it happened.

Dan Walker offered me the generosity of mentorship at a time when it mattered most. When I launched my design studio, it was he who referred me to my first client, Denise Young Smith, a protégé of Dan's who was leading Human Resources for Apple Stores globally. Denise is the very definition of what Dan would call "an overabundance of extraordinary talent." As a professional singer, she listens deeply, and brings her presence to bear by hearing what others don't. Dan's introduction would lead to a lifelong friendship with Denise, as well as a series of projects that would help define the trajectory of my design studio and mature my approach to using design as a social language to help organizational cultures come alive.

When I reached out to Denise for the first time, on October 4, 2011, we explored a project to codify the DNA of the Apple Store employee experience. The very next day, Steve Jobs passed away.

Our inquiry became more important than ever.

We established the Innovation Council—a cross section of both seasoned and emerging leaders, drawn from diverse parts of the organization—and convened its members in a design thinking inquiry to codify, map, and articulate the employee experience. A process meant to see what is, to imagine what could be. Empowering people to better visualize the opportunities and the spaces to propose innovations that could propel the future state of work at Apple Stores. We delivered this program as a series of executive education immersions that functioned as a people-centric R&D lab. A real-time, iterative, holistic view of the employee experience.

This was an era of extraordinary growth for Apple. Between 2009 and 2012, the company opened 117 new Apple Stores. The organization grew 240 percent in two years, adding nearly $100 billion in revenue between 2010 and 2012: a change quotient that is larger than the GDP of nearly 100 countries in the world.

Employees in every corner of the company were doing their life's best work. Yet the growth, the scale, and in turn the expectations of these leaders went beyond typical measure. When the transcendent level of work people deliver is not recognized, honored, and celebrated, there is always a danger that aliveness will be extinguished. It's a funny thing about aliveness. We desire it, we aspire to it, but we rarely point it out and celebrate it when it shows up. Yet there is a direct correlation between how frequently organizations celebrate aliveness and how frequently it shows up. So why do so many organizational cultures not allow the aliveness to, well, come alive? Denise was committed to seeing aliveness.

The importance of seeing and recognizing the aliveness of daily work is one of the most poignant lessons I learned in working with Apple. Denise is a master at seeing people, recognizing their contributions, and marking their aliveness.

In this era dubbed the Great Resignation, at a time when we are radically renegotiating our social contract regarding the purpose and value proposition of work, we need new language to articulate and celebrate when and how people come alive in their work.

When people praise Apple—whether for their sleekly designed devices and interfaces, frictionless customer experience, or ability to churn out new and innovative products year after year—they typically invoke Steve Jobs's unparalleled genius. Rarely, however, do they express such veneration for the tens of thousands of talented, dedicated employees doing the work to turn Jobs's bold vision into reality. In search of the words to celebrate the efforts of those employees who go above and beyond their job descriptions every single day, we stumbled upon a TED Talk titled "Your Elusive Creative Genius," by Elizabeth Gilbert, author of the bestselling memoir *Eat, Pray, Love*. Toward the end of the talk, she describes how, centuries ago in the North African deserts, people used to gather for magnificent moonlight dances that would go on until dawn.

She goes on to recount how on rare occasions, "one of these performers would actually become transcendent. . . . He would be lit from within, and lit from below and all lit up on fire with divinity," and the crowd would chant: "Allah, Allah, Allah, God, God, God." Then Gilbert shares a historical footnote:

> *When the Moors invaded southern Spain, they took this custom with them and the pronunciation changed over the centuries from "Allah, Allah, Allah," to "Olé, olé, olé," which you still hear in bullfights and in flamenco dances. In Spain, when a performer has done something impossible and magic, "Allah, olé, olé, Allah, magnificent, bravo," incomprehensible, there it is—a glimpse of God.*

The moment we heard this, "olé" became our word at Apple. Simple, delicate, and pure. A meaningful gesture to toast excellence, to say "bravo." "Olé" soon came to be shorthand for acknowledging those times when an employee had done something "impossible and magic"—and to let them know they were being seen for doing so. An unexpected moment for aliveness to flourish in the midst of ordinary rituals.

Designing spaces and conditions for human potential to come alive is the primary motivation for experience designers. The problem is, the workplace is filled with countless transactions that are, in a word, boring. Inherited legacies, constraints, and messages reinforcing the soulless autopilot of the production economy. We all know the colloquialism "It's a grind." Do we accept the monotony? Or can we bring a bit of surprise and delight to the least expected rituals of our jobs? How do we create space for experiences to become remarkable? How can a calendar request to join a committee meeting become something joyful, a figurative Willy Wonka Golden Ticket?

The opportunity of the employee experience is to redesign the mundane as magnificent.

This was what our project set out to accomplish. Once Denise carefully selected the members of her Innovation Council, we wanted the very invitation itself to embody the best of what experience design has to offer. Something a little unexpected in such an expected ritual can add mystery and intrigue, propel engagement, and open people up to a process designed with uncertainty in mind. There was only one thing to do: design the invitation to join the Innovation Council as golden-ticket chocolate bars.

Willy Wonka has become a personification of aliveness. An anchored imprint to mean the most absurd level aliveness has to offer. After all, the man lived in a candy factory with rivers of chocolate and would wander his gardens of sweets in a velvet tuxedo. And it was he who said:

If the good Lord had intended us to walk, he wouldn't have invented roller skates.

In a rare interview at the 92nd Street Y, twenty-two years since his last film, the actor Gene Wilder was asked about his iconic role playing Willy Wonka. He described his conversation with the film's director, Mel Stuart, after first reading the script. Wilder told Stuart:

> *It's very good, but there is something missing. If I play that part, I want to come out with a cane. (Performing) That something is wrong with my leg, then come down the stairs slowly, and then have the cane stick into one of the bricks, and then get up, start to fall over, and roll around, and then they all laugh and applaud.*

This is how he shows up. The first impression. His arrival, 44 minutes into the film, is marked by a deliberate subversion of expectations. We are oriented to the character through disorientation. The message: Things are not what they seem.

This is the mindset we wanted to instill in our Innovation Council, as questioners of truths and presenters of alternative possibilities. The golden ticket was meant to convey, even if subconsciously, that what will come next is uncertain and may disorient, yet is sure to be anything but mundane. As we heighten the importance of this gathering, we see you. We appreciate you. You are extraordinary and we are inviting you to do extraordinary things. A golden ticket is a celebration of human potential realized.

In the space where things are not what they seem, ideas come alive.

Apple Stores have historically embraced a credo, a kind of poetic manifesto, that brings this sensibility to the center of the employee experience. One of the stanzas of this credo reads: "We are a community where great relationships, open communication, learning, leading, and growing serve to enrich our daily lives." Apple, in other words, heightens the employee experience into a cause: not just a facet of doing business, but also an explicit social project.

In 2016, when Gene Wilder passed of complications from Alzheimer's disease, the family released the following statement:

> *The decision to wait until this time to disclose his condition wasn't vanity, but more so that the countless young children that would smile or call out to him "there's Willy Wonka" would not have to be then exposed to an adult referencing illness or trouble and causing delight to travel to worry, disappointment or confusion. He simply couldn't bear the idea of one less smile in the world.*

Even in his passing Willy Wonka gifts us wisdom. A silent heroic gesture of human care. What I learned at Apple is that every day is an opportunity for heroic gestures of human care. In fact, we can build organizational cultures around such a wise gift. When an organization's primary objective is money, it designs a customer experience to extract the outcome of money. When an organization's primary focus is extraordinary value creation through human care, it designs an employee experience that naturally delivers customer experiences. The reciprocity of an employee experience and a customer experience mirroring and informing each other produces an enormous number of smiles. Real value, real joy, real care always yield revenue. To design organizations of care is wealth generative leadership.

NATURE

Our Removal from the Natural World Inhibits Humility

How do we define the human relationship with the natural world? How might our daily lives, our business models, and our decision-making evolve if we merged the human condition with the ecological condition? If we developed a greater sense of humility as guests of this planet, rather than its self-appointed masters?

When legacy narratives are left unquestioned, they can have toxic implications. Among the most dangerous legacy narratives, if left untouched for too long, is human beings' relationship with the natural world: one in which we are separate from and dominant over living systems, and therefore entitled to take from them with abandon. Yet we are a part of this world, not separate from it. And human domination over living systems is the greatest threat to our ecological sustainability.

We now know a great deal about the science of climate change. What seem to be less understood are the mental models that have gotten us to the current state. In an astoundingly stark reminder of how easy it is to fall in and out of narratives, Heather Alberro traces how we have woven in and out of a joint identity with nature over the course of human history:

> *Though a varied and complex story, the widespread separation of humans from nature in Western culture can be traced to a few key historical developments, starting with the rise of Judeo-Christian values 2000 years ago. Prior to this point, belief systems with multiple gods and earth spirits, such as paganism, dominated. They generally considered the sacred to be found throughout nature, and humanity as thoroughly enmeshed within it.*
>
> *When Judaism and Christianity rose to become the dominant religious force in Western society, their sole god—as well as sacredness and salvation—were re-positioned outside of nature. The Old Testament taught that God made humans in his own image and gave them dominion over the Earth.*
>
> *In the early 17th century, French father of modern philosophy René Descartes framed the world as essentially split between the realm of mind and that of inert matter. As the only rational beings, Descartes saw humans as wholly separate from and superior to nature and non-human animals, who were considered mere mindless machines to be mastered and exploited at will.*

We tend to rationalize a current narrative as the only narrative. But when we see these narratives with new eyes, with a sense of curiosity, we are empowered to interrogate them as intellectual frames that have informed how we see ourselves and what may be needed to see ourselves anew. We urgently need to reimagine a story in which the human being is simply a stakeholder among many, entangled in a larger whole. Such narratives may, at first, seem irrational because they defy the commonly held beliefs of a Western model of existence. But much of the non-Western world has embraced a different narrative about humans and nature. Leah Penniman writes about the Afro-Indigenous practices that challenge ideas of human supremacy over the natural world. She recalls an inspiring story from her time apprenticing with the Queen Mothers of Kroboland in Ghana, sharing that:

> *Paramount Queen Mother Manye Nartike . . . was particularly animated by a rumor she had heard about our diasporic practices in relation to land. In disbelief she admonished me, "Is it true that in the United States, a farmer will put the seed into the ground and not pour any libations, offer any prayers, sing, or dance, and expect that seed to grow?" Met with my ashamed silence, she continued, "That is why you are all sick! Because you see the Earth as a thing and not a being."*

Heather Alberro also expands our view, pivoting from Judeo-Christian faith frameworks in the West to alternative models in the East, noting that:

> *Eastern philosophies and religions such as Zen Buddhism also entangle humanity and nature, emphasizing that there is no such thing as an independent self and that all things depend on others for their existence and well-being.*

To make significant progress in our fight against climate change will require that we rewrite our Western narratives. This is not merely a scientific challenge but a humanistic one. And addressing it may not be a question of how much carbon we pour into the atmosphere, how many natural resources we use, how much water we consume, or how much is left for us and for future generations. The essential questions may force us to dig deeper and challenge the very mental models that govern how we live. We can't change our behavior if we are unwilling to revisit our beliefs.

The answers to questions of *how much* are abundantly clear. In fact, we measure this quite well. We have ways of quantifying how quickly the Earth's well is running dry. Earth Overshoot Day, for example, is an annual milestone: the point at which humanity has used up more ecological resources than the Earth can regenerate by the end of the year. Like an overdrawn bank account, only in this case, rather than dollars, it's natural resources that are in the red. According to the Global Footprint Network, an international research organization that provides decision-makers with a menu of tools to help the human economy operate within the Earth's ecological limits, in recent years we have been consuming resources 1.75 times faster than the planet can regenerate them. We are living in a state of permanent overdraft.

But an accounting is not enough. We don't need an information campaign; we need a humility campaign.

When we can view ourselves as dependent on, rather than the center of, living systems much bigger than ourselves, we can feel smaller. Not insignificant, but a kind of small that evokes what we have come to call humility.

In his 1995 Harvard commencement address, later published under the title "Radical Renewal of Human Responsibility," the Czech statesman and environmentalist Václav Havel called for a "new humility":

> *The main task in the coming era is something else: a radical renewal of our sense of responsibility. Our conscience must catch up to our reason, otherwise we are lost. It is my profound belief that there is only one way to achieve this: we must divest ourselves of our egotistical anthropocen-*

trism, our habit of seeing ourselves as masters of the universe who can do whatever occurs to us. We must discover a new respect for what transcends us: for the universe, for the earth, for nature, for life, and for reality. Our respect for other people, for other nations and for other cultures, can only grow from a humble respect for the cosmic order and from an awareness that we are a part of it, that we share in it and that nothing of what we do is lost, but rather becomes part of the eternal memory of being, where it is judged.

The hubris of humanity thinking that we are dominant over the planet when our existence is such a tiny blip on its radar is laughable. Consider for a moment that if the history of the Earth were compressed to twenty-four hours, humans would have existed for only one second of time.

Earth scientists use a system of chronological dating to describe the relationship of events in the history of the Earth, with each chapter in that history considered an epoch. For the past 12,000 years, the Earth has been in what is called the Holocene epoch. But recently, scientists have proposed that we have entered a new epoch: a period during which human activity has become the dominant influence on climate and the environment. "The significance of the Anthropocene is that it sets a different trajectory for the Earth system, of which we of course are part," said Professor Jan Zalasiewicz, a geologist at the University of Leicester and chair of the Working Group on the Anthropocene. And according to chemist and Nobel laureate Paul Crutzen, the naming of this new epoch the Anthropocene (from the Greek *anthropos,* meaning "human," and *cene,* meaning "new" or "recent") "stresses the enormity of humanity's responsibility as stewards of the Earth."

Rewriting the narrative on climate will require a large-scale shift across our institutions and businesses. David Orr, the Paul Sears Distinguished Professor of Environmental Studies and Politics Emeritus at Oberlin College, asks the essential question:

Can we imagine education that doesn't alienate us from life in the name of human domination, separate feeling from intellect, and deaden the sense of wonder for the created world?

Companies such as IDEO have developed a professional language for what is called "human-centered design," a practice that seeks design interventions to promote social good. But human-centered design has its limits, and new conversations about the dominant position of human beings are unfolding. The field of design has already migrated from a model in which the product was central to a model in which the user is central. But new questions are arising as to whether there should be a single stakeholder at the center at all. As a result, a new, decentralized model of environment-centered design is emerging, one that designer Monika Sznel, a leader in this movement, describes as:

> *an approach to product or service development that aims to make products or services environmentally, socially and economically sustainable by focusing on the needs, limitations and preferences of target audiences and non-human strategic stakeholders. It involves knowledge and design techniques developed at the intersection of human-centered design, usability, ecology, and sustainability science.*

In his research project, traveling museum exhibition, and bestselling book *Massive Change*, Bruce Mau quotes the historian Arnold Toynbee, who said: "The twentieth century will be chiefly remembered by future generations not as an era of political conflict or technical invention but as an age in which human society dared to think of the welfare of the whole human race as a practical objective." When Bruce once presented these ideas at the Vancouver Gallery of Art, a

HUMAN–CENTERED DESIGN

SYSTEM–CENTERED DESIGN

local high school student spoke up and challenged him to replace the phrase "the whole human race" with "all of life."

We need new narratives that reimagine human identity as being intrinsically linked to the story of our living systems. How might our daily lives, our business models, our decision-making evolve if we fundamentally merged with the ecological condition? If we developed a greater sense of humility as guests of this planet, stewards of the living systems that surround us, rather than their self-appointed masters?

Such a reconfiguration is needed urgently. COVID-19 offers us further evidence that our legacy narratives are costing us dearly. As an article in *The Guardian* notes:

> *The UN environment chief and a leading economist said Covid-19 was an "SOS signal for the human enterprise" and that current economic thinking did not recognise that human wealth depends on nature's health.*

The article goes on to quote Elizabeth Maruma Mrema, head of the UN Convention on Biological Diversity; Maria Neira, the World Health Organization director for environment and health; and Marco Lambertini, head of the World Wildlife Foundation:

> *"We have seen many diseases emerge over the years, such as Zika, Aids, Sars and Ebola, and they all originated from animal populations under conditions of severe environmental pressures." . . . With coronavirus, "these outbreaks are manifestations of our dangerously unbalanced relationship with nature," they said. "They all illustrate that our own destructive behaviour towards nature is endangering our own health—a stark reality we've been collectively ignoring for decades."*

Our natural world grounds us. Keeps us in awe of the spectacular magic in the diversity of life around us. Such awe reminds us that we are a part of something bigger than ourselves. This humility is a fertile garden in which curiosity can grow. We need to be Radically Curious about our relationship with the planet not simply because we live here but because nature brings out the best in us.

22

Walking as a Radical Act

How can we earn trust when we enter a place as an outsider? Do we fully appreciate the alchemy that can take place when we walk alongside others? Are we fully investing in one of the most undervalued assets of our modern economy: slow time?

I'm walking, pacing nervously in a place I never expected to be. Giving a presentation to an audience I never anticipated being in a dialogue with. At the invitation of Don Simpson, founder of the Innovation Expedition, I am the keynote speaker for a special luncheon at the Petroleum Club in Calgary, Canada. I am walking to strengthen my resolve and confidence in what I intend to say to the more than sixty oil executives in the room.

Alberta's oil sands are home to the fourth-largest supply of oil reserves in the world after Venezuela, Saudi Arabia, and Iran—the equivalent of about 165 billion barrels. Depending on the fluctuating price of oil, the total economic value of Alberta's oil reserves may exceed $1 trillion. Most of these resources are found in the Regional Municipality of Wood Buffalo, a government that operates as a network of small towns led by a single mayor and council. The region stretches across a terrain of nearly 24,000 square miles. To put that into perspective, my home state of Rhode Island covers a land area of just over 1,000 square miles.

The luncheon is being held in the relatively nearby city of Calgary, often referred to as the "Houston of Canada" because of the hundred or so oil and gas companies with headquarters or regional offices in the city. I am here to help the assembled executives ask essential questions about the epic challenge they are undertaking regarding the largest industrial projects in human history.

I walk onstage.

The first half of my presentation is backstory. I bring the audience on a walkabout. There aren't many words on my slides; my visuals are mostly rich, high-resolution photographs. I wander between the tables, piercing the typical podium formality.

Soon it's time for the second half of my presentation. The next slide projects a looming image of Darth Vader. I pause and tell the room: "This is how the world sees you. . . . The thing is, I don't think any of you wake up in the morning trying to harm the Earth, your community, or your children's future. And I'd like to see how we might work together to make sense of all this."

And thus began my love affair with Wood Buffalo. It is the largest national park in Canada and the second-largest protected parkland in the world: larger than the entire country of Switzerland.

A few months later, 462 miles north of where I delivered my Darth Vader Petroleum Club talk, I would fly into Fort McMurray, the largest town in Wood Buffalo.

Fort McMurray is a place that is hard to describe. It's part drilling town, born of the explosive growth of the oil sector, an industrial juggernaut. It's been called a modern-day Deadwood. But it also has a seductive beauty, found both in the spirit of its people and in the grandeur of the natural world on display. Forests of a scale that take your breath away. The forests of the Adirondacks, where I grew up, are quite special to me. But this felt different. Not because it was three times the size of the 6-million-acre Adirondacks. But because it was so remote, so sparsely populated, it was as though we were beyond the wall from *Game of Thrones*. I had to take a helicopter ride, arranged by my journey partner, Don Simpson, to experience the vastness of it all.

Over the next twenty-eight months I would visit Wood Buffalo more than twelve times, often staying for more than a week. My studio began a project that we called Nexus North, which utilized the languages of design thinking, social innovation, and community organizing to mobilize a multi-stakeholder collaboration aimed at bringing a new model for sustainability to the region. It is one of those once-in-a-lifetime big hairy audacious goals, with thorny challenges at every turn.

How can we advocate both for the environment and for the people who have come to call this their home? Are these narratives in conflict? How can we create the space for the voices of Indigenous communities to be heard, ensuring their experience shapes the vision for the future of the land? In a community that has struggled with a transient workforce, with thousands of stakeholders being constantly flown in from countries around the world, how can I prove I am not just another consultant here for a payday? These were just a few of the questions I grappled with during my many visits.

But mostly, I walked.

We have a saying in my design studio: "Slow down in order to speed up." Modern life so relentlessly urges us to act, to solve, to win, to make rash decisions in service to speed over quality. What the obsession with speed typically yields is an answer to the wrong question. Deceptively offering value in the short term, only to cost us far more over time. We need to make the up-front investment of slowing down to frame the right questions, and thus arrive at a resilient solution.

Walking slows things down. Walking is a way of moving at the pace of thought. And thought is what is needed in a place with so many contradictions, so many knotted narratives to untangle. A place of incredible wealth creation alongside incredible human degradation. A place being stripped of its natural resources but not of its natural awe, so close to the northern lights it's like you could reach into the glowing sky and scoop them right up.

As I walked, I watched. I listened. I tried to lay the foundation of trust. Then I would wait for it to cement before adding another fragile layer, and then another, slowly shedding my status as an outsider with each one.

As Bayo Akomolafe, the Nigerian chief curator of the Emergence Network, put it in an essay titled "A Slower Urgency":

> Slowing down is thus about lingering in the places we are not used to. Seeking out new questions. Becoming accountable to more than what rests on the surface. Seeking roots. Slowing down is taking care of ghosts, hugging monsters, sharing silence, embracing the weird. . . . The idea of slowing down is not about getting answers, it is about questioning our questions.

I embraced the work in Wood Buffalo. Not because I am pro-oil, but because I am pro–asking new questions. I am pro–seeking the roots of a place, pro–becoming accountable. If we seek change in a place, sometimes we need to go to the origin and investigate fully, with feet on the ground, walking with those whom we believe to be Darth Vader. Sometimes we need to step into haunted spaces and hug the monster.

I didn't know of Akomolafe's voice at the time. I wish I had. But I had enough good sense to linger. And to consult the wisdom of my partner in this initiative, Don Simpson, an eighty-year-old man who spent his life walking across dozens of countries building trust with communities to do things bigger than themselves. We were nearly half a century apart in age, intergenerational co-chairs of the Nexus North initiative, as we walked into the Regional Municipality of Wood Buffalo Council meeting and proposed that the local government itself became a member of the Nexus North project. That they put *themselves* at the nexus of the conversation, instead of ceding their voice to the business leaders down in Calgary, 462 miles south.

Don and I presented this idea to Mayor Melissa Blake, who at the time had led the municipality for more than 50 percent of its existence. A few months later, Mayor Blake and two additional council members joined us near California's Santa Cruz Mountains, just south of Silicon Valley, for a three-day Ideas Salon retreat with forty other stakeholders. It was here that I took a walk with Mayor Blake—literally and metaphorically—in search of new thinking.

Over the years, I have come to understand the power of a walking conversation. But I don't mean the hurried conversation we squeeze in on our way from point A to point B. In her book *Wanderlust: A History of Walking*, Rebecca Solnit, a rare breed of public intellectual, describes intentional walking with precision:

> *Most of the time walking is merely practical, the unconsidered locomotive means between two sites. To make walking into an investigation, a ritual, a meditation, is a special subset of walking, physiologically like and philosophically unlike the way the mail carrier brings the mail and the office worker reaches the train. Which is to say that the subject of walking is, in some sense, about how we invest universal acts with particular meanings. Like eating or breathing, it can be invested with wildly different cultural meanings, from the erotic to the spiritual, from the revolutionary to the artistic. Here this history begins to become part*

of the history of the imagination and the culture, of what kind of plea-
sure, freedom, and meaning are pursued at different times by different
kinds of walks and walkers.

Walking is a radical act in a world of fast-paced transactions and short attention spans. Slowing down time is not easy amid life's endless stream of distraction. We know walking is good for our health, as a form of exercise. But its impact on our entire well-being is only now being better understood. In fact, doctors are moving toward a new practice of prescribing social behaviors, far beyond what we typically think of as medicine. Doctors in Scotland, for example, are literally prescribing nature to their patients, in a new approach to integrated medicine inspired by the popular Japanese practice of *shinrin-yoku,* or "forest bathing."

But a walk is also a context for trust to be forged. Like a handshake or bow, a walk with someone is a gesture of respect. As new research from the University of Hong Kong reveals, the specific dynamics of walking side by side help people build connection, trust, and an affinity to each other:

> *Researchers used sensors to measure how participants walked and found that participants tended to synchronize their walking—"fall into step" with each other—even if they were strangers and even if they weren't allowed to talk. They found that participants' impressions of their partners grew more favorable after the first part of the walk— which took only 3 to 4½ minutes—even though they weren't allowed to speak to each other. Those who were allowed to converse on the return trip got to like each other even more.*

Just twenty-eight miles from the site of my walk with Mayor Blake lies Apple headquarters in Cupertino, a place of some rather well-known walks. It's well documented that Steve Jobs championed walking meetings, and could often be found wandering around the campus, engaged in a conversation in motion. And the science behind his habit is now catching up. Something specific is happening, physiologically, in a walking meeting that often delivers higher-order results. With our bodies engaged in the rhythm of movement, our minds are engaged in the subject of the conversation. It's as though if the body is occupied, our minds can be unoccupied, and open to a more nonlinear set of associations.

The practice of teaching while walking is one that dates back to Aristotle, whose students came to be known as "Peripatetics," from the Greek verb *peripatein,* which means "to walk or stroll about." A reference to Aristotle's practice of teaching while walking with his students. According to Dr. Ted Eytan, former medical director of the Kaiser Permanente Center for Total Health, walking triggers the release of specific neurochemicals that aid executive function, while also serving as a powerful form of bonding: a way to break down the status barriers that inhibit the free exchange of ideas and thoughts.

Months after the Ideas Salon in California, I found myself back in Fort McMurray, spending over seventy-two hours of deep time, walking time, with Mayor Blake and forty others who granted me insight into the complexities of Wood Buffalo that could have taken years to acquire otherwise.

Slow time is an undervalued currency. We aren't as well versed in how to earn it, convert it, and spend it in an economy in which time is literally money.

Slow down in order to speed up.

Mayor Blake lives in a space of patient urgency. She is willing to take a walk if it is in service of getting things done.

In Fort McMurray, new doors have opened. The respect I have earned through the success of our Ideas Salon is evident. The story of what it meant to those who attended is finding its way through the gossip of the small town. And my newfound walking companions are urging others to connect with Don and me, to explore the Nexus North project.

The most significant meeting that emerged as a result of the salon was with one of the five First Nations chiefs of the Athabasca Tribal Council, Chief Vern Janvier from the Chipewyan Prairie First Nation. When I sat down with him, his directness was refreshing. He pulled no punches, courageously saying aloud what many of us were thinking, wondering, suspecting. He shared with me the challenges his people have faced, urgent stories that invoked the complex abuse of land rights and respect. He challenged why I—as a white man, as an outsider, and as an American—was there in the first place. It became clear that I could not have met him before this moment. It took me eighteen months of slowing down, of being present, of lingering in place that earned me the right to sit with Chief Vern, as he asked me to call him. It was perhaps the single most intense conversation I have experienced in my lifetime. And at the end of this conversation, something remarkable happened.

Chief Vern of the Chipewyan Prairie First Nation invited me to take a walk.

23

Big and Small Sauntering

What is the relationship between nature and curiosity? How do we understand ourselves as a part of the natural world? How can nature cultivate the sensibilities of Radical Curiosity? How can we better understand the unique value of rural identities and experiences as different from the value of urban identities and experiences?

I remember trying to locate my sense of place as a child. Asking my parents: "Our house is in Schuyler Falls. I go to the Peru School District. My baseball team is in Morrisonville. But our mailing address is Plattsburgh. So, where do we live?" I couldn't have been more than ten years old, making sense of a rural, regional, distributed identity, with roots in a place so far north that "the city" was Montreal, not the Big Apple. Fifteen years later I'd return to marry my wife on the edge of Lake Champlain, an understudy of the Great Lakes, home of Champy, New York's own Loch Ness Monster. Lake Champlain is nestled in the valley between Vermont's Green Mountains and New York's Adirondack Mountains. With endless space for wandering in between.

Rural life is both big and small. Big was the Peru School District, which stretched out over such a distance that for many kids it was a forty-minute bus ride to school. Small was my graduating class, which struggled to exceed a hundred kids. Small was Peru's population, at a staggering 6,985 people. Big was the farmland: in its acreage and in its footprint on memories. Peru is known for its apple orchards, hundreds of acres of those green-and-red trees in parallel, symmetrical lines. Dotted to the edges of the horizon.

One of the reasons I fell in love with my wife was her love of trees. I grew up in the Adirondacks, a 6-million-acre refuge of trees, and for me forests were like air: everywhere, abundant, mixed into any vista and any breath. It would be difficult to imagine my experience divorced from trees; it would be like interrupting breathing.

This was the backdrop of my childhood. A visual canvas made up of the painted figures of trees, the gestural lines of streams, wrapping around the bends of boulders and rocks grounding their movement. Whatever town, village, or hamlet I was raised in, it was sublime. Big was the space that enabled breathing, thinking, and joy. Acts of freedom unburdened by much of modern life. Big was the forest that seemed to never end. I found my voice under the canopy it provided. Trees held up a kind of spiritual cathedral for curiosity to flourish within me. Nature is perhaps the host of the most compellingly religious experiences I have embraced in my life.

And I am not the only one. Countless voices have sung a chorus of reverence to the awe that our living world presents. Respecting trees is to live with great humility, as Hermann Hesse would say:

Trees have long thoughts, long-breathing and restful, just as they have longer lives than ours. They are wiser than we are, as long as we do not listen to them. But when we have learned how to listen to trees, then the brevity and the quickness and the childlike hastiness of our thoughts achieve an incomparable joy.

In the mid-nineteenth century, among the most critical literary voices in America were Ralph Waldo Emerson, Henry David Thoreau, and Walt Whitman. Some of these figures' most profound writings were journals, poetry, and essays that cumulatively function as a soundtrack of love songs to the majesty of nature. It is their voices that have grounded present-day environmentalism.

Rural life provided me the space, sounds, and pace that allowed curiosity to grow.

Space meant that everything was far apart, and nothing was in between. I used to cup my hand against the glass window of the school bus, imagining that the landscape that passed through my fingers was being selected for an imaginary world. The nothing that was in between was everything. Providing room for the mind to saunter. A scale to remind me of my smallness.

Sounds meant that every day was a concert. Trees sounded like woodwind instruments, blowing in the wind. Storms were like symphonies featuring leaves, water, soil—and you can never mute the white noise of a river. Seasons were more like albums. Providing soundtracks to which the mind could saunter. A rhythm to remind me of my part in something bigger.

Pace meant that time was slow, but not slow motion. It wasn't boring, but born of a rhythm in which nature held the clock. Whether snow came by the foot or by the inch determined if you were late. I once was caught lingering in my friend's long dirt driveway waiting for a bear to finish playing in a puddle. Providing time for the mind to saunter. A speed to remind me that we are not in control.

Thoreau, too, experienced rural life as a reminder of his smallness, his place in something bigger:

> In the street and in society I am almost invariably cheap and dissipated, my life is unspeakably mean. No amount of gold or respectability would in the least redeem it—dining with the Governor or a member of Congress!! But alone in distant woods or fields, in unpretending sprout lands or pastures tracked by rabbits, even on a black and, to most, cheerless day, like this, when a villager would be thinking of his inn, I come to myself, I once more feel myself grandly related, and that the cold and solitude are friends of mine. I suppose that this value, in my case, is equivalent to what others get by churchgoing and prayer. I come to my solitary woodland walk as the homesick go home. . . . It is as if I always met in those places some grand, serene, immortal, infinitely encouraging, though invisible, companion, and walked with him.

Thoreau proposes that his urban life is unspeakably mean—full of the excess of cheap pleasures. Yet alone in the distant woods, in fields, and across land he is present, aligned. His sense of companionship with nature can be compared only to the presence of a kind of secular God. When he describes the immortality, the serenity, the spirituality of nature he can only characterize the bigness of his surroundings in juxtaposition to his own presence, the opposite of big. It's not a smallness that implies something inferior. It is a smallness with grace. He is experiencing humility.

Humility is essential to curiosity.

Thoreau, with inspired clarity, describes one of his most beloved activities within nature as walking. Further invoking the language of religion, he traces the etymological roots of sauntering, celebrating it as a part of a much bigger part of our history:

> I have met with but one or two persons in the course of my life who understood the art of Walking, that is, of taking walks,—who had a genius, so to speak, for sauntering: which word is beautifully derived

"from idle people who roved about the country, in the Middle Ages, and asked charity, under pretense of going à *la Sainte Terre," to the Holy Land, till the children exclaimed, "There goes a* Sainte-Terrer," *a Saunterer,—a Holy-Lander. . . . He who sits still in a house all the time may be the greatest vagrant of all; but the saunterer, in the good sense, is no more vagrant than the meandering river, which is all the while sedulously seeking the shortest course to the sea.*

It shifts our focus on the self to a wider-angle view of the world, full of complexity and wonder. We embrace an interestedness in the world. Nature is a kind of humility aphrodisiac. The bigness of nature draws out an awareness of our smallness, compelling empathy.

The dance between the smallness and bigness is a form of reciprocity. The relationship between human beings and nature is one of embeddedness. It is when we are disconnected from our balanced relationship with nature that we experience disembedding.

In sociology, disembedding refers to a process, associated with modernization, in which social relationships become increasingly dispersed across time and space, leading to a decline in traditional social ties. More significantly, in-person interactions lose their significance in everyday life, people who feel a sense of kinship can live far away from each other, and people sharing the same neighborhood may not even talk to one another.

Early warnings of our disembedding date back to the early 1800s, when Emerson and Thoreau were the central voices of transcendentalism. A literary and philosophical movement of the 1820s and 1830s critical of contemporary society for its conformity, transcendentalism urged people to reclaim their independence, self-reliance, and deep gratitude for nature. In his landmark 1836 essay "Nature," Emerson elucidated four ways that humans use nature: as commodity (to satisfy their basic needs), beauty (to satisfy their desire for delight), language (to communicate with one another), and discipline (to understand the world).

One of the central ideas explored in "Nature" is Emerson's belief that humans, distracted by the demands of modern life, have stepped out of their reciprocity with nature. It's ironic to imagine that the modernity of the 1820s was considered too much of a distraction for Emerson and the transcendentalists.

If only they could see us now! Two centuries later, distraction has become normalized. Our symphony of technology apps from Twitter to Slack to Snapchat aside, there are larger questions about how the way we live determines our connectedness to nature.

According to the most recent U.S. census, rural areas cover 97 percent of the nation's land but contain only 19.3 percent of the population. At a global level, the United Nations projects that 68 percent of the world population will live in urban centers by 2050. By 2030, the world is projected to have forty-three megacities, each with more than 10 million inhabitants.

But the urban/rural dichotomy is about more than demographic data and bar charts for policy wonks to present at conferences. These are two universes in conflict. Big modernity, big city, big opportunities, versus small local, small rural, small ceiling for possibilities. Why have we embraced these narratives? What has contributed to our drifting further and further from nature? How do we reconcile these distinct worlds?

Our culture has glamorized the urban lifestyle. Cities are cosmopolitan, epicenters of culture, hotbeds of commerce. The land of opportunity. What if we've gotten it all wrong? What if the fastness of an urban life has suffocated the space for thinking, for curiosity? And the slowness of the rural identity, embedded within nature, envelops a humility that heightens curiosity?

RURAL COUNTIES ARE THE MAJORITY OF U.S. COUNTIES

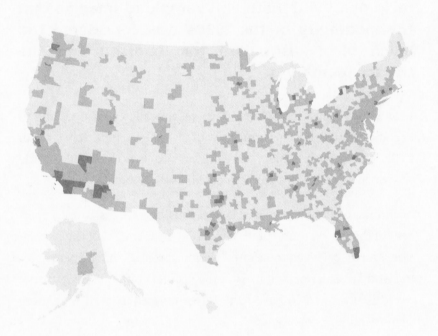

200M   people in the United States **do not** live in urban centers

~46M   Americans live in the nation's rural counties

175M   in its suburbs and small metros

~98M   in its urban core counties

○ Rural

○ Suburbs and Small Metros

● Urban Counties

How we choose to live can cultivate our curiosity or extinguish it. I'll happily visit a city for a quick fix, like a drug. But no sooner do I set foot in the city than I remember why I have fallen in love with the space, the sound, and the speed of a rural life. Too many of us have become addicted to the *doing* that cities are built upon.

Our bias for action has wrongly convinced us that a rural life is one of inaction.

But doing more things that are irrelevant is not better than doing fewer things that are profoundly meaningful. True, embeddedness in nature may conflict with a production economy. But to that I say amen! Let us not blindly accept the mythology of the urban: stories mostly wielded by those with economic interest to convince us to participate in small transactions rather than a big life. Maybe a life of sauntering is the biggest life of all.

Let Us Now Praise Rural Communities

Why have we bought into the dominant narrative asserting the superiority of the urban experience? Where can we find the space and solitude required for radical inquiry if not in the rural landscape? Can we learn to appreciate the quiet retreat that rural life affords us? How might we embrace the countryside as the new frontier for business and cultural innovation?

My studio has had a remote work culture since its inception. We behave more like an informal cooperative network than a formal corporation: a collective of designers, strategists, researchers, educators, and social entrepreneurs dotted across the globe working on cultural change. Over the years the studio has employed or commissioned more than eighty wildly talented team members. About 70 percent of them have been in rural settings, from the farmlands of Wisconsin to the hills of Vermont to our headquarters on the 5,000-person island of Jamestown, Rhode Island.

We redirect the costs saved from our lighter overhead toward seasonal team gatherings we call quarterlies. Typically, quarterlies are held in some bucolic remote environment, like the Berkshire Mountains in Massachusetts or the Ojai Valley in California. But at the end of 2019 we planned to hold our first quarterly of 2020 in an urban setting, in part so we could attend the new Guggenheim exhibition: *Countryside, The Future* by renowned architect Rem Koolhaas.

The New York City quarterly was scheduled for mid-March 2020. But, of course, it never came to pass. By the start of the month, the first coronavirus case reached New York. By the seventh of March the governor declared a state of emergency, as New York City quickly became a hotspot of the pandemic. Then the whole world went into lockdown. Those New Yorkers who had the means and were untethered thanks to new remote work policies flocked to the countryside. An urban exodus, changing the complexion of the city. It's reported that over the course of 2020 approximately 3.57 million people left New York City temporarily or permanently. By spring, according to a national survey conducted by the Harris Poll, 39 percent of urban dwellers across the United States said that the COVID-19 crisis had prompted them to consider leaving for less densely populated, rural areas.

This exodus to the countryside unfolded just as one of the world's greatest museums closed down their exhibition about the future of the countryside in the city that never sleeps.

Prior to *Countryside,* Rem Koolhaas and his firm, the Office for Metropolitan Architecture (OMA), built a reputation for advancing the professional discourse on cities through major publications, iconic buildings, and branded media. The group's skyscrapers defy gravity; looking at their signature works, such as the Seattle Public Library or the CCTV headquarters in Beijing, is like reading a contemporary architecture textbook celebrating city life. Koolhaas was ahead of his time, reviving the urban condition at the height of suburban sprawl and writing the book *Delirious New York* in 1978. Today, he says:

> *I'm interested in the country for the same reason I was paying attention to New York in the 70s. No one else was looking.*

Nearly half a century later, Rem is ahead of the curve one more time. He is looking to the 98 percent of the Earth's surface not occupied by cities. *Countryside, The Future* is the product of nearly a decade of exploration and proposes that "the countryside is now the site where the most radical modern components of our civilization are taking place." One of his partners, Samir Bantal, the director of the think tank within OMA, describes the *Countryside* exhibition as "something that we thought the city was. Countryside is still the place where new ideas and experimentation actually take place."

As someone who has lived most of his life in the countryside, I welcome the awareness he brings to the new ideas and experimentation that take place within the rural landscape. The celebration of rural life is not a new idea. But it has taken a backseat to the dominant narrative asserting the superiority of the urban condition—a narrative often authored by the urban elite, who have spent generations looking down on rural communities and even questioning their right to exist. In 2018, for example, *The New York Times* published an article called "The Hard Truths of Trying to 'Save' the Rural Economy," which posited:

> *For the last quarter century, the story of these places has been one of relentless economic decline. . . . What if nothing really works? Is there really no option but to do nothing and, as some have suggested, return depopulated parts of rural America to the bison?*

This is the fatalist sentiment of an author who has clearly never lived in rural America. The rural-versus-urban debate illustrates our bias against the 60 million Americans populating a landscape representing more than 97 percent of the nation's land.

According to Chris Harris of the Missouri-based Ewing Marion Kauffman Foundation, which champions the rural through its support of non-coastal entrepreneurs:

For anybody seeking to support rural America, and potentially diminish the civic and economic divide, offer trust in the capacity of rural people and listen to new narratives.

Harris, writing the same year that the Guggenheim's *Countryside* exhibition opened and closed its doors, proposes a new, more heightened awareness of the innovation that emerges from rural areas.

> *After generations of disinvestment, rural America might be the most innovative place in the U.S.*
>
> *Rural leaders, governments, and philanthropic funders who aren't afraid to break with long-standing assumptions about the inevitability of rural decline can leverage the potential, talent, and innovative spirit of rural America to build the new Heartland. . . . We must recognize that innovation, diversity of ideas and people, and new concepts don't need to be imported to rural communities—they're already there. Rural entrepreneurs and community leaders have always, by necessity, been innovative.*

The countryside, it turns out, has been a site of radical inquiry all along. What is new, especially in an attention economy, is the waning attention to the rural. Urban areas have enjoyed an avalanche of scholarship, investment, media, infrastructure, and more. As a result, our understanding of the unique condition that defines the rural domain is surprisingly limited. The most significant revelation of *Countryside, The Future* as an exhibition is the fact that it happened at all.

For all the discourse on the city, how well do we understand the countryside? Do we even know what the term "rural" means? The U.S. Census Bureau has defined "rural" in the broadest terms—as "everything not urban." We can do better.

The countryside is a sacred place where we retreat from the burden of the city, immersed in the quiet beauty of nature, to contemplate the human condition and engage with the rural as a significant source of new ideas and experimentation for the future.

The rural landscape has historically been a sacred place for transformative work. Its laboratories for cultural invention deserve praise. In 1907, an artist residency program called MacDowell was founded in Peterborough, New Hampshire. At the time, the town boasted fewer than 2,300 residents. Today, it has grown to 6,200. Built on 450 acres, MacDowell became a popular retreat for influential artists with a mission to "nurture the arts by offering creative individuals of the highest talent an inspiring environment in which they can produce enduring works of the imagination."

Edward MacDowell, a composer, and Marian MacDowell, a pianist, envisioned what became known as the "Peterborough Idea" with the help of former president Grover Cleveland, industrialist Andrew Carnegie, and financier J. P. Morgan. The MacDowells would eventually establish thirty-two studios dotted across the New Hampshire countryside. For more than a century, legendary creatives including James Baldwin, Ta-Nehisi Coates, Audre Lorde, Faith Ringgold, and Leonard Bernstein have nested there for weeks, even months, at a time, making it not unlike a summer camp for the imagination. A staging ground for accomplishments that have included more than 86 Pulitzer Prizes, 31 National Book Awards, 30 Tony Awards, 32 MacArthur Fellowships, 15 Grammys, 8 Oscars, and 828 Guggenheim Fellowships.

MacDowell is one of more than 1,500 artist residency programs globally, places that provide creative thinkers and makers with the time, space, and solitude in the majesty of nature to clear their minds and develop breakthrough ideas. Yaddo, a 400-acre estate in Saratoga Springs, New York, for example, has hosted such guests as Hannah Arendt, Truman Capote, Langston Hughes, Jacob Lawrence, Robert Lowell, and Mario Puzo.

During the height of the pandemic, as cultural institutions faced an existential crisis, MacDowell residents were asked to offer their thoughts on the question "Why MacDowell now?" As Susan Choi, a novelist and Yale University professor, explained in a powerful essay titled "It Has Space to Forge a New National Vision":

> *Why MacDowell now? Because in a society that seems ever more constricted, ever more committed to the single goal of wealth accumulation, ever less interested in freedom and justice and access and affluence for all, MacDowell is a visible resistance, a capacious site of possibility.*

The modern workplace has become a container for the ordinary. Breakthrough impact is best cultivated within extraordinary contexts. Possibility sites are environments designed as remarkable experiences in which people rise to the occasion. Rural communities may very well be these capacious sites of possibility, or at least training grounds for the artistic expression of our highest-order selves. But rural communities have also originated activist movements that have reshaped the nation.

There is no better example than the Highlander Folk School in rural Tennessee, an organization founded in 1932 by Myles Horton, who would be dubbed the "father of the civil rights movement" by James

Bevel, the director of nonviolent education at the Southern Christian Leadership Conference. Horton, who was heavily influenced by Jane Addams and W. E. B. Du Bois while at the University of Chicago, visited Denmark to study their models for folk schools. He founded Highlander out of the belief that an "oppressed people collectively hold strategies for liberation that are lost to its individuals."

Highlander would come to set the stage for some of the most critical milestones of the civil rights movements over the next few decades. Rosa Parks was trained at Highlander, as were Septima Clark, John Lewis, and Martin Luther King Jr.

Congressman John Lewis wrote:

> *Highlander was the place that Rosa Parks witnessed a demonstration of equality that helped inspire her to keep her seat on a Montgomery bus, just a few weeks after her first visit. She saw Septima Clark, a legendary black educator, teaching side-by-side with [Highlander founder Myles] Horton. For her it was revolutionary. She had never seen an integrated team of equals working together, and it inspired her.*

Zilphia Johnson, a musician and community organizer, first visited Highlander in 1935 to attend a workshop. Months later, she married Myles Horton and soon became a major force in the trajectory of the school, where she held the position of music director from 1935 to 1956. In 1945, Zilphia worked with members of the Food, Tobacco, Agricultural, and Allied Workers to lead a five-month strike against the American Tobacco Company. It is said that to keep up the union protesters' morale while on strike, a new interpretation of the gospel hymn "We'll Overcome (I'll Be All Right)" was performed to mark each day's picketing. Zilphia would adapt and refine the song, putting her fingerprints on the version we know today as "We Shall Overcome."

Highlander engaged students in tracing the roots of rural music and adapting them into the songs that would become the soundtrack to the civil rights movements. The intimacy, the critical pedagogy, and the immersive focus turned Horton's classroom into a kind of recording booth where music would become a catalyst for shifting the national narrative.

To develop our voice, we need the quiet retreat that rural life affords us. We need the clean slate, the blank canvas, the immersive focus to make the music that withstands the test of time.

When we believe in the importance of our work, we will travel extraordinary lengths to remove ourselves from distraction and re-embed ourselves in nature.

In 1958, Margo, the mononymous actress who starred in the 1937 film adaptation of *Lost Horizon,* set in the remote paradise of Shangri-La, bought a ranch in Malibu, California. She named it Shangri-La. For the next six decades it would become a destination for some of the most influential figures in popular music seeking solitude and respite from city life. As chronicled in Martin Scorsese's *The Last Waltz,* in the 1970s the property was leased by the Band—contemporaries of Bob Dylan—who turned it into what the band's drummer described as "a clubhouse and studio where we and our friends could record albums and cross-pollinate one another's music." A half a century after leaving Shangri-La, Robbie Robertson, the Band's lead guitarist and songwriter, returned for a stroll down memory lane. He wrote:

> What I was doing with The Band was saying we are going to make a record in here. We are going to make the studio come to us, rather than us going somewhere and we go inside the walls and it's not our place, it's their place. How do we make a comfort zone, so everyone feels comfortable enough to do their best work?

And people did do their best work there; Neil Diamond, ZZ Top, Van Morrison, Pete Townshend, Joe Cocker, and Eric Clapton, among others, all recorded in its iconic studio. In 2012, Shangri-La was purchased by music producer Rick Rubin and became a Zen-like oasis for artists. Rubin, who is perhaps best known for co-founding Def Jam Recordings with Russell Simmons and helping to popularize hip-hop, producing such artists as the Beastie Boys, Public Enemy, Run-DMC, LL Cool J, and Jay-Z, has an almost mythical status in the music industry, where he is considered a kind of spiritual concierge to musicians searching to find their voice. Artists such as Adele, Ed Sheeran, Eminem, Lady Gaga, and Kanye West have worked collaboratively with Rubin and his team. It's noted in a 2019 documentary about Shangri-La that Rubin's minimalist, pared-down design and the absence of any art on the walls were extraordinarily intentional: "The idea is to not have any art on the walls. So, your brain is as empty as possible. So, you aren't thinking about a picture, you have to come up with one."

In contemplating the critical role that one's environment plays in artistic creation, Rubin shares:

> It's like being open to the possibility that these things we don't understand or can't explain happen regularly and that it might even be possible to support them happening. You can't make them happen, but we might be able to create an environment that is conducive to them happening.

I connect with this insight so very deeply. It encapsulates my love affair with the rural landscape. And it reveals Rubin as more than just a producer of hit albums—he is also a producer of the conditions in which possibilities can emerge. How might we begin to celebrate the rural as an environment conducive to extraordinary possibilities?

Samuel Mockbee was a fifth-generation Mississippian who joined Auburn University's School of Architecture in 1992. He co-founded a unique program called the Rural Studio, a design-centric program that aimed to educate emerging architects on sustainable, healthful rural living and the vital systems we must foster to ensure that our communities thrive. The Rural Studio soon became an immersive living laboratory, located 150 miles off campus in Greensboro, Alabama.

Each semester Mockbee and a cohort of students would immerse themselves in the communities of Hale County, one of the most impoverished regions in the nation (the same region where James Agee, the Pulitzer Prize–winning writer, and Walker Evans, the legendary photographer, documented the Great Depression in their 1941 book *Let Us Now Praise Famous Men*), where they built houses and local infrastructure.

Rural Studio students are budding artists who view the local residents not as recipients of a philanthropic service but as clients. As Mockbee would say:

Everyone, rich or poor, deserves a shelter for the soul.

Students of the Rural Studio learn about architecture, materials, construction, and systems. But more than anything else, they learn about civility, civic engagement, and the ethical responsibility we have to one another: the architecture of decency. The Rural Studio is propelled by a social pedagogy shaped by Mockbee's belief that "an architect can help us discover what is noble and help create the opportunity for people to realize their innate nobility."

Mockbee died of leukemia in 2001, at the early age of fifty-seven. But the Rural Studio—his version of Shangri-La—is still flourishing, having completed more than 200 projects and educated more than 1,200 students in rural Alabama. Each year fifty students live and work within the community, forging trust and imagining not just what *could* be done but what *should* be done. Its projects have been exhibited at the Whitney Museum in New York City and at the Venice Biennale of Architecture and featured on *The Oprah Winfrey Show*.

As its current director, Andrew Freear, a champion of the radical inquiry Mockbee initiated, put it: "We encourage aspiring young architects to address the ethical responsibility for the social, political, and environmental consequences of what they design and build."

Whether it is the catalytic writing produced by James Baldwin at MacDowell, the activist training Rosa Parks received at Highlander, the musical maturity Lady Gaga and Adele cultivated at Shangri-La, or the regenerative architecture the Rural Studio built in storied Hale County, the rural provides a setting in which to develop the very best within us. We can all seek out the rural as a retreat from the ordinary: a place to engage in extraordinary creative practices with the promise to advance the human condition.

The rural is indeed the landscape of ideas and experimentation. It may be that the rural is the *only* setting that can provide the space and solitude needed to engage in radical inquiry.

VALUE

Survival Economics Have Made Imagination a Luxury Good

Have we reached a state of imagination inequity? Is imagination a basic human need? How can we make space in our lives for Radical Curiosity when we're struggling just to put food on the table? Can society move beyond survival economics to make imagination available to all?

Inequity has created a preexisting social condition. We are living in an era of survival economics in which imagination has become a luxury good. Survival economics is a merry-go-round difficult to escape when we are prisoners to the demands of capitalism. A system that refuses to be satiated. Demanding all available time, mind space, and stamina to keep our heads above water. The peaceful focus of a meaningful life can be suffocated by the need to feed transactions at a pace that won't slow down. When the primary operating objective is growth, enough is never enough.

The oppressive heartbeat of a not-so-human-centric economy leaves a small arena in which to dream for something better. As a result, we have come to think of inquiry and imagination as luxuries that we "just don't have time for." Sayings like "You can't fix the train while it's moving on the tracks" or "You can't repair the plane while it's flying" are cloaked coping mechanisms: fictions that assume a scarcity of opportunities for imagination. The reality is we are always fixing the plane while flying it.

The mythology that there is no time to imagine keeps us chained to models of living we already know are breaking down, no longer relevant, and likely doing us harm. We perpetuate these fictions, telling ourselves we are too busy feeding the ever-growing volume of transactions to stop and question them. The result being a self-fulfilling prophecy. When everyone believes that a creative life, a Radically Curious life, is for someone else, we inadvertently make imagination a luxury good that is divorced from our identity and always out of reach. Rather than accept defeat, we should fight for the creative life that can be ours. Imagination is a human right.

Radical Curiosity has long been out of reach for too many people, as economic realities have systematically prevented them from exercising their human right of imagination. If a family is struggling to put food on the table, imagination can indeed feel luxurious. An exhaustive effort spent on surviving weakens the potency of our imaginations. And yet, imagination is central to being human.

In 2018, according to the U.S. Census Bureau, 38.1 million Americans were living below the poverty line: a threshold of $12,784 for an individual, $16,247 for a two-person household, and $25,701 for a family of four.

In an underreported key statistic, according to Poverty USA, nearly 29.9 percent of the U.S. population—or 93.6 million people—is considered "close to poverty," defined as having an income that is less than two times the poverty threshold. Meaning that for the year 2018, more than 93 million Americans were making the equivalent of less than $25,500. Let's hold that for a moment. A combined total of 131.7 million people living in or close to poverty in the wealthiest country in the world.

This is just one of the sobering realities that have led MIT economist Peter Temin to claim that the United States has regressed to developing-nation status. In a review of his book *The Vanishing Middle Class: Prejudice and Power in a Dual Economy*, the Institute for New Economic Thinking offers:

> *Temin uses a famous economic model created to understand developing nations to describe how far inequality has progressed in the United States. The model is the work of West Indian economist W. Arthur Lewis, the only person of African descent to win a Nobel Prize in economics. For the first time, this model is applied with systematic precision to the U.S. The result is profoundly disturbing. In the Lewis model of a dual economy, much of the low-wage sector has little influence over public policy. Check. The high-income sector will keep wages down in the other sector to provide cheap labor for its businesses. Check. Social control is used to keep the low-wage sector from challenging the policies favored by the high-income sector. Mass incarceration—check. The primary goal of the richest members of the high-income sector is to lower taxes. Check. Social and economic mobility is low. Check.*

We need to reconcile the distance between our beloved mythologies about the American Dream and the evidence before us. Americans don't have the time to dream anymore.

In 1963, the economist and statistician Mollie Orshansky developed the official measurement of poverty used by the U.S. government.

The Orshansky Poverty Threshold is a model entirely defined by the economics of nutrition—can we afford the sustenance needed to survive? But we know that human beings need more than just basic nutrition and shelter. In fact, we need quite a lot more. Could we envision a new addition to Maslow's hierarchy of needs that includes curiosity?

In Maslow's hierarchy, higher needs can't be satisfied before those below them are met. How can we think and be curious without access to the most basic resources needed for survival? In his rousing TED Talk, the historian Rutger Bregman codifies insights from a Princeton University study that looked at the effects of the scarcity mentality induced by the state of poverty:

The effects of living in poverty, it turns out, correspond to losing 14 points of IQ. Now, to give you an idea, that's comparable to losing a night's sleep or the effects of alcoholism.

In Bregman's discussion of how the all-consuming and distracting nature of poverty prevents long-term thinking and throws us into a survivalist state, he references George Orwell, who once said: "For, when you are approaching poverty, you make one discovery which outweighs some of the others . . . the fact that it annihilates the future."

Without imagination, we cannot think about the future.

Our economic reality has robbed more than 130 million people of the time and space to imagine the future.

We need to reconstruct our moral criteria for what a human experience is and could be. Our economy only works when it serves more of us: not just with subsistence-level resources but also with the opportunity for a better quality of life. We need to move beyond survival economics until imagination is no longer a luxury but a source of essential nutrition available to all.

26

Do We Value Life?

Why do we struggle to protect human life? Have we become desensitized to the loss of life? If we value life, is that inclusive of all living things, all living systems that exist on our planet? And as modern society evolves, how will we continue to take up this age-old conversation regarding what makes a good life?

What is it about the assertion that Black lives do indeed matter that sparks disagreement? What is it about the American psyche that makes this a triggering expression, a source of controversy? There is something absurd about a society in which there is a debate about which lives matter.

Michael Che, co-host of "Weekend Update" on *Saturday Night Live*, highlights this absurdity in his Netflix comedy special, aptly titled *Michael Che Matters*:

We can't agree on anything anymore. As a country, we just can't agree. We just fight about everything. We can't even agree on Black Lives Matter. That's a controversial statement. Black lives matter. Not matters more than you, just matters. Matters. Just matters. That's where we're starting the negotiations. Matters. We can't agree on that shit? What the fuck is less than matters? Black lives exist? Can we say that?... There's people saying, "I think everybody should have the same rights as everyone else." And there's other people like, "No, son, I disagree. I just don't think so."

The power of the gladiator comedian is to wield language and humor as a clarifying device. A gladiator comedian does not directly assert a theory of the case; rather, the comedian invites us, the audience, to come up with that theory ourselves. Inside Che's brilliant monologue are more profound questions. The most essential of them being:

Do we value life?

Such an inquiry propels Raoul Peck, the Haitian filmmaker and political activist, known for the Oscar-nominated documentary film *I Am Not Your Negro*, about the life of James Baldwin and the issue of race in the United States. Peck's follow-up, the HBO docuseries *Exterminate All the Brutes*, is his opus. It offers the most thoroughly convincing answer to the question "Do we value life?" by examining white supremacy across history and nations. The film is an honest and horrifying tour de force. It utilizes animation, reenactment, music, data, historical documents, and Peck's own omniscient narration to confront the repeated genocides perpetrated by our species. He leaves it undeniable: Humanity has not historically valued life.

Too often, this insight is avoided at all costs. Certainly, we don't glamorize the flaws of human history. But we also fail to confront them in ways that are not healthy. What do we write out of the human story? Which stories do we celebrate, and which do we deny? That raises another question: Whose stories are they? This is a central lens Peck asks us to look through as he guides us through history, raising to our attention the fact that whoever "wins" in the end gets to frame the story. *Exterminate All the Brutes* not only deconstructs the official narrative of history but also offers a critical commentary on how stories have been rewritten to reinforce a narrative of supremacy.

> *Peck asks if it's knowledge that we lack—if ignorance is what accounts for the travesties of history. But "the Western world is panicking, a delirious spiraling panicking, talking about the 'clash of civilizations.'"* . . . *So no,* Exterminate All the Brutes *concludes, it's not knowledge we lack. Peck spends four hours scrupulously laying out that case, and by the end it's undeniable. Since the Crusades, it's been "profitable to deny or suppress such knowledge." We've always known what was happening; white supremacy has been in plain sight, not even hiding. The question is, what does the world lack when humanity-denying arrogance goes unconfronted? And where is our courage?*

And where *is* our courage? What a human question. What a Radically Curious sensibility. James Baldwin famously said, "I imagine one of the reasons people cling to their hates so stubbornly is because they sense, once hate is gone, they will be forced to deal with pain." But we've clung to hate for so long, grown too comfortable, that we can't seem to part with it, like a tattered old baby blanket. It seems we've turned a corner in the contemporary conversation. Unfortunately, that turn is not an improvement, but a kind of numbness.

In the United States, the question is no longer whether racism and hate-based violence are present in the national identity.

The question is why a nation with such spectacular resources, ingenuity, and self-proclaimed morality struggles to protect human life.

Charles M. Blow wrote a powerful op-ed in the spring of 2021 titled "Rage Is the Only Language I Have Left." In it, he presents a case that is impossible to argue with: Society has become horribly desensitized to police killings of Black people.

> *So, it becomes hard to write about this in a newspaper because it is no longer new. The news of these killings is not that they are interruptions of the norm, but a manifestation of the norm. There is no new angle. There is no new hot take. There is very little new to be revealed. These killings are not continuing to happen due to a lack of exposure, but in spite of it. Our systems of law enforcement, criminal justice and communal consciousness have adjusted themselves to a banal barbarism.*

The hate is all around us, in plain sight. The evidence is not even subtle. According to the Southern Poverty Law Center, there are more than 1,000 hate groups active in the United States, a 30 percent increase from 2014 to 2018. Even more alarming is that these are among the very same groups that in early 2016 helped propel President Trump to the White House.

Trump was a president who thrived on being noticed. After all, the overwhelming, omnipresent voice of the tweeter in chief was a signature of his presidency. In 2019, David Remnick, editor of *The New Yorker*, put it plainly: This president is an unapologetic racist. He reminds us:

> *The President's views are clear: black athletes who dare to protest police violence are "sons of bitches"; African countries are "shitholes"; and there are some "fine people" among the bigoted thugs who carried tiki torches and chanted "Blood and soil" and "Jews will not replace us" in Charlottesville.*

The impact of a racist in the White House cannot be underestimated. When the elected leader of the American government, the commander in chief of the nation, holds such blatant disregard for human life, we must ask: Do the people of the United States, as a group, value life?

And when the leader of the free world acts, again and again, in ways that perpetuate a less free world, it eventually forces us to ask: Have we come to be desensitized by the "othering" of human life across the world?

Let's take the case of gun violence. According to the Gun Violence Archive, a nonprofit that tracks shootings in the United States, there were 340 U.S. mass shootings in 2018, which means there were nearly as many shootings as days in the year. The United States has the thirty-second-highest rate of deaths from gun violence in the world: 3.96 deaths per 100,000 people in 2019. That was more than eight times the rate in Canada, which had 0.47 deaths per 100,000 people—and nearly a hundred times higher than in the United Kingdom, which had 0.04 deaths per 100,000 people. More shocking yet is the comparison with nations that are at war. In 2019, the United States had over 300 percent more deaths from gun violence than Afghanistan. At what point do we consider America a war zone?

We have become so desensitized to death that we may not be aware of the toll it is taking on our mental health. Due to COVID-19, the estimated death rate increased by 15.9 percent from 2019 to 2020. This kind of leap in the death rate in a single year is a tragedy that affects the entire nation—a nation already struggling to find healthy ways to navigate collective trauma. And yet our epidemic of gun violence and police shootings continues to add to our death toll.

Our disregard for life is an expression not just of *white* supremacy but of *human* supremacy: that is, our belief in the supremacy of humans over the natural world.

If we are asking whether we value life, we must stretch our active definition of the term "life" to be inclusive of all living things, all living systems. Do we value the health of our planet?

If Raoul Peck's documentary deconstructed the predominant historical narratives concerning supremacy as an act of violence against other humans, in recent years we are seeing more storytellers beginning to reframe the narrative of the human relationship to nature. Our technological ability to capture stunning imagery showing the majesty of life—from *Our Planet,* narrated by David Attenborough, to *One Strange Rock,* presented by National Geographic—has, perhaps, heightened our awareness of it. Yet, clearly, the ability to see and experience the miracles of our planet from the comfort of our living rooms is not enough. Even in our revived respect for the natural world we are "othering" it. The further we remove ourselves from others' experiences, distancing ourselves from others' suffering, the less empathy we have for life beyond our own. And witnessing the spectacle of nature through a screen has only distanced us further, reinforcing the notion of the human experience as separate from the natural world.

In the film *Kiss the Ground,* Joshua and Rebecca Tickell shine a light on the practices of our agricultural sector that accelerate erosion and undermine our complex micro-ecosystems. The film also illuminates the link between our devaluing of human life and our disregard for living systems by examining the history of farming and the industrialization of agriculture. In it we encounter a German chemist and Nobel laureate named Fritz Haber. As the film recounts:

> *Haber invented a process for making synthetic nitrogen fertilizer that increased food production. His other scientific breakthrough was the creation of poisons known as pesticides. Haber used his pesticides as the first chemical weapons in history. Then he developed the poison used in the gas chambers in the Holocaust. When the war ended, US chemical companies brought Haber's poisons back to America and rebranded his toxic chemicals as pesticides for American farmers.*

Haber, sometimes referred to as "the father of chemical warfare," was a contemporary of Einstein. His life, chronicled in the play

Einstein's Gift, paints a portrait of a man in deep conflict between his own Jewish heritage and his choice to convert to Christianity, his career and nationalistic pride, and the immoral application of knowledge—a theme that would lead Haber's wife to suicide after she discovered how he had used for evil the science they developed together.

This is the prehistory to the invention of pesticides. The story of the degradation of our planet's soil is entangled within the same narrative as Nazi genocide. The poisons of chemical warfare retrofitted to wage war against our ecosystems. Spraying some of the same chemicals utilized for mass killing in World War I and World War II, at scale, on the source of our food, our vegetation, our living systems. The degradation of life is not merely an expression of our rage and indifference but force of habit. In plain sight.

It's not only that farmers still spray pesticides—one of the major causes of ungrowable topsoil in our country—across hundreds of millions of acres of agriculture. Today, pesticides can be found on the shelves of grocery stores, having made their way into countless consumer products, like a spray called Roundup, developed by the agrochemical giant Monsanto. Roundup kills weeds. But it kills other living systems as well. In 2020, when Bayer, the pharmaceutical company, acquired Monsanto for $63 billion, it had to settle class-action lawsuits totaling $11 billion because so many people around the country had become ill from its use. In further evidence that the world values profits over life, when the news that the Bayer lawsuits had been settled was announced, the company's stock climbed 3 percent.

Our past makes us imperfect, but it also motivates the best within us. Even amid the most horrifying examples of humanity's active extermination of life, we also find reasons for hope—those people who endorse the only seemingly rational answer to the question "Do we value life?" *Yes to life, in spite of everything.*

This is literally the title of a book of collected lectures and essays by Viktor Frankl, a Viennese survivor of the Holocaust. A witness to and victim of the legacy of "the father of chemical warfare." After the Holocaust, Frankl became a globally recognized thought leader, advocating for the search for a meaningful life as central to the human experience. He spent nearly a century engaged with the question "Do we value life?" Few voices have arrived to this inquiry with such profound credentials: Frankl survived three years in four Nazi concentration camps, where his mother, father, wife, and brother all died. Frankl lived through one of the most significant tragedies in modern history and went on to advance the field of mental health, paving the way for positive psychology as the scientific study of what makes life most worth living.

Frankl speaks a great deal about questions. In *Yes to Life: In Spite of Everything*, he says:

> The question can no longer be "What can I expect from life?" but can now only be "What does life expect of me?" What task in life is waiting for me? . . . The question of the meaning of life is not asked in the right way, if asked in the way it is generally asked: it is not we who are permitted to ask about the meaning of life—it is life that asks the questions, directs questions at us. . . . We are the ones who must answer, must give answers to the constant, hourly question of life, to the essential "life questions." Living itself means nothing other than being questioned; our whole act of being is nothing more than responding to—of being responsible toward—life.

Frankl introduces another layer to the discussion, proposing a shift in the human-centered worldview we have long adopted. Beyond the question of whether we should exert dominion over each other and over nature, Frankl questions whether we should see ourselves as the primary actor at all. Maybe the question is not whether we value life, but whether life values us.

Flipping the question may provide a useful humility. We cannot value life, all of life, without recalibrating our notion of flourishing. Valuing life may require us to release our current preoccupation with economic growth and embrace the value of multiple living systems' well-being.

The concept of flourishing is rooted in the Greek term *eudaimonia*, meaning "happiness, welfare, prosperity, and blessedness." The term dates to Aristotle, who first used the term *ethics* to name a field of study developed by Socrates and Plato, meant to question how humans should best live. For Aristotle, eudaimonia is the highest human good. In philosophical discourse there is an agreement that eudaimonia represents a kind of ideal, a flourishing of living well. I would propose that this may be the Radically Curious point of departure.

Umair Haque, a London-based thought leader and head of Bubblegeneration, a strategy and innovation group, contrasts how we have intermingled economics and eudaimonia. In his popular blog, aptly titled *Eudaimonia & Co.*, he writes:

> If I were to ask you, "what are the economics of this country?," you'd probably point to GDP, income, and productivity. If I were to ask you, "what are the economics of this company?," you'd point me to unit revenues and costs per employee and so on. But if I were to ask you, "wait a minute. How is this country or company or town or city, this organization, really doing? are people's lives really growing, developing, flourishing?," then you'd probably frown, and draw a blank. The two aren't the same, are they? Today we're seeing that whole economies can "grow"—but somehow, human possibility, life as a quest for self-realization, doesn't. The old paradigm—where organizations exist only for an economic purpose, maximizing income—is deeply, badly broken. So let's change it. The economics of a thing is about the speed and quantity of income a thing generates. But the eudaimonics of a thing is about how much life a thing produces: how well-being, possibility, and

ECONOMICS

(n.) The social science
that studies how people
interact with value; in
particular, the production,
distribution, and
consumption of goods
and services.

EUDAIMONICS

(n.) Well-being. The type
of happiness or contentment
that is achieved through
self-actualization and
having meaningful purpose
in one's life.

wealth is created. Life is a quest for self-realization. Yours, mine, our grandkids', our planet's. And eudaimonics asks: is that quest reaching fruition? Are lives flourishing, blossoming, transforming, realizing their fullest possibilities? In the same way that lottery winners end up paradoxically unhappier than before, so an organization's financial success, whether that organization is a city, a company, or a country, is no sure guarantee that it's creating better lives. Eudaimonics, in contrast to economics, is the art of creating genuinely good lives. Every bit of eudaimonia that we fail to create in time comes back to us as a cost we will have to pay.

Valuing life is necessary for economies and societies to flourish, just as it is for human beings to flourish. In business we discuss the notion of opportunity cost. The essential concept is that there is a value, an economic quotient, that represents the forgone benefit that would have been derived with different decision-making, different scenarios. I think about this all the time.

What has been the opportunity cost of our decisions? Of the trillion-dollar war in Afghanistan? Of the $11 billion in lawsuits over a single pesticide? Of racism? Of climate change? Of underinvesting in public health? It has become extraordinarily expensive to not value life. How much has been wasted in service of ideas that are no longer serving us well? When we seek utopian moonshots, we are often told there is not enough money. But I believe we may discover an abundance of resources if we rewired the operating system of our economy as one that values life. That cares for living things, human or otherwise. What would our GDP leap to if we recommitted to an economics of care?

Until we recalibrate our notion of flourishing to include eudaimonia, rather than just economic well-being, we will pay dearly. Yet eudaimonia doesn't show up in Excel spreadsheets, GDP calculations, or stock dividends. Eudaimonia needs to be in plain sight.

What would our nation look like if eudaimonia was the primary design goal?

27

Utopia Is Worth Fighting For

Is our aspiration for a utopian ideal no longer present? Temporarily dormant? Have we eradicated the civic imagination, and in turn our collective ability to imagine a better future? Why have we lost interest in stories about world-building and become obsessed with stories about the world's collapse? Is utopia still worth fighting for?

In 1989, my father and I went to the Strand Theatre in the Adirondacks to see the premiere of the film *Field of Dreams*. The theater was built in 1924 in the Classical Revival style, with a mezzanine auditorium, a front entrance that cantilevered over the downtown street—backlit, with individual letters hung by hand—and red velvet seats that had borne witness to a century of cinema. I remember how proud I was to see the movie with my dad. It felt like a secret field trip with a grown-up.

Field of Dreams, starring Kevin Costner, is a classic American story: of a midwestern farming community, the nostalgia of baseball, a midlife crisis, and a leap of faith. In it, Costner's character, Ray Kinsella, heeds a mysterious voice urging him to cut down his corn crop to build a baseball field, where he will reunite and reconcile with the ghost of his father, John, who died years earlier. In the final scene, this meeting comes to pass. With minimal dialogue they perform the quintessential bonding ritual of father and son: they play catch. The scene concludes with one of the more memorable conversations in cinema:

> **John:** Is this heaven?
> **Ray:** No, it's . . . Iowa.
> **John:** Iowa?
> **Ray:** Yeah . . .
> **John:** I could have sworn it was heaven.
> **Ray:** Is . . . is there a heaven?
> **John:** Oh, yeah. It's the place where dreams come true.

With these words, the frame of the film glides across the glow of the sunset on the farmland. Costner's wife and daughter are in the distance, tickling, giggling, swinging on the wraparound porch of an *American Gothic*–style farmhouse. The music hits just the right note. Costner's character pauses and says:

Maybe this is heaven.

Roger Ebert said of the film: "*This is the kind of movie Frank Capra might have directed, and James Stewart might have starred in—a movie about dreams.*"

Indeed, it is about dreams. But it is also about possibility. About living a life guided by curiosity. About daring to ask, "What is it all about?"

Costner's character is the quintessential romantic who sacrifices his family's sole source of income to realize his dream, regardless of whether it is congruent with common sense. He builds a baseball diamond as a cathedral to his faith in the impossible, and in doing so takes a risk, a big leap of faith. Illustrating to the ordinary person that audacious, wonderful, fantastical things are possible. More than a movie about dreams, it's a story of boundless optimism. You cannot help but leave the theater with a starry eye and the renewed confidence that perhaps anything *is* possible—however absurd that ideal may be.

Where does optimism come from? How do we form our own expectations for what seems or does not seem possible? How do we discern what is in or out of reach for us individually in our own lives, or collectively as nations? How do we, as a society, conjure the dream so big, we're willing to risk it all? Do we know how to imagine ideal alternatives to our current reality? To protect the deeply optimistic experience of believing that a utopian ideal was possible?

Long before we had Iowa, we believed the ideal was possible.

The concept of utopia—an ideal society—dates to 375 B.C., when Plato authored *The Republic*. In it, he explores the meaning of justice and the essence of happiness, and invites us to imagine a utopian city-state ruled by a philosopher-king.

Nearly 800 years later in China, the poet Tao Yuanming wrote *The Peach Blossom Spring*, a fable about a chance discovery of an ethereal utopia where the people live in harmony with nature, unaware of the outside world for centuries.

In 1516, Thomas More published a work of fiction called *Utopia*. It enshrined the term "utopia" in our modern lexicon as an imaginary society that "possesses highly desirable or nearly perfect qualities for its citizens."

The word "utopia" comes from the Greek prefix *ou,* meaning "not," and *topos,* meaning "place." Utopia is indeed not a place. It is aspirational. Just out of reach. It is nowhere but holds the promise to be anywhere.

Utopia is not geographically linked to the place inhabited by a people.

But utopia is morally and philosophically linked to the values of a people.

Utopias are laboratories for imagining new ways to be in the world. They are also moral dilemmas. Presenting us with scenarios to test what we value: *If I value economic security, should I continue harvesting my cornfield to pay my mortgage? Or if I value dreaming, can I turn the act of dreaming into value?*

The importance of actively asking ourselves what we value, what we hold up as our ideal in the contemporary moment, cannot be overstated. Especially in the in-between times. During a cultural interregnum, the active pursuit of utopia is not a vehicle to ferry us to a destination but an iterative process of discovery into what that destination might look like. How do we build worlds of tomorrow? Can we normalize the pursuit of utopia? We once did.

There may be a clue in the phrase "worlds of tomorrow."

One of the grand experiments in utopic ideals began in 1939, when New York hosted the World's Fair, which had the theme "the World of Tomorrow."

World's Fairs (sometimes called expositions, or expos for short) are utopian expressions—opportunities for participating nations to present their ideal portraits of themselves. "The World of Tomorrow" did not disappoint. The 1939 World's Fair was a veritable campus of ideas totaling 1,202 acres. Opening day featured a talk by Albert Einstein. Thirty-five galleries featured great works from master painters, from Leonardo da Vinci and Michelangelo to Rembrandt. A copy of the Magna Carta left Britain for the first time, to be displayed in the British Pavilion. "Futurama," a featured exhibit and ride sponsored by General Motors, envisioned what automotive travel would look like twenty years into the future and introduced the idea of highways to Americans for the first time. RCA introduced the first-ever television. By the time the fair reached the end of its run in October 1940, more than 44 million people had attended.

World's Fairs are the Olympics of ideas. They act as simulators in which to test our evolving visions for the future.

There is just one problem. Around the same time that Americans were going to the movies to watch *Field of Dreams*, Congress was preparing legislation that eventually established a law preventing public resources to be spent on participation in World's Fairs. In part, this is the legacy of the last World's Fair held in the United States. This World's Fair took place in 1984—an ominously ironic year for a failed utopia—and drew only 7 million total visitors, a decrease of more than 80 percent from the 1939 "World of Tomorrow" event, even as the country's population had increased nearly 200 percent in the forty-five years between the two. For the final nail in the coffin, the fair went bankrupt, unable to pay many of its contractors and vendors, causing the United States such embarrassment that it prompted a call for the legislation that would ultimately ban participation in World's Fairs moving forward. But World's Fairs haven't gone anywhere; it's just America that has moved on.

In 2005, 22 million visitors attended the World's Fair in Japan with the theme "Nature's Wisdom." In a visionary statement the expo organizers declared:

We must come together and share our experience and wisdom, in order to create a new direction for humanity which is both sustainable and harmonious with nature.

In 2008, Spain hosted an expo with the theme of "Water and Sustainable Development." The legendary Iraqi British architect Zaha Hadid designed the Bridge Pavilion, and Cirque du Soleil put on a daily parade called The Awakening of the Serpent. Bob Dylan even recorded a new version of his 1963 classic "A Hard Rain's a-Gonna Fall" exclusively for the water-themed expo. More than a hundred countries presented pavilions. But the United States was nowhere to be found.

Since the United States last held an expo in 1984, the rest of the world has staged twenty-three different World's Fair expositions, several of which were billion-dollar endeavors. While a great many Americans may assume that the World's Fair is extinct, it is in fact the country's civic imagination that has all but disappeared.

What is it about the idea of utopian experiments that has fallen out of the American dialect? Do we no longer desire to engage in the project of imagining, or are we simply too busy doing other things? As we approach four decades since the last World's Fair on American soil, two generations of citizens have grown up without the opportunity to experience this display of civic imagination. Have we forgotten how to imagine what a better future can look like?

It is healthy to think about the future. To struggle with it, to contemplate it, to safely build up and tear down models—both literal and figurative—for the kind of society we strive to become. These are acts of design. The World's Fair, then, is perhaps the ultimate design project.

As Herbert Simon, recipient of the 1978 Nobel Prize in economics, said:

Everyone designs who devises courses of action aimed at changing existing situations into preferred ones. . . . The natural sciences are concerned with how things are. Design, on the other hand, is concerned with how things ought to be.

Yet in a production economy, our definition of "design" has become reduced to the creation of products, the fabrication of things as objects. But design is also a practice of transforming existing situations into preferred ones. At its best, design is a practice of storytelling, of imagining utopian potential. We need these stories of what the future might look like. After all, we often live the stories that we tell ourselves.

We are still telling ourselves stories. Apocalyptic ones.

Just six years after playing the dreaming American farmer in Iowa, Kevin Costner directed and starred in the film *Waterworld,* a post-apocalyptic story set on an endless ocean after the polar ice caps melted, and in 1997 went on to star in *The Postman,* a kind of neo-Western set in a fictional future America that has been besieged by a sixteen-year period of war, plagues, and the collapse of government. Since Costner's *Field of Dreams* in 1989, there have been more than 200 major Hollywood films categorized as apocalyptic stories: *Snowpiercer, Mad Max, Oblivion, After Earth, Armageddon, End of Days, Deep Impact, 2012, The Day After Tomorrow, I Am Legend, World War Z, A Quiet Place,* and *Don't Look Up* to name a few. In total, these fifteen films alone earned more than $5 billion in revenue, and one can easily peg the film industry's cut from this business of dystopian storytelling at tens of billions over the last thirty years.

We have lost interest in stories about world-building. But we have built a thriving economy around telling the story of civilization's collapse.

Our rebuff of the World's Fair and our obsession with stories about the destruction of the world are just two examples of our rejection of utopian thinking.

Our country's leaders don't articulate big, bold visions. We leave it to Google to carry on the legacy of JFK's moonshots. We get lost in debates like single-payer versus dual-payer healthcare rather than articulate what it might look like if we were all healthier. A difficult question we may need to ask is whether we have eradicated utopian thinking as a national policy.

We have been inadvertently whittling away at our collective ability to imagine the future. As a result, we have set our expectations so low, we're satisfied by incremental change. We've come to view compromise as a victory rather than a defeat. In America we believe we are the greatest country in the world. Yet we seem to have lost faith in our capacity for human achievement and moral integrity.

In 2012, the short-lived but beautifully written Aaron Sorkin HBO series *The Newsroom* premiered with one of the most powerful opening scenes in television history. In it, the mercurial news anchor (played by Jeff Daniels) is onstage in a large auditorium where he is appearing as a panelist for a university event. When they reach the Q&A portion of the program, a student stands up and asks: *"Why is America the greatest country in the world?"*

After a dramatic pause, Daniels's character spots a woman in the audience. She is holding up a sign that reads: IT'S NOT. BUT IT CAN BE.

This gives him just the confidence he needs, and he launches into a passionate tirade on the decline of American exceptionalism:

> *There is absolutely no evidence to support the statement that we're the greatest country in the world. We're seventh in literacy, twenty-seventh in math, twenty-second in science, forty-ninth in life expectancy, 178th in infant mortality, third in median household income, number four in labor force, and number four in exports. We lead the world in only three categories: number of incarcerated citizens per capita, number of adults who believe angels are real, and defense spending, where we spend more than the next twenty-six countries combined, twenty-five of whom are allies. . . . So when you ask what makes us the greatest country in the world, I don't know what the hell you're talking about.*

The auditorium falls silent. The audience—and viewers—are left speechless. It knocks the wind out of you. A Mike Tyson punch. Over the course of the next three minutes, his cynicism will be transformed into an optimistic vision for a nation that can become great once again.

In 1933, six years prior to "the World of Tomorrow"–themed World's Fair, a group of rebels convened in the rural outskirts of Asheville, North Carolina. Inspired by John Dewey's notion of education as a holistic practice, they had decided to reject the hierarchy of traditional universities and create a college hidden on 667 acres in the mountains along a lake. Founded by John Andrew Rice, it was a radical experiment. A utopian learning, living, creative community. Over the course of its mere twenty-four years of existence, it hosted artists Josef and Anni Albers, architect Walter Gropius, painter Robert Motherwell, abstract expressionist Cy Twombly, interdisciplinary artist Robert Rauschenberg, dancer and choreographer Merce Cunningham, poet and musician John Cage, design visionary Buckminster Fuller, painter Franz Kline, painters Willem and Elaine de Kooning, Harlem Renaissance legend Jacob Lawrence, scientist Albert Einstein, and poet William Carlos Williams. It became known as Black Mountain College.

Joseph and Anni Albers were some of the earliest and most influential faculty to join the experimental school. They had been central to its predecessor, the Bauhaus school in Germany, which had closed under Nazi pressure the year Black Mountain College was founded. As Anni would later describe the experience of immigrating to the United States from Nazi Germany:

> *Our world goes to pieces. . . . We have to rebuild our world. . . . Wholeness is not a Utopian dream. It is something that we once possessed and now seem largely to have lost, or to say it less pessimistically, seem to have lost were it not for our inner sense of direction which still reminds us that something is wrong here because we know of something that is right.*

Utopian dreams can happen in the mountains of North Carolina. They can happen in the cornfields of Iowa. And they can happen in Osaka, Japan, where the 2025 World's Fair will be staged. For these stories to become our reality, we must decide that utopia is worth fighting for.

Imagination Is the Most Valuable Natural Resource on Earth

Why does society fail to recognize creativity and imagination as powerful tools for value creation? As societies and businesses face a diverse landscape of seemingly hopeless challenges, how can the language of imagination help us to respond? Considering that we've imagined the current state of the world, can't we also reimagine our way out of it?

In 2010, IBM produced a landmark study involving more than 1,500 CEOs from sixty countries across thirty-three industries, exploring what they believed to be the most crucial factor for future success in business. A surprising result emerged. More than any other skill traditionally associated with business, the number one quality CEOs cited was creativity. In the interviews, these executives indicated that in an environment of increased complexity and ambiguity that required business model change and the ability to invent and navigate disruptive innovation, creativity should be prioritized above all else.

Yet society does not prioritize creativity above all else. Not in business, government, or education. The evidence of this from real-world behavior is staggering.

In 2020, for the fourth consecutive year, the Trump administration announced that its proposed federal expenditure, ironically titled "Budget for America's Future," would eliminate funding for the National Endowment for the Arts (NEA) and the National Endowment for the Humanities (NEH). The final federal budget ultimately included an allocation of approximately $160 million for the NEA, similar to the insufficient sum the agency has struggled with for more than a decade. In contrast, that same year, the federal allocation for the Department of Defense exceeded $700 billion, making the federal arts budget .02 percent of the military budget. Let's just hold this in the air for a moment.

The tools of imagination were two-hundredths of a single percent of the tools of war.

The most significant indicator of a nation's values is how it allocates its resources. In other words, money talks. To make this more tangible, consider that the overhyped and problematic F-35 fighter jet program alone will cost nearly $1.5 trillion over a fifty-five-year period. A number so astronomical that if amortized at approximately $28 billion annually, this single war plane's annual allocation would equal nearly 175 NEA entire budgets every single year.

We invest in what we value. So why do we not value the arts? Why do we not value creativity? *Do we really understand creativity?*

Although imagination and creativity are hallmarks of our most iconic achievements throughout history, and even a defining feature of

$700 Billion

$160 Million

**DEPARTMENT OF
DEFENSE (DOD)**

**NATIONAL ENDOWMENT
FOR THE ARTS (NEA)**

what it means to be human, we're wildly suspicious of it, deeply uncomfortable with those who live it, and confused about the role it can play in society, business, and civic life. And this lack of understanding is holding us back.

Imagination and creativity have been pigeonholed as soft skills, the extracurricular pursuits that business subsidizes rather than the key drivers of business success. Part of the problem is that imagination, creativity, and the arts have long been defined within the narrative of the production economy. This is itself a misconception. Too often when we speak of "the arts" or "art," we do so in terms of commerce and money. Even Americans for the Arts, whose mission is to "build recognition and support for the extraordinary and dynamic value for the arts," makes their case through an analysis of economic data. Their press release reads:

> *Arts & Economic Prosperity 5 is the fifth study of the nonprofit arts and culture industry's impact on the economy. . . . Nationally the nonprofit arts and culture industry generated $166.3 billion of economic activity during 2015—$63.8 billion in spending by arts and cultural organizations and an additional $102.5 billion in event-related expenditures by their audiences. This activity supported 4.6 million jobs and generated $27.5 billion in revenue to local, state, and federal governments (a yield well beyond their collective $5 billion in arts allocations).*

This focus on return on investment is an extraordinarily limited way of defining the value of the arts. Consider the absurdity of asking how much *profit* is generated by this *nonprofit sector*. It's the wrong question. Do we think that the reason we invest in the arts is to create revenue and replenish the government coffers with taxes? Do we believe that the arts and culture industry is the sole domain of imagination in our society? To rewrite these narratives, we need to acknowledge that "the arts" are not tangible objects but *processes* that can be applied diversely. And we need to recognize that the objects, performances, and productions that represent "the arts" are just outputs of such processes.

When we set forth to tackle big, wicked problems, we tend to focus on two key factors: what the outcome is and how much it will cost. These are not the right questions. A better question may be: *What are the processes we will use to solve the challenges in front of us? If imagination is a process, this question can also be framed as: How, who, when, and where will we deploy our imaginations toward any problem to be solved?*

To make the case for imagination, we need better arguments. Smarter framing of imagination and creativity as processes: methods for seeing, methods for problem-solving, and methods for expression across multiple languages. Not unlike, for example, the scientific method. Yet we don't feel the need to justify the existence of the scientific method as we do with creativity. Instead we ask how the scientific method might be applied. Can it help us cure cancer? Can it help us end or ease suffering? We should be asking the same of imagination. And, in fact, these questions are related. Because without the imagination to understand the experience of suffering, we cannot ease it through science alone.

We need to become fluent in the languages of the imagination in order to unleash it. Our ability to understand imagination, unlock its value, and adopt it as a leadership and daily practice is what we call *creativity*.

As Sir Ken Robinson, author and prominent advocate for arts and culture education, offers, "I think of creativity as putting your imagination to work. . . . Creativity is the process of having original ideas that have value."

Today, the most competitive tools in business come from a variety of languages located within the broad category of imagination. Leaders are beginning to acquire these languages and translate them into the context of business. One of the most significant figures in the field of design thinking, for example, has been not a designer but the former dean of the Rotman School of Management in Toronto, Roger Martin, who published a book called *The Design of Business: Why Design Thinking Is the Next Competitive Advantage*. Similarly, a major champion of the broad applications of imagination has been not an artist but the business thinker Dan Pink, who provocatively declared in his book *A Whole New Mind: Why Right-Brainers Will Rule the Future* that "the MFA is the new MBA."

While steps have been taken to implement the practice of creativity at scale, efforts to deeply mine the languages of imagination and unleash the powerful potential imagination can enable are still in their infancy. What interests me is the role imagination and creativity can have in the questioning process. The way that creative people see, hear, and invert the origins of a problem is intrinsically linked to the Radical Curiosity mindset. Examining how creatives, in the broadest definition of the term, challenge and question assumptions can illuminate insights that will yield impact in line with what the times demand.

Consider the powerful description by James Baldwin from a lesser-known essay called "The Creative Process":

> The artist is distinguished from all other responsible actors in society—the politicians, legislators, educators, and scientists—by the fact that he is his own test tube, his own laboratory, working according to very rigorous rules, however unstated these may be, and cannot allow any consideration to supersede his responsibility to reveal all that he can possibly discover concerning the mystery of the human being. Society must accept some things as real; but he must always know that visible reality hides a deeper one, and that all our action and achievement rest on things unseen. A society must assume that it is stable, but the artist must know, and he must let us know, that there is nothing stable under heaven. . . . The artist cannot and must not take anything for granted,

but must drive to the heart of every answer and expose the question the answer hides.

Baldwin presents creativity as a dialogue of questions and answers, a kind of unfolding dance. As we strive for better answers we must strive for better questions. Most answers come with a bias, an ideology, a set of intellectual assumptions that need to be shaken off. Baldwin makes a case that the role of an artist in society is to become an interrogator of those answers. Answers are themselves fluid and unstable because wisdom is always growing. And so it is a responsibility of the artist to reveal the fractures, biases, and outdated assumptions in the answers we have. To restlessly demand more of those answers, stretching them until they snap, so that we may find the limits of our existing knowledge—and then expand them.

Because nothing—not even knowledge—is stable under heaven.

The world faces significant challenges. Big, overwhelming, wicked problems. It may be natural to default to a defeatist position: What can a painter or composer or designer bring to the complexity of problems like economic inequality, a global public health crisis, or the destruction of our planet?

How frivolous might it seem to bring a paintbrush to a courtroom, a boardroom, or an emergency room? Yet as our world struggles with wicked problem after wicked problem, it has begun to feel as though we've turned to every profession—politicians, doctors, lawyers, management experts, and philanthropists—for solutions. So maybe it's time we looked to artists, creatives, and all professional wielders of imagination to take a serious crack at these intractable challenges.

We may need to shake things up a bit, break some rules, and cross some traditional boundaries to see the seemingly immovable obstacles anew.

Take, for example, climate change. An economic crisis as well as an existential one, according to a recent report estimating that the risks associated with climate change are anticipated to cost businesses $1 trillion over the next five to ten years.

The narrative that is unfolding is a case study in complexity. Our ability to collect the scientific data on a host of interconnected variables exceeds our ability to communicate the situation in familiar storytelling. We struggle to translate the science of climate change in such a way that more of us can wrap our heads around the concepts. The subject is heavily burdened by inaccessible language, further widening the disconnect between how each of us individually lives and the holistic picture delivered by scientists and policy wonks. The scale of the crisis is difficult to imagine. And who really wants to imagine the scenarios that science tells us are likely to come to pass?

The United Nations Framework Convention on Climate Change released its initial synthesis report, "Nationally Determined Contributions," in early 2021 to evaluate progress toward achieving the goals of the Paris Agreement. This landmark international agreement seeks to limit climate change to a 1.5°C temperature increase by the year 2030. A date that may have felt far into the future—the stuff of science fiction, even—only moments ago. Let us remember that the flying cars of *Back to the Future II* were to be found in the imagined year 2015, and that reality disappointingly has yet to emerge. But the year 2030 is more accessible to our imaginations as time crawls on. Easier to conceptualize as the date that my daughter will be considering college.

It has become more urgent to anchor our understanding of future climate scenarios, recognizing that climate change will be a significant threat in our children's lifetimes. A Gallup Poll indicated that 56 percent of people fifty-five years and older worry about climate change, while 70 percent of their children and grandchildren, people ages eighteen to thirty-four, worry about it. A generational gap illustrated by the courageous Greta Thunberg, who at sixteen years of age looked in the eyes of her elders, leaders of nations, at the 2019 United Nations General Assembly and declared:

This is all wrong. I shouldn't be up here. I should be back in school, on the other side of the ocean. Yet you all come to us young people for hope. How dare you! You have stolen my dreams and my childhood with your empty words. . . . The popular idea of cutting our emissions in half in 10 years only gives us a 50% chance of staying below 1.5 degrees [Celsius] and the risk of setting off irreversible chain reactions beyond human control. . . . So, a 50% risk is simply not acceptable to us—we who have to live with the consequences.

In the ever-increasing lexicon used to understand the narratives about the consequences of our warming planet we now find the term "climate anxiety." As one recent national survey revealed, climate change makes 57 percent of American teens feel afraid and 43 percent feel hopeless. In another survey, 87 percent of respondents reported such severe anxiety about the impending climate crisis that it impaired their ability to perform at least one activity of daily living.

Hope is in short supply, as we are bombarded with information that is cause for despair. Rationally, there may not be much evidence for hope.

But *hope* is a state that transcends rationality. Hope, as Václav Havel articulated it, is a state of mind, not a state of the world. He described hope as

an orientation of the spirit, an orientation of the heart; it transcends the world that is immediately experienced, and is anchored somewhere beyond its horizons. . . . Hope is definitely not the same thing as optimism. It is not the conviction that something will turn out well, but the certainty that something makes sense, regardless of how it turns out. . . . It is also this hope, above all, which gives us the strength to live and continually to try new things, even in conditions that seem as hopeless as ours do, here and now.

Hope requires imagination: the ability to conceive of things that we can't see or that may not exist at all. As societies and businesses face a diverse landscape of seemingly hopeless challenges ranging from widespread inequity and a mental health epidemic to the looming climate crisis, it will take the language of imagination to respond.

The challenges of climate change are real. Using data from the U.S. Geological Survey, we can see timetables for extinction events, both for living things and for minerals and materials that we will consume to the point of depletion. It is currently predicted, for example, that copper will be extinct by 2027, gold by 2043, platinum by 2049, and lithium by 2053. Earth is made up of thousands of essential non-renewable resources. Imagination is not one of them.

Imagination is a renewable natural resource.

Imagination is rooted in a phenomenon known in neuroscience as mental synthesis: our brain's ability to combine known images or concepts to make new ideas. This capability is considered a uniquely human trait, something that differentiates us from other living beings.

The application of mental synthesis, moving it from theory to action, is where imagination and business meet. If the function of business is to link infrastructure, to mobilize people, and to execute value creation, business and imagination are intertwined in a marriage that bridges theory and practice (praxis), left-brain and right-brain thinking (synthesis or integrative thinking), and planning and doing (full life-cycle development).

The wicked challenges we face are, for better or for worse, outcomes of our own success. Considering that we've imagined the current state of the world, we can reimagine our way out of it.

Consider, for example, Weather Makers, a Dutch firm dedicated to "holistic engineering." Its co-founder Ties van der Hoeven is a voice in the rapidly growing new field of regenerative agriculture and eco-systems. The term "regenerative agriculture" describes farming and grazing practices that, among other benefits, reverse climate change by rebuilding the soil's organic matter and restoring its degraded biodiversity—resulting in both carbon drawdown and an improved water cycle.

Van der Hoeven was inspired by examples such as the Loess Plateau, an area of northern China almost the size of France that had become a dry, barren, heavily eroded landscape. Over a twenty-year period, regenerative approaches led by pioneering Chinese scientist Li Rui transformed the desert into a green oasis and productive farmland, as chronicled in a documentary called *Green Gold* by filmmaker John D. Liu.

Can we imagine this? A geographic region the size of France as brown desert one day and a lush green ecosystem in a single generation? Can we free ourselves of the constraints that may prevent us from even entertaining such a possibility? The logic that drives us to believe this is impossible—irrational, even—is preventing us from considering alternative opportunities to do extraordinary things. Maybe common sense isn't so common.

Certainly, there are moral questions regarding not simply what we *can* do but what we *should* do with the advances in science now shared across humanity. These are critical dialogues that should accompany our embrace of imagination. Should we live forever, even if we could? Should we build a settlement on Mars, even if we could? Our technological capabilities exceed our moral literacies.

But regenerative agriculture is not the science fiction terraforming of a "Genesis planet," as imagined on the big screen more than forty years ago in *Star Trek III: The Search for Spock*. It is simply a shift in the prevailing narrative regarding how human beings can become stewards of living systems rather than exerting our dominion over these ecologies. We should strive not to play God and test the moral boundaries, but rather to remove our own God-like complex in the first place.

This kind of thinking, and the resulting interventions, raise a question: How many of the challenges that we face are of our own making?

What freedom might we enjoy if we were to view so many problems that appear intractable as manageable—if only we were to retire the commonly held assumptions that hold the problem in suspension? Imagination can be a catalyst of this freedom.

Imagination doesn't merely operate as a language for smarter solutions. It can also inspire others to believe. As Bruce Mau used to say back when I led his design thinking creative studio:

The only way to effect real change is to show people a future more exciting than their past, and inspire them to work together on the journey.

Time, labor, and money, too, are nonrenewable resources. And we've wasted decades, lifetimes, and trillions of dollars on flawed processes. But imagination is regenerated when harvested. As Maya Angelou said: "Creativity cannot be used up. The more you use, the more you have."

Imagination may be the most valuable natural resource in the world.

PRACTICE

28 Building Blocks for Radical Curiosity

1. RADIUS OF EXPOSURE

The distance we travel expands and diversifies our worldview. Exposing ourselves to new experiences extends our lived knowledge, leading to the retiring of assumptions and birthing of new beliefs. We literally and metaphorically expand the radius of possibility.

2. INTENTIONAL LEISURE

Intentional leisure is not the absence of labor but the presence of purpose. The freedom to practice active rest that heals, and exploration that cultivates meaning. When we blend education and vacation our work/life balance is generative.

3. UNLEARNING

Learning has come to mean the acquisition of new skills. Unlearning is the skill of stepping outside of existing mental models and embracing new ones. Metacognition is the most important skill of the twenty-first century.

4. UPENDING INDICATORS

When new values emerge in society, the narratives we live by are upended. Upending indicators are events, behaviors, and patterns signaling that a narrative is shifting—like early detection sonar.

5. SOCIAL CONTRACT

As an implicit agreement to share power with governance structures responsible for the well-being of its stakeholders, a social contract is fueled by trust and successful outcomes. When trust is broken, such agreements may become irrelevant.

6. POLARIZATION DISORIENTATION

Diverse views are healthy. But polarization across many issues sustained over time creates disorientation and triggers emotional chaos. The cohesion of our narrative falls apart.

7. OUTSIDENESS AWARENESS

It is difficult to see ourselves when swimming in our own aquarium. Understanding a perspective outside our own requires dialogue with another person. As relational actors, we derive our awareness from others.

8. VISION, VEHICLE, IMPACT

Strategy is a plan to achieve goals under conditions of uncertainty. Developing strategic frameworks demands an inquiry-based method that codifies the vision, vehicle, and impact of ambitious cultural change.

9. SLOW WORK

Today, perpetual interruption is the standard climate—and it is eroding our ability to accomplish meaningful work. Just as we need REM sleep to experience deep, healthy, and restorative rest, we need slow work to experience the uninterrupted time that untangles complexity for deep clarity.

10. TIME READINESS DILATION

We all experience time differently. Cultural contexts have a gravitational pull that impacts how we receive and embrace new ideas. Time readiness dilation accounts for this variation to help us better understand the rate at which we absorb change.

11. LISTENING TO SLOW TIME

Counterintuitively, we need to slow down to speed up. Slow time offers new kinds of soundscapes that bring forward much-needed clarity, allowing us to hear our own voice through the cacophony of noise.

12. THE PRESENT FUTURE

Events in time are not merely history but prototypes for possible futures. The Present Future draws upon an Afrofuturist model of collapsing past, present, and future to forge alternative possibilities.

13. AWE-BASED LEADERSHIP

Awe violates our understanding of the world. Awe-based leadership welcomes wonder into our lives by calling beloved truths into question and adjusting our mental models to allow for the assimilation of profound ideas.

14. YOUTH MINDSET

Youth is the stage in between childhood and adulthood when everything is in a state of newness. A youth mindset allows us to encounter the world through a lens of wonder, to view the future as full of potential, and to rediscover the joy of discovery.

15. SENSORY EXPERIENCES

Life isn't a schedule, it's a collection of encounters. And sensory encounters are packed with knowledge and accelerate insights—but only if we receive, translate, and unpack the diverse languages that surround us.

16. FOURTH PLACES

Meaningful conversations require distinct physical places. Our first place is home, our second place is work. Third places are community spaces. Fourth Places are where we shape the future with dialogue and civic imagination.

17. MEANING AS MEDICINE

Languishing is the absence of well-being. In an era defined by the comprehensive loss of normalcy, meaning is the medicine to prevent an epidemic of languishing.

18. COLLECTIVE ACTUALIZATION

Self-actualization is an experience of becoming the best version of ourselves. But today, our social systems are so deeply entangled and interdependent that for me to flourish, we all must flourish. Thriving requires collective actualization.

19. INCONGRUITY HUMOR

We find humor in the space between our expectations of the world and our experience of it. Observing and articulating life's many contradictions is a central tenet in comedy, and a powerful way to deliver and receive cultural critique.

20. OLÉ

A deeply religious and cultural term used to express appreciation for when people accomplish extraordinary things. In the contemporary workplace context, "olé" is a way to name and acknowledge remarkable talent. "Olé" embodies an empathy-based style of leadership.

21. ECOLOGICAL HUMILITY

A reoriented mental model that views humans as guests of the planet, rather than its self-appointed extractors. Ecological humility removes humanity from the center of the diagram and grounds us as a part of—not separate from or superior to—the complexity of living systems.

22. TRUST WALKING

The practice of being present for another person by sharing a walk. An activity that relaxes the mind to stimulate nonlinear thinking, cultivates trust by breaking down status barriers, and eliminates distractions through multisensory immersion.

23. DISEMBEDDING

A process by which social relationships become increasingly dispersed across time and space. Global cultural mobility, digital social communities, and access to real-time information are disembedding social ties from physical location.

24. POSSIBILITY SITES

The modern workplace has become a container for the ordinary. Breakthrough impact is best cultivated within extraordinary contexts. Possibility sites are environments intentionally designed for remarkable experiences in which people rise to the occasion.

25. QUESTION INEQUITY

For those living in poverty, survival becomes the all-consuming narrative. As a result, imagination becomes a luxury, unaffordable to wide swaths of society. When large populations do not have the power to imagine, we all lose.

26. EUDAIMONIA

An ancient Greek philosophical concept valuing the highest human good: ethics, virtue, happiness, well-being. In contemporary life, positive psychology has interpreted eudaimonia as a state of flourishing associated with a sense of purpose in life.

27. CIVIC IMAGINATION

Activism requires not only protesting how things are but also imagining what they could become. Civic imagination is the capacity to articulate alternatives to existing conditions. We must see, experiment, and prototype if we are to realize better futures.

28. REGENERATIVE RESOURCES

Imagination is the most valuable natural resource in the world. Too often, we focus on managing nonrenewable resources. Instead of trying to maximize fixed variables, we can regenerate the intangible resources that can unleash unexpected solutions.

ACKNOWLEDGMENTS

This book is the result of a robust life filled with Radical Curiosity, long before I knew to call it such. The trajectory of learning, working, and experimenting with ideas has brought me into contact with an extraordinary community of talent that has shown me generosity, mentorship, and GPS coordinates on a journey whether they realize it or not. For the wayfinding signals, I am in deep gratitude to Deba Patnaik, Peter Hocking, Suzanne Lacy, Bruce Price, Jessie Shefrin, David Adjaye, Ann Hamilton, Krzysztof Wodiczko, DJ Spooky, Daniel Peltz, Charlie Cannon, Luke Dubois, Chris Coleman, Laleh Mehran, Erin Trapp, John Hickenlooper, Bruce Mau, Randi Fiat, Alex Bogusky, Oprah Winfrey, Christina Norman, Steve Groth, Barb Groth, Maya Cohan, Kate Thiel, Dan Walker, Alex Jadad, Martha Garcia, Dawn Danby, Ivy Ross, Bruce Vaughn, Barney Pell, Nadya Direkova, Tim O'Reilly, Saul Griffith, Anne Bergeron, Beth Comstock, Barry Frew, Don Simpson, Melissa Blake, Chief Vern Janvier, Gregory Johnson, Denise Young Smith, Rex Bothwell, Stephanie Fehr, Marian Salzman, Stefan Pryor, Nicholas Felton, Benjamin Bratton, Dondeena Bradley, Kurt Graves, Trung Lee, Anna Cano-Morales, Alison Croney, Saul Kaplan, Sasha Dichter, Esther Dyson, Ron O'Hanley, Andrew Zuckerman, Tamen Garcia, Kris Geekie, Bob Mitchell, Brian Goldner, Quinten Hardy, Cheline Jaidar, Larry Kopald, Miwa Matreyek, Bill Moggridge, Morris Nathanson, Emily Norton, Morgwn Rimel, Jay Rogers, Ricardo Pitts-Wiley, David McConville, Ayesha Khanna, Amanda Rock, Jay Rogers, Decker Rolph, Leslie Schrock, Sanyu Dillon, Michael Ventura, Andrew Yang, and many more.

A special thanks to David Drake, who moved quickly from being a publisher to a friend and whose patience and intellectual curiosity gave me the time and confidence to complete this project; Talia Krohn, whose editing and intellectual dance partner skills strengthened clarity of thought; Matt Inman, whose clarity to navigate this project to the finish line made all the difference; Nicholas Rock, Sarah Rabinovich, Daria Nikolaeva, and Tamara Grusin, who comprised a design team that translated the vision of *Radical Curiosity* and its words into a visually elegant expression.

Deep gratitude to Henry and Mona Goldenberg, whose love, comedy, and civic care modeled for me an ethical life of service to something bigger than yourself that became a foundation for my imagination to soar.

NOTES

FRAMING

CURIOSITY IS AN ENDANGERED SPECIES

2 *"In larger groups our conversations"* "Jony Ive on What He Misses Most About Steve Jobs," *Wall Street Journal*, October 4, 2019.

5 *"There is no such thing as"* Audre Lorde, "Learning from the 60s," in *Sister Outsider: Essays & Speeches by Audre Lorde* (Berkeley: Crossing Press, 2007).

12 *first-principles thinking is applied to innovation* Tim Urban, "The Cook and the Chef: Musk's Secret Sauce," *Wait But Why* (blog), November 6, 2015, https://waitbutwhy.com /2015/11/the-cook-and-the-chef-musks-secret -sauce.html.

LEARNING

1. LIMITED EXPOSURE TO DIVERSE EXPERIENCES

19 *"I've learned that people will forget"* Maya Angelou, www.mayaangelou.com/2018/04/04 /dr-maya-angelous-90th-birthday.

20 *"If I'm an advocate for anything"* Anthony Bourdain, https://twitter.com/PartsUnknown CNN/status/1005094991029415936.

20 *In 2019, 37.79 million Americans . . . traveled abroad* "Number of United States Residents Traveling Overseas from 2002 to 2020," Travel, Tourism & Hospitality, Statista, June 2021, https://www.statista.com/statis tics/214774/number-of-outbound-tourists -from-the-us/#:~:text=In%202019%2C%20 there%20were%20approximately,of%20%20 41.77%20million%20overseas%20travelers .&text=Excluding%20visitors%20to%20 Canada%20and,in%202018%20at%2041.77 %20million.

21 *"Fascism is cured by reading"* Miguel de Unamuno, https://www.azquotes.com/quote /691301.

21 *"We will not be free if we do not imagine freedom"* Ursula K. Le Guin, *The Wave in the Mind: Talks and Essays on the Writer, the Reader, and the Imagination* (Boston: Shambhala, 2004).

22 *"If photography can bring these things to life,"* "The Family of Man," Wikipedia, last modified, August 12, 2021, https://en.wikipe dia.org/wiki/The_Family_of_Man#cite_note -39.

22 *"decided to quit my ordinary life"* "About Mihaela Noroc," The Atlas of Beauty, https:// theatlasofbeauty.com/about.

23 *"We have to start from early age with children"* Meghan Collins Sullivan, "Photos: A 4-Year Mission to Present a New Vision of Beauty," *Goats and Soda*, NPR, September 24, 2017, https://www.npr.org/sections/goatsand soda/2017/09/24/552863777/photos-a-4-year -mission-to-present-a-new-vision-of-beauty.

24 *"I recently spoke at a university"* Chimamanda Ngozi Adichie, https://www.ted.com /talks/chimamanda_ngozi_adichie_the _danger_of_a_single_story?language=en.

25 *are we also ready to acknowledge* Bayo Akomolafe, How to Make Sense of This Moment? | Bayo Akomolafe & Charles Eisenstein at the Concrete Love Summit, House of Beautiful Business.

25 *"I wonder if he has ever really learned how to love"* "From the Archives: Chief Dan George Teaches Understanding," *North Shore News*, August 26, 2019, https://www .nsnews.com/nsn-50th/from-the-archives -chief-dan-george-teaches-understanding -3105824.

2. EDUCATION IS TOO BIG TO FAIL, BUT MAYBE IT SHOULD

28 *According to the U.S. Bureau of Labor Statistics* Investopedia, updated October 23, 2020, reviewed by Michael J. Boyle, fact-checked by Amanda Bellucco-Chatham.

28 *The United States spends more than $2 trillion annually* "2019 State of the Indus-

try: Talent Development Benchmarks and Trends," ASTD DBA Association for Talent Development, 2019.

29 *When educators debate the purpose of education* Steven Mintz, "11 Lessons from the History of Higher Ed," *Higher Ed Gamma* (blog), Inside Higher Ed, May 7, 2017, https:// www.insidehighered.com/blogs/higher-ed -gamma/11-lessons-history-higher-ed.

30 *"all students should acquire the same information at the same pace"* Mintz, "11 Lessons from the History of Higher Ed."

33 *"educators took on the problem of 'education for leisure'"* Livia Gershon, "The Rise and Fall of 'Education for Leisure,'" *JSTOR Daily,* December 3, 2014, https://daily.jstor .org/rise-fall-education-leisure/.

3. UNLEARNING AS A FORM OF ACTIVISM

38 *"The academy is not paradise"* bell hooks, *Teaching to Transgress: Education as the Practice of Freedom* (New York: Routledge, 1994).

38 *"The more radical the person is"* Paolo Freire, *Pedagogy of the Oppressed,* trans. Myra Bergman Ramos, 30th anniversary edition (New York: Bloomsbury, 2014).

40 *"Beyond the inequities of digital access"* Valerie Vande Panne, "Is Unschooling the Way to Decolonize Education?" Next City, July 6, 2020, https://nextcity.org/features /view/is-unschooling-the-way-to-decolonize -education.

41 *"school prepares for the alienating institutionalization of life"* Ivan Illich, *Deschooling Society* (London: Marion Boyars, 2000).

42 *"The only thing that interferes with my learning"* Lee T. Silber, *Career Management for the Creative Person* (New York: Three Rivers Press, 1999).

43 *"For apart from inquiry, apart from the praxis"* Paolo Freire, *Pedagogy of the Oppressed.*

44 *"radically shift how communities imagine, problem solve, heal, and connect"* Ashley

McCall, "What If We Radically Reimagined the New School Year?" *Chicago Unheard* (blog), July 30, 2020, https://chicagounheard .org/blog/what-if-we-radically-reimagined -the-new-school-year/.

44 *Activism is defined as* "Activism," Wikipedia, last modified April 24, 2021, https://en .wikipedia.org/wiki/Activism.

45 *"I don't mean to say that being wrong is the same thing as"* Sir Ken Robinson, "Do Schools Kill Creativity?" TED Talk, https:// www.ted.com/talks/sir_ken_robinson_do _schools_kill_creativity/transcript?language =en.

46 *"I don't feel frightened not knowing things"* Eric Weiner, "Preparing Your Mind for Uncertain Times," *The Atlantic,* August 25, 2020.

47 *"Education is the point at which we decide"* Hannah Arendt, "The Crisis of Education," in *Between Past and Future* (New York: Viking Press, 1961).

48 *"How can we introduce moral principles"* "Education of the Heart," His Holiness the 14th Dali Lama of Tibet, October 22, 2014, https://www.dalailama.com/news/2014 /education-of-the-heart.

4. STORIES AS REGENERATIVE CATALYSTS

50 *become prepared for any eventuality* Ramin Settodeh, "Exclusive: A Talk with the 'Wild Things' Creator," *Newsweek,* October 8, 2009.

51 *"The human mind is addicted to stories"* Maria Konnikova, "The Storytelling Animal: A Conversation with Jonathan Gottschall," *Literally Psyched* (blog), *Scientific American,* April 19, 2021, https://blogs.scientificameri can.com/literally-psyched/the-storytelling -animal-a-conversation-with-jonathan -gottschall/.

52 *"binding society together by reinforcing a set of common values"* Jonathan Gottschall, *The Storytelling Animal: How Stories Make Us*

Human (New York: Houghton Mifflin Harcourt, 2012).

53 *"I think of the act of naming as diagnosis"* Rebecca Solnit, *Call Them by Their True Names: American Crises (and Essays)* (Chicago: Haymarket Books, 2018).

54 *the gender binary is out of date* Daniel Reynolds, "Study: Half of Gen Z Believes the Gender Binary Is Outdated," *Advocate,* February 24, 2021.

54 *at least fifty-eight gender identities that users can* Russell Goldman, "Here's a List of 58 Gender Options for Facebook Users," ABC News, February 13, 2014, https://abc news.go.com/blogs/headlines/2014/02/heres -a-list-of-58-gender-options-for-facebook -users.

54 *recognizing not three but five genders* Emily Krempholtz, "Some Native Americans Recognized Not Two, Not Three . . . but Five Genders," *Buzzworthy,* no date, https://www .buzzworthy.com/native-americans-five -genders/.

55 *in a recent Gallup Poll* Jeffrey M. Jones, "LGBT Identification Rises to 5.6% in Latest U.S. Estimate," Gallup, February 24, 2021, https://news.gallup.com/poll/329708/lgbt -identification-rises-latest-estimate.aspx.

55 *"I am literally open to every single thing"* Karen Mizoguchi, "Everything Miley Cyrus Has Said About Her Sexuality: 'I Am Literally Open to Every Single Thing,'" *People,* August 12, 2019.

55 *criticizing the church's "overzealous morality"* Jeremy Blum, "Pope Francis Says Having Sex and Eating Good Food Is 'Simply Divine,'" *HuffPost,* September 11, 2020, https:// www.huffpost.com/entry/pope-francis-sex -food-divine-pleasure_n_5f5bd9c3c5b67602f 6051a6e.

56 *adopting indefinite hybrid or full work-from-home policies* Emily Courtney, "30 Companies Switching to Long-Term Remote Work," *Articles on Finding a Job* (blog), Flex-Jobs, no date, https://www.flexjobs.com/blog /post/companies-switching-remote-work -long-term/.

56 *700+ staff a simultaneous paid week off* Soo Youn, "America's Workers Are Exhausted and Burned Out—and Some Employers Are Taking Notice," *Washington Post,* June 29, 2021.

56 *they are looking for a reset* Raghu Krishnamoorthy, "Is It the Great Resignation . . . or the Great Reset?" *The Future of Working* (blog), LinkedIn, July 18, 2021, https://www .linkedin.com/pulse/great-resignationor -reset-raghu-krishnamoorthy/?trackingId =JWZGzESDIyz1jd28oiSBkw%3D%3D.

56 *"working fewer hours can make a country"* Patrick Thomas, "Is a Four-Day Week the Future of Work?" *Wall Street Journal,* July 31, 2021.

57 *protests were organized across the United States* "George Floyd Protests," Wikipedia, last modified August 3, 2021, https://en .wikipedia.org/wiki/George_Floyd_protests #Elsewhere_in_the_United_States.

57 *"the largest movement in U.S. history"* Larry Buchanan, Quoctrung Bui, and Jugal K. Patel, "Black Lives Matter May Be the Largest Movement in U.S. History," *New York Times,* July 3, 2020.

57 *for police officers who engage in* Derek Major, "Police Unions Sue New York City Over Anti-chokehold Bill," *Black Enterprise,* August 8, 2020, https://www.blackenterprise .com/police-unions-sue-new-york-city-over -anti-chokehold-bill/?test=prebid.

57 *"racism is not a matter of individual bigotry"* Lauren Jackson, "What Is Critical Race Theory?" *New York Times,* July 20, 2021.

58 *Even the global investment firm* Yusuf Khan, "Goldman Sachs Released a 34-Page Analysis of the Effects of Climate Change. And the Results Are Terrifying," *Business Insider,* September 25, 2019, https://markets .businessinsider.com/news/stocks/goldman -sachs-climate-change-threatens-new-york -tokyo-lagos-cities-2019-9.

58 *call for civil disobedience to force institutions* Jeff McMahon, "Former UN Climate Chief Calls for Civil Disobedience," *Forbes*, February 24, 2020.

58 *"fire clouds" sparked 710,117 lightning strikes* Amy Graff, "Fire Clouds Spark 710,117 Lightning Strikes in Western Canada in 15 Hours," *SF Gate*, July 1, 2021.

58 *"more than 90 percent of all climate scientists"* Pam Wright, "87 Percent of Americans Unaware There's Scientific Consensus on Climate Change," The Weather Channel, July 11, 2017, https://weather.com/science /environment/news/americans-climate -change-scientific-consensus.

59 *during a hearing held by the House Committee* William Cummings, "Rocks Falling into Oceans, Not Climate, Causing Seas to Rise, Congressman Suggests," *USA Today*, May 17, 2018.

60 *"We often tell our students"* Ocean Vuong, "Ocean Vuong: A Life Worthy of Our Breath," *On Being with Krista Tippett* (podcast), April 30, 2020, https://onbeing.org/programs /ocean-vuong-a-life-worthy-of-our-breath/.

60 *calling them "palaces for the people"* Emmett FitzGerald, "Palaces for the People," *99% Invisible* (podcast), episode 346, March 19, 2019, https://99percentinvisible.org/epi sode/palaces-for-the-people/.

60 *"Libraries are the kinds of places where"* "Palaces for the People Quotes," Goodreads, last modified 2021, https://www.goodreads .com/work/quotes/59341203-palaces-for-the -people-how-social-infrastructure-can-help -fight-inequal.

61 *"We wouldn't need books quite so much"* Alain de Botton, quoted in eds. Maria Popova and Claudia Bedrick, *A Velocity of Being: Letters to a Young Reader* (New York: Enchanted Lion Books, 2018).

62 *"This is precisely the time when artists go to work"* Toni Morrison, "No Place for Self-Pity, No Room for Fear," *The Nation*, March 23, 2015.

COHESION

5. THE DECLINE OF PARTICIPATION IN PUBLIC LIFE

67 *With only 55.7 percent of* Drew Desilver, "In past elections, U.S. trailed most developed countries in voter turnout," Pew Research Center, November 3, 2020, https:// www.pewresearch.org/fact-tank/2020/11/03 /in-past-elections-u-s-trailed-most-devel oped-countries-in-voter-turnout/.

67 *66.3 percent of the voting-age population* Kevin Schaul, Kate Rabinowitz, and Ted Mellnik, "2020 Turnout Is the Highest in Over a Century," *Washington Post*, November 5, 2020.

69 *There are four theories on the origins of government* "Theories on the Origin of Government," *Students of History* (blog), Medium, September 20, 2017, https://medium .com/@StudentsHistory/theories-on-the -origin-of-government-2150325b7bfd.

70 *nearly 20,000 incorporated towns and cities* "How Many Cities Are in the US 2021," World Population Review, last accessed October 22, 2021, https://worldpopulation review.com/us-city-rankings/how-many -cities-are-in-the-us.

70 *adult makes more than 35,000 decisions per day* Heidi Zak, "Adults Make More Than 35,000 Decisions Per Day. Here Are 4 Ways to Prevent Mental Burnout: Don't Let Decision Fatigue Get the Best of You," *Inc.*, June 24, 2021.

71 *Democracy is the worst form* Winston Churchill, International Churchill Society, November 11, 1947, https://winstonchurchill .org/resources/quotes/the-worst-form-of -government/.

72 *such a contract requires amendments* "Amending the Constitution," U.S. Senate, last accessed October 22, 2021, https://www .senate.gov/reference/reference_index_sub jects/Constitution_vrd.htm#:~:text=It%20 has%20become%20the%20landmark,11%2C

000%20amendments%20proposed%20since %20178.

72 *two edits are made every second* "Wikipedia:Statistics," Wikipedia, last modified August 27, 2021, https://en.wikipedia.org /wiki/Wikipedia:Statistics#:~:text=This%20is %20an%20information%20page.&text=While %20you%20read%20this%2C%20Wikipedia ,598%20new%20articles%20per%20day.

72 *As soon as any man* Jean-Jacques Rousseau, *The Social Contract,* trans. Rose M. Harrington (New York: G. P. Putnam's Sons, 1893).

74 *"Two-thirds of adults think"* Lee Rainie, Scott Keeter, and Andrew Perrin, "Trust and Distrust in America," Pew Research Center, July 22, 2019, https://www.pewresearch.org /politics/2019/07/22/trust-and-distrust-in -america/.

75 *"We're less interested in big government vs. small government"* "When It Comes to Politics, Do Millennials Care About Anything?" *The Atlantic,* citing a 2013 report by the Roosevelt Institute titled "Government by and for Millennials," https://www.theatlantic .com/sponsored/allstate/when-it-comes-to -politics-do-millennials-care-about-anything /255/.

75 *"I'm a great believer in community"* Nicholas Kristof, "The Friendships Trump Pulled Apart," *New York Times,* November 1, 2020.

6. WE DON'T TALK ANYMORE

78 *our brain waves might synchronize as people interact* Conor Feehly, "Brains Might Sync as People Interact—and That Could Upend Consciousness Research," *Discover,* July 26, 2021.

79 *"our political system seems to only be working for the insiders"* Carrie Dann, "'A Deep and Boiling Anger': NBC/WSJ Poll Finds a Pessimistic America Despite Current Economic Satisfaction," *Meet the Press,* NBC News, August 25, 2019, https://www.nbcnews .com/politics/meet-the-press/deep-boiling

-anger-nbc-wsj-%20poll-finds-pessimistic -america-despite-n1045916.

79 *"there are stark contrasts between voters"* "Voters' Attitudes About Race and Gender Are Even More Divided Than in 2016," Pew Research Center, last modified September 10, 2020, https://www.pewresearch.org /politics/2020/09/10/voters-attitudes-about -race-and-gender-are-even-more-divided -than-in-2016/.

79 *there are essentially two Americas* Chuck Bonfig, "America Is Over: Let's Just Split into Different Countries," *Philadelphia Inquirer,* September 18, 2020.

80 *A study asking about the use of, trust in, and distrust of thirty* Mark Jurkowitz, Amy Mitchell, Elisa Shearer, and Mason Walker, "U.S. Media Polarization and the 2020 Election: A Nation Divided," Pew Research Center, January 24, 2020, https://www.jour nalism.org/2020/01/24/u-s-media-polari zation-and-the-2020-election-a-nation -divided/.

80 *A new study from Princeton and Northwestern* Zachary Davies Boren, "The US Is an Oligarchy, Study Concludes," *The Telegraph,* April 16, 2014.

80 *Americans with ideologically consistent values has increased* "The Shift in the American Public's Political Values: Political Polarization 1994–2017," U.S. Politics & Policy, Pew Research Center, last modified October 20, 2017, https://www.pewresearch.org/politics /interactives/political-polarization-1994 -2017/.

82 *the Latin root of the term "polarization"* "UGM-27 Polaris," Wikipedia, last modified May 3, 2021, https://en.wikipedia.org/wiki /UGM-27_Polaris.

82 *the word of the day was "truthiness"* Ben Zimmer, "On Language: Truthiness," *New York Times Magazine,* October 13, 2010.

82 *"We are divided between those who think with their head"* *The Colbert Report,* season 1, episode 1, "The Word—Truthiness," Stephen

Colbert, aired October 17, 2005, in broadcast syndication, Comedy Central, https://www.cc.com/video/63ite2/the-colbert-report-the-word-truthiness.

83 *"at the point of decision, emotions are very important for choosing"* Jim Camp, "Decisions Are Largely Emotional, Not Logical: The Neuroscience Behind Decision-Making," Big Think, June 11, 2012, https://bigthink.com/experts-corner/decisions-are-emotional-not-logical-the-neuroscience-behind-decision-making.

84 *"We want to know if it's possible to live on the earth, peacefully"* bell hooks and Dr. William Turner, "Appalachian Heritage: Summer 2008 Issue—Public Reading and Discussion," Berea College, YouTube video, 55:52, April 21, 2009, https://www.youtube.com/watch?v=BEPEtcqPOyE&t=5s.

85 *"What does trauma do to us"* Umair Haque, "Americans Don't Know How to Talk to Each Other Anymore," *Eudaimonia & Co.* (blog), March 24, 2021, https://eand.co/americans-dont-know-how-to-talk-to-each-other-anymore-ed7f0fb6ea97.

7. BETWEEN OUTSIDENESS AND OTHERNESS

88 *a story structure that features* "Polyphony (literature)," Wikipedia, last modified January 12, 2021, https://en.wikipedia.org/wiki/Polyphony_(literature).

88 *"it is immensely important for the person"* Mikhail Bakhtin, "Response to a Question from the *Novyi Mir* Editorial Staff," quoted in Gary Saul Morson and Caryl Emerson, *Mikhail Bakhtin: Creation of a Prosaics* (Stanford: Stanford University Press, 1990).

89 *If outsideness is the humility to depend on others* Jean-François Staszak, "Other/otherness," in *International Encyclopedia of Human Geography*, ed. Rob Kitchin et al., 12 vols., 1st ed. (Oxford: Elsevier Science, 2009), available online at https://archive-ouverte.unige.ch/unige:77582.

90 *"unless we can manage to establish some kind of dialogue"* James Baldwin, "Pin Drop Speech," Cambridge University, YouTube video, 8:14, July 26, 2017, https://www.youtube.com/watch?v=NUBh9GqFU3A.

91 *"They each had different 'systems of reality'"* Gabrielle Bellot, "The Famous Baldwin-Buckley Debate Still Matters Today," *The Atlantic*, December 2, 2019.

92 *"she argued against a monochromatic literary canon"* Nell Irvin Painter, "Long Divisions: The History of Racism and Exclusion in the United States Is the History of Whiteness," *New Republic*, October 11, 2017.

93 *"Those who are 'them' can be described in the negative language of disgust"* Painter, "Long Divisions."

94 *"it wasn't until the advent of traveling minstrel shows"* Natalie Escobar, "An Ice Cream Truck Jingle's Racist History Has Caught Up to It," *Code Switch* (podcast), August 14, 2020, https://www.npr.org/sections/codeswitch/2020/08/14/902664184/an-ice-cream-truck-jingles-racist-history-has-caught-up-toit?utm_term=nprnews&utm_medium=social&utm_source=facebook.com&utm_campaign=npr&fbclid=%20IwAR1knMe1Id6kPa7TTotKbJ7NHrfy7RjFVPJV_D1nXwABH2-lOUC7Hw_.

94 *but the company wanted to be "part of the solution"* Escobar, "An Ice Cream Truck Jingle's Racist History Has Caught Up to It."

95 *We are each other's* Gwendolyn Brooks, "Paul Robeson," The Essential Gwendolyn Brooks (New York: Library of America, 2005).

8. HOW TO ASK AN ESSENTIAL QUESTION

99 *In 2019, the United States spent $3.8 trillion on healthcare* "Historical National Health Expenditure Data," Centers for Medicare & Medicaid Services, last accessed October 22, 2021, https://www.cms.gov/Research-Statistics-Data-and-Systems/Statistics-Trends

-and-Reports/NationalHealthExpendData
/NationalHealthAccountsHistorical#:~:text
=The%20data%20are%20presented%20by
,spending%20accounted%20for%202017.7%20
percent.

99 *more than double the per capita spending* Rabah Kamal, Giorlando Ramirez, and Cynthia Cox, "How Does Health Spending in the U.S. Compare to Other Countries?" Healthy System Tracker, December 23, 2020, https:// www.healthsystemtracker.org/chart-collec tion/health-spending-u-s-compare-countries /#item-spendingcomparison_gdp-per-capita -and-health-consumption-spending-per-cap ita-2019.

TIME

9. THE DIGITIZATION OF OUR SELF-INTERESTS

108 *"If time and reason are functions"* Ursula K. Le Guin, *The Dispossessed: An Ambiguous Utopia* (New York: HarperCollins, 1974).

109 *nearly two decades before the internet became mainstream* Timothy B. Lee, "The Internet, Explained," *Vox,* May 14, 2015, https:// www.vox.com/2014/6/16/18076282/the-inter net.

110 *"email-, Facebook- and Twitter-checking constitute a neural addiction"* Daniel J. Levitin, "Why the Modern World Is Bad for You," *The Guardian,* January 18, 2015.

110 *"the whole population is subject to a degree of behavior modification"* Jaron Lanier, "How We Need to Remake the Internet," TED video, 14:46, April 2018, https://www.ted.com /talks/jaron_lanier_how_we_need_to_remake _the_internet.

111 *When you play with* Tristan Harris, "A Path to Humane Technology," YouTube video, November 14, 2019, https://www.you tube.com/watch?v=-oFcGfQ8bWM.

112 *"People go to work"* Jason Fried, "Why Work Doesn't Happen at Work," TED video, 02:30, October 2010, https://www.ted.com /talks/jason_fried_why_work_doesn_t_hap pen_at_work?language=en.

113 *interruptions and information overload eat up* Brigid Schulte, "Work Interruptions Can Cost You 6 Hours a Day. An Efficiency Expert Explains How to Avoid Them," *Washington Post,* June 1, 2015.

10. TIME TRAVEL IS NOT RESERVED FOR DELOREANS

116 *Some sources point to the U.S. military* "Ahead of the Curve," The Idioms, https:// www.theidioms.com/ahead-of-the-curve /#:~:text=The%20idiomatic%20%20expres sion%20is%20most%20probably%20origi nated%20from%20the%20%20US%20 military.&text=Other%20sources%20sug gest%20that%20%20the,phrase%20also%20 refer%20to%20flying.

118 *"the gravity of a large mass, like Earth"* Stephen Johnson, "'Time Is Elastic': Why Time Passes Faster atop a Mountain Than at Sea Level," Big Think, December 31, 2019, https://bigthink.com/surprising-science/time -perception?rebelltitem=1#rebelltitem1.

120 *"The future is already here"* Wade Gibson, quoted in Scott Rosenberg, "Virtual Reality Check, Digital Daydreams, Cyberspace Nightmares," *San Francisco Examiner,* April 19, 1992.

120 *"Is it doubted, then, that the plan I propose"* Abraham Lincoln, "Annual Message to Congress—Concluding Remarks," December 1, 1862, Abraham Lincoln Online, http:// www.abrahamlincolnonline.org/lincoln /speeches/congress.htm.

11. BEFRIENDING THE SOUNDS OF SLOW TIME

122 Jimson Weed/White Flower No. 1 *holds the record* "The 15 Most Expensive Female Artists," *Bbys Magazine,* June 9, 2020, https://www.barnebys.com/blog/15-most -expensive-female-artists.

123 *"to see takes time, like to have a friend takes time"* Elizabeth Hutton Turner, *Georgia O'Keeffe: The Poetry of Things* (Washington, D.C.: Phillips Collections, 1999).

124 *"heavy multi-screeners find it difficult to filter out irrelevant stimuli"* Kevin McSpadden, "You Now Have a Shorter Attention Span Than a Goldfish," *Time*, May 14, 2015.

124 *"Remember that Time is Money"* Benjamin Franklin, "Advice to a Young Tradesman, [21 July 1748]," Founders Online, National Archives, https://founders.archives .gov/documents/Franklin/01-03-02-0130.

125 *"What I have done and what I enjoy doing feels closer to a walk"* "Harvard GSD Virtual Commencement 2020," YouTube video, 3:25:38, May 2020, https://www.youtube.com /watch?v=Exx28NlLhro&t=4229s.

126 *"The idea is to balance linear thinking"* Emma Seppälä, "Happiness Research Shows the Biggest Obstacle to Creativity Is Being Too Busy," *Quartz*, May 8, 2017, https://qz .com/978018/happiness-research-shows-the -biggest-obstacle-to-creativity-is-being-too -busy/?utm_source=qzfb.

127 *power of silence has long been* Alex Ross, "Searching for Silence: John Cage's Art of Noise," *New Yorker*, September 27, 2010.

128 *pushed the boundaries of listening for silence* Mark Swed, "How Gay Feminist Composer Pauline Oliveros Taught Us to Hear with More Than Ears," *Los Angeles Times*, August 5, 2020.

128 *Rensselaer Polytechnic Institute is home to* Center for Deep Listening at Rensselaer home page, last accessed October 22, 2021, https://www.deeplistening.rpi.edu/.

128 *"Are there any places on Earth left untouched by noise pollution"* Victoria Jaggard, "Are There Any Places on Earth Left Untouched by Noise Pollution?" *Smithsonian*, September 15, 2015, https://www.deeplisten ing.rpi.edu/.

128 *Within this 1-million-acre forest is a spot* "About," One Square Inch, last accessed October 22, 2021, https://www.google.com/url ?q=https://onesquareinch.org/about/&sa=D &source=docs&ust=1634932519600000&usg =AOvVaw2K37X9VrfAspyoNhFkPkgV.

128 *Dadirri is an inner, deep listening and quiet, still awareness* "Dadirri Our Greatest Gift to Australia, Says Indigenous Elder and 2021 Senior Australian of the Year," *Living Water* (blog), January 26, 2021, https://www .thelivingwater.com.au/blog/dadirri-our -greatest-gift-to-australia-says-indigenous -elder-and-2021-senior-australian-of-the -year?fbclid=IwAR3fByBz-H9R23TmQT3Rg1 XeFmM6guaDQvu4ckqagoMt4Q9VrTg-kcX ULRQ.

129 *"the Lebron James of touching stuff"* "Gibi ASMR," Wikipedia, last accessed October 21, 2021, https://en.wikipedia.org/wiki /Gibi_ASMR.

129 *ASMR itself gained mainstream notoriety during the 2019 Super Bowl* "ASMR," Wikipedia, last accessed October 21, 2021, https:// en.wikipedia.org/wiki/ASMR#In_pop_cul ture.

130 *"Musicians know how to create moments that break patterns"* "What Musical Mindsets Can Teach Us About Business Innovation," *Irving Wladawsky-Berger* (blog), July 2, 2021, https://blog.irvingwb.com/blog/2021/07/what -musical-minds-teach-us-about-innovation .html?fbclid=IwAR0oDGBo2odJuZAReJC26 q6VPYW7JnGIOt3cwg6oxikekDwOHO7qRE 9PaYM.

12. AFROFUTURIST TIME: MS. PRESIDENT 2036

132 *Terra Nova, a new large-scale performance* "Terra Nova: Sinfonia Antarctica," DJ Spooky, last accessed September 10, 2021, http://djspooky.com/terra-nova-sinfonia -antarctica/.

133 *The eight installations that constituted Dialog:City* Julie Bloom, "Your (Nonparti-

san) Message Here," *New York Times,* August 15, 2008.

134 *The artist is always* Wyndham Lewis, quoted in Marshall McLuhan, *Understanding Media: The Extensions of Man* (Cambridge, Mass.: The MIT Press, 1994).

134 *"the past and the future are very much about the present"* Essence Harden, quoted in Elissaveta M. Brandon, "Inside the Fantastical World of Afrofuturism, from P-Funk's Mothership to 'Black Panther,'" *Fast Company,* August 17, 2021.

134 *"Futurists ask* what *tomorrow's hover-boards"* C. Brandon Ogbunu, "How Afrofuturism Can Help the World Mend," *Wired,* July 15, 2020.

136 *"Ms. Payton took the process public"* Carol Kino, "A Museum Rises, but Not the Usual Way," *New York Times,* November 12, 2007.

137 *The inaugural exhibition of MCA Denver* "Selected Exhibitions & Writings," Cydney Payton, last accessed September 10, 2011, http://www.cydneypayton.com/star-power -exhibition.

138 *"She creates whole new mythologies"* Carrie Mae Weems, "Wangechi Mutu and Carrie Mae Weems on the Profound Impulse to Make Art," *Interview,* December 7, 2020.

138 *"Nka" is an Igbo word that means "to make, to create"* Zeke Turner, "How Okwui Enwezor Changed the Art World," *Wall Street Journal,* September 8, 2014.

139 *"We are large containing multitudes"* Washington Post Staff, "Full Transcript of President Obama's Speech at the Opening Ceremony of the African American Museum," *Washington Post,* September 24, 2016.

139 *"This place is more than a building"* Washington Post Staff, "Full Transcript of President Obama's Speech at the Opening Ceremony of the African American Museum."

140 *"It's meant to suggest the link"* Michael Kimmelman, "David Adjaye on Designing a Museum That Speaks a Different Language," *New York Times,* September 21, 2016.

141 *"to make the impossible more proximate"* Clover Hope, "Why Poet Amanda Gorman Wants to Be President," *WSJ.,* August 24, 2021.

YOUTH

13. INNOVATION AS A PRACTICE OF AWE

146 *"it can provoke an attempt to change the mental structures"* Summer Allen, "The Science of Awe," Greater Good Science Center, UC Berkeley, September 2018, https://ggsc .berkeley.edu/images/uploads/GGSC-JTF _White_Paper-Awe_FINAL.pdf.

147 *"they need to make a leap, not knowing where they will land"* Helen De Cruz, "The Necessity of Awe," *Aeon,* July 10, 2020, https://aeon.co/essays/how-awe-drives-sci entists-to-make-a-leap-into-the-unknown.

148 *"let go of our certainty and expect ourselves to be confused"* Margaret J. Wheatley, *Turning to One Another: Simple Conversations to Restore Hope to the Future* (San Francisco: Berrett-Koehler, 2002).

148 *"mostly used as a slogan with no substance"* Michael O'Bryan, "Innovation: The Most Important and Overused Word in America," *Wired,* https://www.wired.com /insights/2013/11/innovation-the-most -important-and-overused-word-in-america/.

149 *"sentenced to a life in prison and worse—a life without ears"* Emma Green, "Innovation: The History of a Buzzword," *The Atlantic,* June 2013.

149 *"meddle not with them that are given to change"* "Compare Translations for Proverbs 24:21," Bible Study Tools, https://www.bible studytools.com/proverbs/24-21-compare .html.

150 *"Studies have found that awe"* Summer Allen, "The Science of Awe."

150 *"from computers you control with levitating orbs"* Mark Wilson, "The Head of the World's Coolest Innovation Lab Wants to Focus on . . . Public Policy," *Fast Company*, August 20, 2021.

150 *launched more than 2,000 companies* Y Combinator home page, https://www.ycombinator.com.

151 *"What causes innovation? Why does it happen, and how might we nurture it?"* Walter Isaacson, "Inventing the Future," *New York Times*, April 6, 2012.

151 *"That's the magic, the genius, that means our entire community"* Wilson, "The Head of the World's Coolest Innovation Lab Wants to Focus on . . . Public Policy."

152 *"to collectively imagine a better, bolder future"* Peter Dizikes, "Dava Newman Named Director of MIT Media Lab," *MIT News*, December 22, 2020, https://news.mit.edu/2020/media-lab-director-newman-1222.

152 *"we have a once-in-a-century opportunity to hit the reset button"* Astro Teller, "The Secret Superpower of the Class of 2020," *X Company* (blog), May 15, 2020, https://x.company/blog/posts/the-secret-superpower-of-the-class-of-2020/.

14. MAY WE NEVER GROW UP

155 *"Home is that youthful region where a child is"* Maya Angelou, "Home," in *Letter to My Daughter* (New York: Random House, 2008).

156 *"Imagineering is letting your imagination soar"* Alcoa, "The Place They Do Imagineering," ad, *Time*, February 16, 1942.

158 *"when an experience comes into conflict"* Albert Einstein, *Autobiographical Notes* (Peru, Ill.: Open Court, 1999).

158 *"sense of wonder" is defined as* Jeff Prucher, ed., *Brave New Worlds: The Oxford Dictionary of Science Fiction* (Oxford: Oxford University Press, 2007).

159 *the term "amateur" is rooted in the French* Joe Moran, "Beginners by Tom Vanderbilt Review—It's Never Too Late to Learn," *The Guardian*, December 31, 2020.

160 *"The child sees everything in a state of newness"* Charles Baudelaire, *The Painter of Modern Life and Other Essays* (New York: Phaidon Press, 1995).

161 *"This world demands the qualities of youth"* Robert F. Kennedy, "Day of Affirmation" (speech, University of Cape Town, South Africa, June 6, 1966), Robert F. Kennedy Center for Justice and Human Rights, https://web.archive.org/web/20110227110620/http:/rfkcenter.org/lifevision/dayofaffirmation/.

162 *"I am convinced that most people do not grow up"* Angelou, "Home."

162 *"Growing up is such a barbarous business"* *Peter Pan*, directed by Clyde Geronimi, Wilfred Jackson, and Hamilton Luske (Walt Disney, 1953), film.

15. COMING TO OUR SENSES

166 *a state beyond the possibility of calculation* "Sublime (philosophy)," Wikipedia, last modified June 27, 2021, https://en.wikipedia.org/wiki/Sublime_(philosophy).

166 *"an experience of such perceptual vastness"* Raya Bidshahri, "Let Me Blow Your Mind: The Importance of Awe in Education," Singularity Hub, December 4, 2017, https://singularityhub.com/2017/12/04/let-me-blow-your-mind-the-importance-of-awe-in-education/.

166 *"experience the world with naïve, pure eyes"* Elisabeth Leopold, *Egon Schiele: Poems and Letters, 1910–1912* (New York: Prestel, 2008).

166 More than 80 percent of the information that our brains process Barbara Wilmes et al., "Coming to Our Senses: Incorporating Brain Research Findings into Classroom Instruction," *Education* 128, no. 4 (2008), https://go.galegroup.com/ps/i.do?p=AONE

&u=googlescholar&id=GALE%7CA30364282 5&v=2.1&it=r&sid=AONE&asid=7c026e82.

167 *humanity shot 1.2 trillion photographs* Eric Perret, "Here's How Many Digital Photos Will Be Taken in 2017," Mylio, October 26, 2017, https://focus.mylio.com/tech -today/heres-how-many-digital-photos-will -be-taken-in-2017-repost-oct.

167 *more photos than existed in total 150 years ago* Rose Eveleth, "How Many Photographs of You Are Out There in the World?" *The Atlantic*, November 2, 2015.

167 *simulation of more than 100 million neurons* "FAQ About the Blue Brain Project," EPFL, last accessed July 19, 2021, https:// www.epfl.ch/research/domains/bluebrain /frequently_asked_questions/.

167 *string theory has proposed that* Matt Williams, "A Universe of 10 Dimensions," Phys.org, December 11, 2014, https://phys.org /news/2014-12-universe-dimensions.html.

167 *our brain creates neural structures with up to eleven dimensions* Paul Ratner, "The Human Brain Builds Structures in 11 Dimensions, Discover Scientists," Big Think, June 14, 2017, https://bigthink.com/paul -ratner/our-brains-think-in-11-dimensions -discover-scientists.

168 *a series of ephemeral phenomena* "Take Your Time: Olafur Eliasson," April 20– June 30, 2008, MoMA, last accessed July 19, 2021, https://www.moma.org/calendar/exhi bitions/31.

168 *Eliasson engineered a floor-to-ceiling curtain* "Beauty, 1993," Olafur Eliasson, last accessed July 18, 2021, https://olafureliasson .net/archive/artwork/WEK101824/beauty.

168 *phenomenology is the study of how individuals* Brian E. Neubauer et al., "How Phenomenology Can Help Us Learn from the Experiences of Others," *Perspectives on Medical Education* 8 (2019), https://doi.org/10 .1007/s40037-019-0509-2.

169 *"connect businesses with their customers"* B. Joseph Pine II and James H. Gilmore, *The Experience Economy*, updated edition (Boston: Harvard Business Review Press, 2011).

171 *happiness derived from experiences is found in the anticipation prior* James Hamblin, "Buy Experiences, Not Things," *The Atlantic*, October 7, 2014.

171 *"Storytelling is a tool"* Maria Popova, "Iris Murdoch on Storytelling, Why Art Is Essential for Democracy, and the Key to Good Writing," *The Marginalian*, July 18, 2018, https://www.brainpickings.org/2018/07/18 /iris-murdoch-existentialists-mystics-philos ophy-literature-art/?fbclid=IwAR2WaORtVU BNPOPvbm_FF1CoMD3lfW3Zyc5gsax1qtwK 7rItzK75vjSLcDU.

16. THE JOY OF CONVERSATION

172 *The Compromise of 1877* "Compromise of 1877," The History Channel, last modified November 27, 2019, https://www.history.com /topics/us-presidents/compromise-of-1877.

173 *introducing the idea of social distancing* bioMérieux Connection Editors, "How Public Health Policies Saved Citizens in St. Louis During the 1918 Flu Pandemic," bioMérieux Connection, October 25, 2018, https://www.biomerieuxconnection.com /2018/10/25/how-public-health-policies -saved-citizens-in-st-louis-during-the-1918 -flu-pandemic/.

173 *"talk which burst forth"* "Rombauer, Irma (1877–1962)," Harvard Square Library, last accessed October 22, 2021, https://www .harvardsquarelibrary.org/biographies/irma -rombauer/.

174 *the recipes were composed as narratives* "Joy of Cooking," Wikipedia, last modified September 10, 2021, https://en.wikipedia.org /wiki/Joy_of_Cooking.

175 *in the Paris salons* Jennifer Llewellyn and Steve Thompson, "The Salons," Alpha History, October 5, 2020, https://alphahistory .com/frenchrevolution/salons/.

176 *Jefferson hosted perhaps the most signifi-cant* "The Dinner Table Bargain, June 1790," PBS, last accessed October 22, 2021, https://www.google.com/url?q=https://www.pbs.org/wgbh/americanexperience/features/hamilton-dinner-table-bargain-june-1790/&sa=D&source=docs&ust=1634928791143000&usg=AOvVaw2JiFIsYjLC6Rmxi_F5B3QR.

176 *"stimulate dialogue, imagine a better society"* Kyle Harris, "Why Denver's Museum of Contemporary Art Skipped the Anti-Trump Art Strike," *Westword*, January 20, 2017.

177 *what sociologist Ray Oldenburg called "third places"* Stuart M. Butler and Carmen Diaz, "'Third Places' as Community Builders," *Up Front* (blog), Brookings, September 14, 2016, https://www.google.com/url?q=https://www.brookings.edu/blog/up-front/2016/09/14/third-places-as-community-builders/&sa=D&source=editors&ust=163262771796 6000&usg=AOvVaw0stKuDf5YZodYwowg81YWo.

177 *"we will succeed in changing this world"* Margaret J. Wheatley, *Turning to One Another: Simple Conversations to Restore Hope to the Future* (San Francisco: Berrett-Koehler, 2002).

179 *"A small group of thoughtful, committed citizens"* Attributed to Margaret Mead in Donald Keys, *Earth at Omega: Passage to Planetization* (Boston: Branden Press, 1982).

ALIVENESS

17. THE FLOURISHING STATE OF LANGUISHING

185 *On July 30, 1997, there were two consecutive suicide bombings* Serge Schmemann, "Suicide Bombers Kill 13 in Jerusalem Market," *New York Times*, July 31, 1997.

186 *Psychologists find that one of the best strategies* Adam Grant, "There's a Name for the Blah You're Feeling: It's Called Languishing," *New York Times*, April 19, 2021.

188 *there is scientific value in not going at full speed* Lauren Bedosky, "What Is Active Recovery? 11 of the Best Activities to Do on Your Rest Day," *Self*, January 7, 2021.

188 *"and the things you own end up owning you"* Fight Club, directed by David Fincher (Fox 2000 Pictures, 1999) film.

190 *"Feeling good about life is not enough"* Dani Blum, "The Other Side of Languishing Is Flourishing. Here's How to Get There," *New York Times*, May 4, 2021.

190 *By the fall of 2021, more than 700,000 Americans had* Julie Bosman and Lauren Leatherby, "U.S. Coronavirus Death Toll Surpasses 700,000 Despite Availability of Vaccines," *New York Times*, October 7, 2021.

190 *nearly one out of every five Americans* Mike Labrum, "Nearly One-Fifth of Americans Know Someone Who Has Died of Covid-19, Survey Says," UChicago News, March 11, 2021, https://news.uchicago.edu/story/nearly-one-fifth-americans-know-someone-who-has-died-covid-19-survey-says.

190 *a picture of the emerging mental health tsunami* Alejandro (Alex) Jadad and Tamen Jadad Garcia, "Protecting Talented People Working from Home in the Age of COVID-19, and Beyond: Curbing the 'Echo Pandemic of Mental Illness'" Medium, May 15, 2020, https://medium.com/@ajadad/protecting-talent-working-from-home-in-the-age-of-covid-19-and-beyond-9dbe588148b9.

191 *"It turns out there's a name for that: languishing"* Grant, "There's a Name for the Blah You're Feeling: It's Called Languishing."

192 *"It gave us a familiar vocabulary"* Grant, "There's a Name for the Blah You're Feeling: It's Called Languishing."

193 *a landmark survey of the state of global happiness* "World Happiness Report 2021," World Happiness Report, last accessed October 10, 2021, https://worldhappiness.report/ed/2021/.

194 *"Americans are less happy"* John Helliwell, Richard Layard, and Jeffrey D. Sachs, "World Happiness Report 2019," last accessed October 22, 2021, https://s3.amazonaws.com/happiness-report/2019/WHR19.pdf.

194 *Loneliness has been estimated to shorten* Claire Pomeroy, "Loneliness Is Harmful to Our Nation's Health," *Scientific American,* March 20, 2019, https://blogs.scientificamerican.com/observations/loneliness-is-harmful-to-our-nations-health/.

194 *a staggering 47 percent of Americans often feel alone* Pomeroy, "Loneliness Is Harmful to Our Nation's Health."

194 *a new cabinet-level position, the minister for loneliness* Ceylan Yeginsu, "U.K. Appoints a Minister for Loneliness," *New York Times,* January 17, 2018.

194 *loneliness is about "the subjective perception of isolation"* Jane E. Brody, "The Surprising Effects of Loneliness on Health," *New York Times,* December 11, 2017.

18. ALIVENESS AS A MORAL RESPONSIBILITY

197 *Bailey, who believed she was too old* The X Factor UK, "Sam Bailey Sings Listen by Beyonce—Room Auditions Week 1—The X Factor 2013," YouTube video, 6:25, August 31, 2013, https://www.youtube.com/watch?v=mCylXy-IRGU.

197 *delivers a devastating rendition of Etta James's "At Last"* The X Factor UK, "Jahmene Douglas' Audition—Etta James' At Last—The X Factor UK 2012," YouTube video, 7:36, August 18, 2012, https://www.youtube.com/watch?v=V-xndZZjM4A.

197 *"some are amazing singers, some are just enthusiastic"* Britain's Got Talent, "Flakefleet Primary School Gets First GOLDEN BUZZER of 2019! | Auditions | BGT 2019," YouTube video, 7:00, April 6, 2019, https://www.youtube.com/watch?v=itSbV3YiRkI.

197 *It's about the pure joy of Revelation Avenue* Britain's Got Talent, "Revelation Avenue Roar Straight into the Semi-finals! | Britain's Got Talent 2015," YouTube video, 6:00, April 25, 2015, https://www.youtube.com/watch?v=oXhNIS4nKL8.

197 *A concept of self-actualization* A. H. Maslow, "A Theory of Human Motivation," *Psychological Review* 50, no. 4 (1943): 370–396, https://doi.org/10.1037/h0054346.

198 *what Maslow called a peak experience* Raymond J. Corsini, "Peak Experience," in *Concise Encyclopedia of Psychology,* 2nd ed. (New York: John Wiley & Sons, 1998).

203 *"extractive and exploitative, like the settler colonialism that enabled it"* Jennifer Szalai, "'The Sum of Us' Tallies the Cost of Racism for Everyone," *New York Times,* February 23, 2021.

204 *"A new Federal Reserve Bank of San Francisco study calculated"* Heather C. McGhee, "The Way out of America's Zero-Sum Thinking on Race and Wealth," *New York Times,* February 13, 2021.

204 *"many life examples of cooperation and sociability"* Marlene Cimons, "'Friendliest,' Not Fittest, Is Key to Evolutionary Survival, Scientists Argue in Book," *Washington Post,* July 20, 2020.

205 *"We must learn to reawaken"* Henry David Thoreau, *Walden* (New York: Thomas Y. Crowell & Co. Publishers, 1910).

19. THE COMEDIAN AS GLADIATOR

207 *There are three philosophical frameworks* John Morreall, "Philosophy of Humor" last revised August 20, 2020, Stanford Encyclopedia of Philosophy Archive, https://plato.stanford.edu/archives/fall2020/entries/humor/.

208 *when we experience a concept and a perception* PhilosoFun, "The Philosophy of Comedy: The Three Theories of Humor," Youtube video, 5:19, July 14, 2017, https://www.youtube.com/watch?v=KHRhvMJAg8E.

210 *"There is too much hysteria around gender"* Hannah Gadsby, *Nanette,* directed by Madeleine Parry and John Olb (Netflix, 2018), film.

211 *"a kind of meta self-interrogatory anticomedy"* Wired Staff, "Seriously, We Really Need to Talk About *Nanette,*" *Wired,* July 31, 2018.

211 *Netflix has brought the stand-up special* Jason Zinoman, "The Netflix Executives Who Bent Comedy to Their Will," *New York Times,* September 9, 2018.

212 *"50 percent of its 130 million subscribers have watched"* Zinoman, "The Netflix Executives Who Bent Comedy to Their Will."

212 *it's no surprise that Nishimura has been celebrated* Serena Kim, "Neflix's Lisa Nishimura Is One of the Most Powerful Asian Americans in Hollywood," Character Media, November 28, 2018, https://charactermedia.com/netflixs-lisa-nishimura-is-one-of-the-most-powerful-asian-americans-japanese-in-hollywood/.

212 *"the best documentarians and comedians"* Kim, "Netflix's Lisa Nishimura Is One of the Most Powerful Asian Americans in Hollywood."

213 *"An artist's duty"* Nina Simone, "Nina Simone: An Artist's Duty," YouTube video, February 21, 2013, https://youtu.be/99VomMNf5fo.

214 *"I still don't understand, all these fuckin' police"* Dave Chappelle, *8:36* directed by Julia Reichert and Steve Bognar (Netflix, 2020), YouTube video, 27:20, June 11, 2020, https://www.youtube.com/watch?v=3tR6mKcBbT4.

214 *"'8:46' is most impactful if received as a workshop"* Lauren Michele Jackson, "Dave Chappelle's Rough-Cut Humorlessness in '8:46,'" *New Yorker,* June 18, 2020.

215 *"Everybody is mad at me"* David Chappelle, *Dave Chappelle: The Kennedy Center Mark Twain Prize for American Humor,* directed by Chris Robinson (Netflix, 2020), film.

216 *"This is sacred ground"* David Chappelle, *Dave Chappelle: The Kennedy Center Mark Twain Prize for American Humor.*

217 *"emotionally stunted partial world view"* Caitlin Cassidy, "Hannah Gadsby Condemns Netflix as an 'Amoral Algorithm Cult' Amid Dave Chappelle Controversy," *The Guardian,* October 16, 2021.

217 *"The negative reaction"* Helen Lewis, "Dave Chappelle's Rorschach Test," *The Atlantic,* October 13, 2021.

218 *77 percent of millennials* Kendall Breitman, "Poll: Majority of Millennials Can't Name a Senator from Their Home State," *Politico,* February 3, 2015.

20. OLÉ, WILLY WONKA

221 *This was an era of extraordinary growth for Apple* "Number of Apple Stores Worldwide from 2005 to 2015," Statista, last modified October 2015, https://www.statista.com/statistics/273480/number-of-apple-stores-worldwide-since-2005/.

221 *The organization grew 240 percent* "Global Revenue of Apple from 2004 to 2020," Statista, last modified October 2020, https://www.statista.com/statistics/265125/total-net-sales-of-apple-since-2004/.

222 *In search of the words to celebrate* Elizabeth Gilbert, "Your Elusive Creative Genius," TED video, 19:15, February 2009, https://www.ted.com/talks/elizabeth_gilbert_your_elusive_creative_genius?language=en.

224 *"If the good Lord had intended"* Willy Wonka & the Chocolate Factory, directed by Mel Stuart (Paramount Pictures, 1971), film.

224 *In a rare interview at the 92nd Street Y* 92nd Street Y, "Gene Wilder on Willy Wonka Remake, Young Frankenstein, Mel Brooks, and More," YouTube video, 28:40,

June 20, 2013, https://www.youtube.com
/watch?v=ezfVc5MGmIU.

225 *"He simply couldn't bear the idea of one
less smile in the world"* Marissa Martinelli,
"Gene Wilder Kept His Alzheimer's Secret
So Kids Wouldn't Know That Willy Wonka
Was Sick," *Slate,* August 30, 2016, https://
slate.com/culture/2016/08/gene-wilder-s
-family-issues-a-statement-on-his-alzheimer
-s-and-circumstances-of-death.html.

NATURE

21. OUR REMOVAL FROM
THE NATURAL WORLD
INHIBITS HUMILITY

229 *"separation of humans from nature in
Western culture can be traced"* Heather Alberro, "Humanity and Nature Are Not
Separate—We Must See Them as One to Fix
the Climate Crisis," *The Conversation,* September 17, 2019, https://theconversation.com
/humanity-and-nature-are-not-separate-we
-must-see-them-as-one-to-fix-the-climate
-crisis-122110?fbclid=IwAR3ZTb2r7BuVmrHe
LtriuWruAtgOiDLEKJNeAoy2J3xlVFJYDZ
1D3MzyUgI.

230 *"you see the Earth as a thing and not a
being"* Leah Penniman, "The Gift of Ecological Humility," *Yes!* February 16, 2021.

230 *"all things depend on others for their exis-
tence and well-being"* Alberro, "Humanity and
Nature Are Not Separate—We Must See
Them as One to Fix the Climate Crisis."

231 *"Our conscience must catch up to our reason"* Maria Popova, "The Search for a New
Humility: Václav Havel on Reclaiming Our
Human Interconnectedness in a Globalized
Yet Divided World," *The Marginalian,* September 28, 2017, https://www.brainpick
ings.org/2017/09/18/vaclav-havel-harvard
-commencement/.

232 *"it sets a different trajectory for the Earth
system"* Damian Carrington, "The Anthropocene Epoch: Scientists Declare Dawn of

Human-Influenced Age," *The Guardian,* August 29, 2016.

233 *Can we imagine education* David W. Orr,
*Earth in Mind: On Education, Environment,
and the Human Prospect* (Washington, D.C.:
Island Press, 1994).

233 *"techniques developed at the intersection of
human-centered design"* Monika Sznel, "The
Time for Environment-Centered Design Has
Come," UX Collective, May 5, 2020, https://
uxdesign.cc/the-time-for-environment
-centered-design-has-come-770123c8cc61?gi
=89f4ffbc536a.

233 *"The twentieth century will be chiefly re-
membered"* Arnold Toynbee, quoted in Bruce
Mau, *Massive Change* (New York: Phaidon
Press, 2004).

235 *"'manifestations of our dangerously unbal-
anced relationship with nature'"* Damian Carrington, "Pandemics Result from Destruction
of Nature, Say UN and WHO," *The Guardian,* June 17, 2020.

22. WALKING AS A RADICAL ACT

237 *the equivalent of about 165 billion barrels*
"Oil Sands Facts and Statistics," Alberta
website, last accessed September 22, 2021,
https://www.alberta.ca/oil-sands-facts-and
-statistics.aspx.

237 *total economic value of Alberta's oil reserves* "Average Annual OPEC Crude Oil
Price from 1960 to 2021," Statista, last
modified September 13, 2021, https://www
.statista.com/statistics/262858/change-in
-opec-crude-oil-prices-since-1960/.

239 *"slowing down is not about getting answers"* Bayo Akomolafe, "A Slower Urgency,"
https://www.bayoakomolafe.net/post/a
-slower-urgency.

240 *"it can be invested with wildly different
cultural meanings"* Rebecca Solnit, *Wanderlust: A History of Walking* (New York: Penguin
Putnam, 2000).

241 *literally prescribing nature to their patients* Peter Dockrill, "Doctors in Scotland Are Literally Prescribing Nature to Their Patients," ScienceAlert, October 9, 2018, https://www.sciencealert.com/doctors-in-scotland-are-literally-prescribing-nature-to-patients-shetland-gps-pilot-benefits-health-mental.

241 *"impressions of their partners grew more favorable after the first part of the walk"* Minda Zetlin, "Steve Jobs Loved Walking Meetings. New Research Shows Why He Was Right," *Inc.*, February 24, 2020.

23. BIG AND SMALL SAUNTERING

246 *"But when we have learned how to listen to trees"* Hermann Hesse, *Wandering: Notes and Sketches* (New York: Farrar, Straus and Giroux, 1972).

247 *"I come to myself, I once more feel myself grandly related"* Richard Higgins, *Thoreau and the Language of Trees* (Berkeley: University of California Press, 2017).

247 *"I have met with but one or two persons"* Henry David Thoreau, "Walking," *The Atlantic*, June 1862.

248 *"no more vagrant than the meandering river"* Henry David Thoreau, "Walking," in *The Making of the American Essay,* ed. John D'Agata (Minneapolis: Graywolf Press, 2016).

248 *In sociology, disembedding refers to a process* Oxford Reference, s.v. "disembedding," accessed September 2, 2021, https://www.oxfordreference.com/view/10.1093/oi/authority.20110803095721556.

248 *in-person interactions lose their significance in everyday life* Christoph Henning, "Distanciation and Disembedding," in *The Blackwell Encyclopedia of Sociology*, 3rd ed. (Malden, Mass.: Blackwell, 2007).

248 *Emerson elucidated four ways* Ralph Waldo Emerson, "Nature," in *The Oxford Companion to American Literature*, ed. James D. Hart (Oxford: Oxford University Press, 1995).

249 *rural areas cover 97 percent of the nation's land* "New Census Data Show Difference Between Urban and Rural Populations," press release, U.S. Census Bureau, last modified December 8, 2016, https://www.census.gov/newsroom/press-releases/2016/cb16-210.html#:~:text=%E2%80%9CRural%20areas%20cover%2097%20percent,Thompson%20said.

249 *the world is projected to have forty-three megacities* "2018 Revision of World Urbanization Prospects," United Nations Department of Economics and Social Affairs, last modified May 16, 2018, https://www.un.org/development/desa/publications/2018-revision-of-world-urbanization-prospects.html.

24. LET US NOW PRAISE RURAL COMMUNITIES

253 *approximately 3.57 million people left New York City* Jonnelle Marte, "Fleeing New Yorkers Resulted in an Estimated $34 Billion in Lost Income—Study," Reuters, December 15, 2020, https://www.reuters.com/article/usa-economy-nyc-idINKBN28P1Q8.

253 *39 percent of urban dwellers across the United States* Ruth Bender, "Escape to the Country: Why City Living Is Losing Its Appeal During the Pandemic," *Wall Street Journal*, June 21, 2020.

254 *"I'm interested in the country"* Oliver Wainwright, "'The Countryside Is Where the Radical Changes Are': Rem Koolhaas Goes Rural," *The Guardian*, February 11, 2020.

254 *"the countryside is now the site where the most radical"* "Questioning the Future: Rem Koolhaas at the Guggenheim," Guggenheim video, 7:18, September 18, 2020, https://www.guggenheim.org/video/questioning-the-future-rem-koolhaas-at-the-guggenheim.

254 *"Is there really no option but to do nothing"* Eduardo Porter, "The Hard Truths of Trying to 'Save' the Rural Economy," *New York Times*, December 14, 2018.

255 *"offer trust in the capacity of rural people"* Chris Harris, "After Generations of Disinvestment, Rural America Might Be the Most Innovative Place in the U.S.," Ewing Marion Kauffman Foundation, December 14, 2020, https://www.kauffman.org/currents/rural -america-most-innovative-place-in-united -states/.

255 *"Rural entrepreneurs and community leaders have always"* Harris, "After Generations of Disinvestment, Rural America Might Be the Most Innovative Place in the U.S."

256 as *"everything not urban"* Michael Ratcliffe, Charlynn Burd, Kelly Holder, and Alison Fields, "Defining Rural at the U.S. Census Bureau," U.S. Department of Commerce Economics and Statistics Administration, U.S. Census Bureau, December 2016, https://www2.census.gov/geo/pdfs/reference /ua/Defining_Rural.pdf.

257 *"ever less interested in freedom and justice"* Susan Choi, "Why MacDowell NOW? It Has Space to Forge Vision," MacDowell, July 27, 2020, https://www.macdowell.org /news/why-macdowell-now-it-has-space-to -forge-a-new-national-vision.

257 *Myles Horton, who would be dubbed the "father of the civil rights movement"* "Myles Horton," Wikipedia, last accessed October 21, 2021, https://en.wikipedia.org/wiki /Myles_Horton.

258 *Horton, who was heavily influenced by Jane Addams* Robin D. G. Kelley and Makani Themba, "Why the Highlander Attack Matters," *The Nation,* April 12, 2019.

258 *"oppressed people collectively hold strategies for liberation"* "Myles Horton."

258 *"Highlander was the place that Rosa Parks witnessed"* Travis Dorman, "Knoxville Desegregation Leader Recalls Friendship with Civil Rights Icon John Lewis," *Knoxville News Sentinel,* July 18, 2020.

258 *while on strike, a new interpretation of the gospel hymn* "We Shall Overcome: Role of the Highlander Folk School," Wikipedia, last accessed October 21, 2021, https://en.wikipe dia.org/wiki/We_Shall_Overcome#Role_of _the_Highlander_Folk_School.

259 *"a clubhouse and studio where we and our friends"* Zillow, "Adele Went 'Rolling in the Deep' at Shangri-La Studio," *Forbes,* February 14, 2012.

259 *"How do we make a comfort zone"* *Shangri-La,* directed by Morgan Neville and Jeff Malmberg, (Showtime, 2019), documentary series.

260 *"So, you aren't thinking about a picture"* *Shangri-La.*

260 *"You can't make them happen"* *Shangri-La.*

260 *Rural Studio, a design-centric program* Rural Studio home page, last accessed October 22, 2021, https://ruralstudio.org/.

261 *But more than anything else, they learn about civility* Andrea Oppenheimer Dean, *Rural Studio: Samuel Mockbee and an Architecture of Decency* (New York: Princeton Architectural Press, 2002).

261 *"an architect can help us discover what is noble"* "4.1 History and Philosophy," SamuelMockbee.net, last accessed October 21, 2021, http://samuelmockbee.net/rural -studio/about-the-rural-studio/.

261 *forging trust and imagining not just what could be done* "Becoming the Town Architect," Rural Studio, last accessed October 21, 2021, http://ruralstudio.org/about/.

VALUE

25. SURVIVAL ECONOMICS HAVE MADE IMAGINATION A LUXURY GOOD

268 *nearly 29.9 percent of the U.S. population . . . is considered "close to poverty"* "Poverty Facts," Poverty USA, last accessed, September 25, 2021, https://www.povertyusa .org/facts.

268 *"a famous economic model created to understand developing nations"* Lynn Parramore, "America Is Regressing into a Developing Nation for Most People," Institute for New Economic Thinking, April 20, 2017, https://www.ineteconomics.org/perspectives/blog/america-is-regressing-into-a-developing-nation-for-most-people.

269 *scarcity mentality induced by the state of poverty* Rutger Bregman, "Poverty Isn't a Lack of Character; It's a Lack of Cash," TED video, 14:49, 2017, https://www.ted.com/talks/rutger_bregman_poverty_isn_t_a_lack_of_character_it_s_a_lack_of_cash/transcript?language=en#t-944986.

26. DO WE VALUE LIFE?

272 *"We can't agree on anything anymore"* Michael Che, *Michael Che Matters*, directed by Osmany Rodriguez (Netflix, 2016), film.

273 *"it's been 'profitable to deny or suppress such knowledge'"* Alissa Wilkinson, "It's Astounding That HBO's New Docuseries 'Exterminate All the Brutes' Even Exists," *Vox*, April 9, 2021, https://www.vox.com/platform/amp/22373647/exterminate-all-the-brutes-review-hbo?fbclid=IwAR0GOuzBvzQOGCGa5YBvkuAwkARjs8cazVNhtmIxl7brFMnjudqAqRdSmuA.

274 *"The news of these killings is not that they are interruptions"* Charles M. Blow, "Rage Is the Only Language I Have Left," *New York Times*, April 14, 2021.

274 *there are more than 1,000 hate groups* Liam Stack, "Over 1,000 Hate Groups Are Now Active in United States, Civil Rights Group Says," *New York Times*, February 20, 2019.

274 *"The President's views are clear"* David Remnick, "A Racist in the White House," *New Yorker*, July 15, 2019.

275 *there were nearly as many shootings as days in the year* Melia Robinson and Skye Gould, "There Were 340 Mass Shootings in the US in 2018—Here's the Full List," *Business Insider*, December 31, 2018.

275 *The United States has the thirty-second-highest rate* Nurith Aizenman, "Gun Violence Deaths: How the U.S. Compares with the Rest of the World," NPR, March 24, 2021, https://www.npr.org/sections/goatsandsoda/2021/03/24/980838151/gun-violence-deaths-how-the-u-s-compares-to-the-rest.

275 *death rate increased by 15.9 percent from 2019 to 2020* Farida B. Ahmad et al., "Provisional Mortality Data—United States, 2020," *CDC Morbidity and Mortality Weekly Report* 70, no. 24 (June 2021), https://www.cdc.gov/mmwr/volumes/70/wr/pdfs/mm7014e1-H.pdf.

276 *"Haber invented a process for making"* *Kiss the Ground*, directed by Rebecca Harrell Tickell and Josh Tickell (Beneson Productions, 2020), film.

277 *when the news that the Bayer lawsuits had been settled* Jessica Sier, "Bayer Shares Climb After $11B Roundup Settlement," *MarketWatch*, June 25, 2020, https://www.marketwatch.com/story/bayer-shares-climb-after-11b-roundup-settlement-2020-06-25.

278 *"The question can no longer be"* Viktor E. Frankl, *Yes to Life: In Spite of Everything* (Boston: Beacon Press, 2020).

279 *"If I were to ask you"* Umair Haque, "The Fundamentals: The Five Essentials of Eudaimonics," *Eudaimonia & Co.* (blog), September 14, 2017, https://eand.co/the-fundamentals-370db41b2958.

280 *Of the trillion-dollar war in Afghanistan* Reality Check Team, "Afghanistan: What Has the Conflict Cost the US and Its Allies?" BBC News, September 3, 2021, https://www.bbc.com/news/world-47391821#:~:text=According%20to%20the%20US%20Department,bn%20spent%20on%20reconstruction%20projects.

27. UTOPIA IS WORTH FIGHTING FOR

283 *"Maybe this is heaven" Field of Dreams,* directed by Phil Aiden Robinson (Universal Pictures, 1989), film.

283 *"This is the kind of movie Frank Capra"* Roger Ebert, "Reviews: Field of Dreams," RogerEbert.com, April 12, 1989, https://www.rogerebert.com/reviews/field-of-dreams-1989.

284 *the meaning of justice and the essence of happiness* "Republic (Plato)," Wikipedia, last modified July 15, 2021, https://en.wikipedia.org/wiki/Republic_(Plato).

284 *an ethereal utopia where the people live in harmony with nature* "The Peach Blossom Spring," Wikipedia, last modified March 26, 2021, https://en.wikipedia.org/wiki/The_Peach_Blossom_Spring.

285 *"possesses highly desirable or nearly perfect qualities"* Henry Giroux, "Utopian Thinking Under the Sign of Neoliberalism: Towards a Critical Pedagogy of Educated Hope," *Democracy & Nature* 9, no. 1 (2003), https://www.tandfonline.com/doi/abs/10.1080/1085566032000074968.

285 *participating nations to present their ideal portraits of themselves* "1939 New York World's Fair," Wikipedia, last modified August 3, 2021, https://en.wikipedia.org/wiki/1939_New_York_World%27s_Fair.

286 *more than 44 million people had attended* Alan Taylor, "The 1939 New York World's Fair," *The Atlantic,* November 1, 2013.

286 *established a law preventing public resources to be spent* Fred A. Bernstein, "Is America Poised for Another World's Fair Embarrassment?" *Architect,* January 28, 2020.

286 *the fair went bankrupt* Harry Swartout, "How the 'World of Tomorrow' Became a Thing of the Past," *Time,* April 29, 2014.

287 *"in order to create a new direction for humanity"* "Expo 2005," Wikipedia, last modified June 2, 2021, https://en.wikipedia.org/wiki/Expo_2005.

287 *Bob Dylan even recorded a new version* Howell Llewellyn, "Dylan Reworks 'Hard Rain's' for Spanish Expo," Reuters, November 23, 2007, https://www.reuters.com/article/music-dylan-dc/dylan-reworks-hard-rains-for-spanish-expo-idUSN2358049520071123.

288 *"Design, on the other hand, is concerned with how things"* Howard Silverman, "Herbert Simon: Design for Understanding," Solving for Pattern, June 15, 2013, https://www.solvingforpattern.org/2013/06/15/herbert-simon-design-for-understanding/.

290 *"There is absolutely no evidence to support the statement"* Lance Masina, "The Newsroom (Epic Opening Scene)," Vimeo video, 7:55, June 25, 2012, https://vimeo.com/44645929.

291 *"Wholeness is not a Utopian dream"* Holland Cotter, "The Short and Long Legacy of Black Mountain College," *New York Times,* December 17, 2015.

28. IMAGINATION IS THE MOST VALUABLE NATURAL RESOURCE ON EARTH

292 *more than 1,500 CEOs from sixty countries* "IBM 2010 Global CEO Study: Creativity Selected as Most Crucial Factor for Future Success," news release, IBM, last modified May 18, 2010, http://www-03.ibm.com/press/us/en/pressrelease/31670.wss.

293 *F-35 fighter jet program alone* Valerie Insinna, "Inside America's Dysfunctional Trillion-Dollar Fighter-Jet Program," *New York Times Magazine,* August 21, 2019.

295 *"study of the nonprofit arts and culture industry's impact on the economy"* "Arts & Economic Prosperity 5: The Economic Impact of Nonprofit Arts & Cultural Organizations & Their Audiences," Americans for the Arts, https://www.americansforthearts.org/by-program/reports-and-data/research-studies

-publications/arts-economic-prosperity
-5#:~:text=Arts%20%26%20Economic%20
Prosperity%205%20is,and%20the%20Dis
trict%20of%20Columbia.

296 *"I think of creativity as"* Sir Ken Robinson, "Do Schools Kill Creativity?" TED Talk, https://www.ted.com/talks/sir_ken_robinson _do_schools_kill_creativity/transcript?lang uage=en.

297 *"the MFA is the new MBA"* Daniel H. Pink, *A Whole New Mind: Why Right-Brainers Will Rule the Future* (New York: Riverhead Books, 2005).

297 *"The artist is distinguished from all other responsible actors in society"* James Baldwin, *The Price of the Ticket: Collected Nonfiction, 1948–1985* (London: St. Martin's Press, 1985).

298 *An economic crisis as well as an existential one* "World's Biggest Companies Face $1 Trillion in Climate Change Risks," CDP, last modified June 4, 2019, https://www.cdp.net /en/articles/media/worlds-biggest-companies -face-1-trillion-in-climate-change-risks.

299 *56 percent of people fifty-five years and older worry about climate change* RJ Reinhart, "Global Warming Age Gap: Younger Americans Most Worried," Gallup, May 11, 2018, https://news.gallup.com/poll/234314/global -warming-age-gap-younger-ameri-%20cans -worried.aspx.

300 *"This is all wrong"* Greta Thunberg, "Transcript: Greta Thunberg's Speech at the U.N. Climate Action Summit," NPR, September 23, 2019, https://www.npr.org/2019 /09/23/763452863/transcript-greta-thunbergs -speech-at-the-u-n-climate-action-summit #:~:text=%22You%20are%20failing%20us .,We%20will%20never%20forgive%20you.

300 *we now find the term "climate anxiety"* Brian Barnett and Amit Anand, "Climate Anxiety and Mental Illness," *Scientific American*, October 10, 2020.

300 *57 percent of American teens feel afraid and 43 percent feel hopeless* Barnett and Anand, "Climate Anxiety and Mental Illness."

300 *"Hope is definitely not the same thing as optimism"* Paul Rogat Loeb, *The Impossible Will Take a Little While: A Citizen's Guide to Hope in a Time of Fear* (New York: Basic Books, 2014).

301 *It is currently predicted* Fernando Alcoforado, "Planet Earth and Its Limits on Use of Natural Resources," World Resources Forum, July 8, 2015, https://www.wrforum .org/opinion/planet-earth-limits-natural -resources/.

302 *reverse climate change by rebuilding the soil's* "Why Regenerative Agriculture?" Regeneration International, last modified 2019, https://regenerationinternational.org/why -regenerative-agriculture/.

302 *transformed the desert into a green oasis* Steve Rose, "'Our Biggest Challenge? Lack of Imagination': The Scientists Turning the Desert Green," *The Guardian*, March 20, 2021.

303 *show people a future more exciting than their past* Bruce Mau, *MC24 Bruce Mau's 24 Principles for Designing Massive Change in Your Life and Work,* ed. Jon Ward (New York: Phaidon Press, 2020).

303 *"Creativity cannot be used up"* Maya Angelou, quoted in Mary Ardito, "Creativity: It's the Thought That Counts," *Bell Telephone Magazine*, 61, no. 1 (1982).

ABOUT THE AUTHOR

Seth Goldenberg is an artist, curator, entrepreneur, and activist who has spent his life harnessing the practice of questioning to catalyze audacious business innovation and cultural change. He is the founder and CEO of Curiosity & Co., an experience design group based on the island of Jamestown, Rhode Island. Goldenberg founded the Ideas Salons, invitational thought leader retreats that have been attended by more than 2,500 VIP guests to take on the essential questions of our time.

Since founding Curiosity & Co., Goldenberg has led a series of high-profile projects with organizations such as Apple, American Express, Boston University, and ConocoPhillips to help build their capacity for ambitious change. He was previously the interim chief marketing officer for tourism of the state of Rhode Island; chief design officer of the biotech Intarcia Therapeutics; vice president of Bruce Mau Design, where he led major client engagements with the Oprah Winfrey Network, Walt Disney Imagineering, and the city of Denver; founder and curator of the digital media festival for the President Obama 2008 Democratic National Convention; deputy director of the Museum of Contemporary Art Denver; and founder of the Center for Public Engagement at the Rhode Island School of Design.

Goldenberg has been a featured speaker to audiences such as SXSW, the College Art Association, Brown University, Duke University, Virginia Tech University, and Florida State University. His work has been featured in *The New York Times*, *Fast Company*, *Wired*, *The Chronicle of Higher Education*, and *The Boston Globe*.

www.curiosityand.company

To inquire about booking Seth Goldenberg for a speaking engagement, please contact the Penguin Random House Speakers Bureau at speakers@penguinrandomhouse.com.

ABOUT THE TYPE

This book was set in Freight Text, a stylish yet sturdy humanist serif typeface drawn by the type designer Joshua Darden and published by GarageFonts in 2005. Darden, who published his first typeface at age fifteen, is also the designer of the award-winning typeface Jubilat. Freight Text is a member of the Freight "superfamily" of fonts prized for their versatility and suitability for use both in print and online.